# A PLACE
# CALLED
# PRINCETON

## ALSO BY SAMUEL A. SCHREINER, JR.

Angelica
Pleasant Places
The Possessors and the Possessed
Thine Is the Glory
The Van Alens: First Family of a Nation's First City

# A PLACE CALLED PRINCETON

Samuel A. Schreiner, Jr.

*Illustrated with Photographs*

ARBOR HOUSE ○ NEW YORK

To Doris Boon, a Finch College girl,
who shared my Princeton experience
with me and fortunately the rest of
my life, including the part we both
gave to the writing of this book.

Library of Congress Cataloging in Publication Data

Schreiner, Samuel Agnew.
  A place called Princeton.

  Includes index.
1. Princeton University. I. Title.
LD4610.S37   1984      378.749'67      84–3007
ISBN 0–87795–573–5

Text design by Rueith Ottiger/Levavi & Levavi

Manufactured in the United States of America

10 9 8 7 6 5 4 3 2 1

This book is printed on acid-free paper. The paper in this book
meets the guidelines for permanence and durability of the
Committee on Production Guidelines for Book Longevity of the
Council on Library Resources.

# CONTENTS

# Preface

# THE NATURAL ELITISM OF PRINCETON

When I first started out on this book, a fellow Princetonian and fellow journalist challenged me: "What's your point of view about the old place?"

"Well," I said, "I see Princeton as a historic and unique American institution, and people are always fascinated by the unique."

"It won't fly," he said. "Not these days. You've got to say something irritating or even shocking to sell books."

"Like what?"

He grinned. "How about this? Princeton's unique all right—unique in that it always turns out failures in life."

"How so?"

"Well, consider John Foster Dulles or Adlai Stevenson. Or take a look at James Forrestal, who killed himself. And what happened to that greatest Princetonian of them all—Woodrow

Wilson? Compare them to Harvard's Teddy Roosevelt and FDR and Kissinger and . . . "

He was joking, of course. It was one of those *in vino veritas*–type conversations that are easily forgotten, and yet I couldn't get it out of my mind. At least we both agreed that Princeton was unique. If I could decide what made it so, I would have my point of view. It wasn't all that hard. After I had read fifty books and talked to as many members of the Princeton community, a point of view simply thrust itself upon me—a point of view, moreover, that may prove irritating to large numbers of people.

Yes, Princeton is unique because, more than any other institution of its kind in the United States, it remains an unconquered citadel of the elite. Through nearly 250 years of shifting social sands, this smallish educational institution in the middle of New Jersey has plodded steadily along a straight course: the selection and shaping of that shadowy presence in society that is sometimes called "the old boy (now girl, too) network" or "the establishment." *Elite* is probably a dirty word in this egalitarian era, but it would be hard to invent a more satisfactory one to describe the Princeton product, still carefully crafted at the rate of only a thousand or so a year, in view of the word's dictionary definition: "1 *a:* the choice part; *esp:* a socially superior group; *b:* a powerful minority." As applied to Princeton, however, *elite* has an important connotation that doesn't appear in the dictionary: an elite is under heavy obligation to exert leadership, presumably in an approved direction.

From the days when its seething young patriots led the way to revolution against British colonialism, clear through to tomorrow, when its scientists may well supply the world with unlimited fusion energy, Princeton has been, and will continue to be, an influence on the affairs of men out of all proportion to its small size and seemingly soft nature. The reason, of course, is the leavening effect of its manufactured elite. It may seem self-serving and even tasteless for a Princetonian to make these assertions, but the truth remains that how Princeton works and the kind of people it produces do make a difference, for good or ill, to the nation and the world. A failed Princetonian—at the helm of a large corporation, say—is likely to take a great many other people down with him, or her. Although it would be too much to claim that as Princeton goes, so goes the nation—there *are,* of course, other cradles for the nurturing of the elite, though none so perfectly fashioned for the job—it would not be too much to argue that a look inside Princeton today gives a sharp glimpse of America's ideals and aspirations in the making.

Unfortunately, the public isn't often treated to a clear look at Princeton. Although its prominence has been amply acknowledged throughout its history by a disproportionate amount of press coverage, this coverage, aside from notices of Nobel Prize awards and scientific breakthroughs, has seldom concentrated on Princeton's real business. Once upon a time, most of the headlines on the sports pages were devoted to Princeton's championship football teams and, until recently, to its unbeatable basketball teams. Perhaps astonishment had something to do with headlining this athletic prowess, since Princetonians, breaking out into occasional riot, were otherwise pictured as spoiled brats. This public image of the young Princeton "gentleman" as having more money than sense became an important political factor early this century when the press dramatized the effort of Princeton's president to take over his students' exclusive eating clubs as a symbolic clash between the people and the privileged. Riding that wave of publicity, Woodrow Wilson was swept right out of Princeton—and into the White House.

Princeton is still in the news, and most of it is still trivial. Accounts of Princeton's athletic contests have shrunk to a few paragraphs on the inside sports pages, but other peripheral happenings keep its name steadily before the public. Among them: the admission of "the face of the eighties"—Brooke Shields—into the class of 1987, and the fictional admission into Princeton of a young man who turned his parents' home into a brothel in a recent movie called *Risky Business.* Then there are the lawsuits: one by an angry young woman against Princeton's few, but still exclusive, all-male clubs (some things never change); one—a first in ninety-one years—by an angry young man against Princeton's sacrosanct honor system (some things *do* change). A disgruntled alumni group persistently manages to attract public attention by attacking the university for diluting its elite with women and blacks, for banishing God from the campus, for undergraduate wallowing in sex and drugs, for voting Democratic, and for generally going to hell.

The thought that Princeton just *might* be going to hell was one of the intriguing factors in my decision to undertake this project. Whether this is so or not will, I hope, emerge from the chapters that follow. I have made no effort to be either exhaustive or scholarly in this work. Indeed, it would be folly for a journalist and novelist to make such an effort in the face of a community of scholars—an elite at that. But, as I write, I take comfort in a witticism of a longtime *Reader's Digest* colleague, Charles Ferguson, that "scholarship is only plagiarism with footnotes." There will be no footnotes here, although attribution will be given when necessary. Unless in quotation, the opinions expressed will be my own as, I fear, will be the errors, too.

It would be impossible to disentangle my experience of Princeton from my observations, but I have tried to be objective within that limitation. It would be impossible, too, to write this at all without the generous gifts of time and honest opinion from students, faculty, members of the administration, and fellow alumni. I owe a particular debt of gratitude to George B. Eager, director of communications/publications for the university, and his staff. But I must emphasize that this book has been conceived, researched, and written without a shred of authorization or critical review by anyone at Princeton University. As something of a special pleader, I cannot sit in judgment on my argument for Princeton's elitism. My arguments will be more implicit than explicit, and the reader will have to decide whether I am right and whether it matters as much to the society as a whole as I believe it does.

Samuel A. Schreiner, Jr.
Darien, Connecticut
January 1984

# Chapter One

# BROOKE SHIELDS'S PRINCETON

The more honorable segments of the popular press called her "the student princess," and they might have been right if she had matriculated at almost any other educational institution than Princeton University. She certainly had what it takes to aspire to a crown. Hers was one of the most recognized faces and bodies of the early 1980s. Her name, Brooke Shields, was a synonym for sex appeal, and one would have had to be an ostrich or diehard recluse not to have heard it—or seen her photograph—anywhere around the globe. Yet weeks after she walked through the tall iron gates fronting Princeton's Nassau Hall in September 1983, one could talk to any Princeton undergraduate and get the same response: "Shields? You wouldn't know she's here."

In view of the potency of modern publicity, this swift and silent disappearance in a relatively small place of one of the most touted personalities on the American scene is little less than

astonishing. It probably says more about the institution she entered than the girl herself. Shields chose the fourth oldest (after
Harvard, Yale, and William and Mary) and academically fourth-
ranked (after Stanford, Harvard, Yale) university in America. But
if one had followed Shields onto the campus on her first day one
would have received the impression of entering a small college.

When you step off Nassau Street, the town of Princeton's
main commercial artery, the first building you see through arches
of elms is ivy-covered Nassau Hall, practically all there was of
Princeton when it was built in 1756, and a group of smaller
colonial structures flanking it on the right. Behind Nassau Hall
is an open grassy area surrounding a Revolutionary cannon buried
muzzle down in the ground, the scene of tumultuous victory
bonfires, and beyond the green two miniature Greek temples,
Whig and Clio halls, where James Madison and Aaron Burr,
Woodrow Wilson and Norman Thomas refined their debating
skills. A long stone's throw to the left is the Gothic cluster of
library, chapel, and classrooms, and an equal distance to the right
stand the towered Gothic dormitory quadrangles that give
Princeton its overall Oxonian architectural character. Stroll
down a gentle slope behind Whig and Clio, through a conglomerate of building styles, and you come to acres of courts and playing
fields and finally to the shore of placid Lake Carnegie. Although
some important university installations lie just off campus, you
have been through the heart of Princeton—a fifteen-minute
stroll. Much of it is obviously old, and most of it looks hand-
somely livable; it would be hard to get lost in such a small and
pleasant place.

But the challenge of Princeton is psychological, not physical.
As one recent Princeton graduate said: "The thing about Princeton is that you may be a hot shot when you go there, but then
you suddenly find yourself surrounded by a couple of thousand
people who are stars in *something,* and it's very humiliating." Yet,
although it has blithely absorbed for centuries the sons (now
daughters, too) of celebrities and nurtured the famous of many
eras, Princeton for a time seemed overcome by a tall, dazzling girl
called Brooke Shields.

It began in the spring of 1983 when the renowned actress-model simply said she *wanted* to go to Princeton. Although it had been dented by Revolutionary cannon, acted as host to the United States Congress, served as classroom and platform for presidents, poets, and Nobel laureates, old Nassau Hall had undoubtedly never been the focus of so many curious eyes as when Brooke Shields, still a prospective student, flung herself for the benefit of cameras caressingly on the statue of a tiger guarding Nassau Hall. When, shortly after this incident, the university sent her a letter of acceptance—mailed from Florida, presumably so the postman wouldn't know it first—she and the university became fair game for the prurient, the outraged, and the astonished both inside and outside the Princeton community.

Underneath the reaction caused by the news lay the question: "Why does she *need* it?" Already possessed by a dismaying income and with her foot apparently on the first rungs of the ladder leading to screen stardom, Brooke Shields seemed to be living the classic version of the American dream. Those who view a college education as a preparation for a lucrative career found it particularly hard to understand her avowed desire to give up four years of high-six-figure income to become an undergraduate. In an interview with Shields, artist–publicity connoisseur Andy Warhol said flatly: "If I were you, I wouldn't go to school at all. I would just worry about modeling and becoming a very serious actress." To which Shields replied: "I'm not doing it for anybody but myself. I know how I feel about myself, and I know what I want to do." Apparently Warhol didn't know the off-camera Shields, the girl who was such a conscientious student at Dwight-Englewood School in New Jersey that people jokingly said of one of her endorsed products, the Brooke doll: "You wind it up and it goes to school."

As for Princetonians, their reaction to the news was more or less: "Who needs *her?*" Among Princeton alumni there were quite a few old boys who were still smarting over the admission of females to their once all-male bastion, and the idea of accepting *that girl,* whose only known talent was posing in the altogether, was—well, preposterous. Ironically, it was one of Princeton's first female graduates, Barbara Dash, '73, who sounded the sourest note about Shields in a letter to the *Princeton Alumni Weekly:*

Who, one wonders, is the talented and intellectually superior student who has not been admitted to Princeton this year so that Brooke Shields might be? It seems doubtful that Ms. Shields's particular film and modeling experience gives her an advantage over the unusually articulate freshmen I remember. Nor does it seem likely to enrich campus life.

Not that long ago undergraduate coeducation was introduced with some hardship. Many of the difficulties experienced by students of both sexes, and by faculty, were owed, I think, to the attitudes which shape careers such as Ms. Shields's, and which such careers perpetuate. What value does the Admission Office see in exposing students to the kind of tasteless publicity which her admission immediately engendered? . . . Finally, one wonders what harm is done the university's public image when the country's "most overpaid personality" becomes Princeton's best-known student.

In view of the hullabaloo in the press and in anticipation of such reactions as Ms. Dash's, Princeton's then dean of admission, James W. Wickenden, Jr., was undoubtedly courageous in sending Brooke Shields a welcoming letter from his Florida vacation spot. Since there is such an element of mystery to the Princeton admission process, he could easily have turned her down. But, as Wickenden said: "There is a vibrancy to her, an enthusiasm that is not in any way affected. She's a genuine and enjoyable person to be around, rather than being impressed with her own achievements." Knowing Princeton well—he graduated with the class of 1961—Wickenden might also have anticipated that the university could cope with Shields if she could cope with it.

There was a time, though, in the spring of 1983 when such anticipation seemed questionable. Carried away by the prospect of rubbing elbows with the sex symbol of their generation, the editors of the campus humor magazine, the *Princeton Tiger,* went a bit haywire. They turned out a version of another Shields-endorsed product, *The Brooke Book,* which was so crude and libelous that their graduate board forced them to trash it at considerable cost to an always-struggling publication. In an effort to recoup, they spiced up—in a manner of speaking—the March issue with an article meant to skirt libel by calling the subject "Brook Shell." Entitled "The Princeton Man's Guide to Impressing and Sleeping with Brook If and When She Gets Here," the article achieved a certain glory: it was the most tasteless example of sophomoric humor in the long history of a magazine frequently in trouble for indecency and irreverence. Not only did the editors manage to offend the real Brooke Shields, if she cared to read their tripe, but their sexist bias also put off all the women undergraduates. A sample: "Yes, we know: it's relatively difficult to get good ass at Princeton, and this little celebrity could very well be the Ivy League bitch to the twentieth power." The outraged graduate board sent the editors packing and virtually closed down the *Tiger* until a more responsible group could be recruited. Still, if Princetonians were going to keep pulling stunts like this, wasn't her admission a ghastly mistake?

Though it was an unusually hot summer, things seemed to cool off by fall. For one thing, the first issues of the *Princeton Alumni Weekly* carried letters from alumni of both sexes and all ages spanking Ms. Dash for her inhospitable treatment of the new freshman on campus. Worth quoting by reason of the author's age and evident disgruntlement with other aspects of Princeton's admission policy is this one from Fred Doolittle, '32:

> Thank you for the hearty guffaw ignited by the letter from a middle-aged alumna decrying the admission of Brooke Shields to the Class of 1987. Is women's liberation too good for some women?
>
> My information is that Miss Shields is intelligent, attractive and of good lineage. She has achieved professional distinction at an early age, which testifies to character. She opted for Princeton, thus demonstrating ambition. It is not her fault that (apparently) she does not belong to one of the ethnic minorities now favored by the university.
>
> The big problem for Princeton is whether the current administration, faculty and student body can summon up enough good taste and common decency (as was customary with "famous" students in the past) to give this earnest freshman an equal opportunity to partake of all the goodies that Princeton, *mirabile dictu,* still offers.

It would now seem that Mr. Doolittle had no cause for concern. As zero hour approached, university officials met with Mrs. Teri Shields, their stellar pupil's mother and manager, and decided to hold one big press conference when Brooke arrived on campus to let all the media blow off some steam. Brooke herself vetoed the suggestion; she wished, she said, to be treated like any other student. And she was—to the surprise of nearly everybody. Campus security forces made sure that outsiders were kept away from her, but there was no trouble at all from students. Much of the credit for this might well go to T. Richard Waechter, Jr., a senior and chairman of the *Daily Princetonian,* and his staff. Though editorially unrestrained by the administration, the *"Prince"* editors obviously showed more sophistication and a better understanding of their audience than those at the *Tiger.*

"We did run a couple of stories in the spring, but they didn't get such a good reception," Waechter told me, "so we decided to have a real hands-off policy on Shields when she arrived. I'm very pleased with the results. You really don't hear anything about her on campus, and you don't think about it. I've passed by her a few times, and it's not that great a moment. Of course if she does something here, like getting on the hockey team, we'll write about her like any other student. It remains to be seen how much talent she has compared to other students, and so you've got to admire her for coming to Princeton in the first place. It's great that she really has been able to blend in—so far. Actually, the only time you do talk about her is when you call your folks and they ask, 'Have you met Brooke yet?' "

However cool the campus, interest among "the folks" was hot enough that a number of publications felt obliged to record Shields's advent at Princeton despite the security measures. *People* magazine, for example, made up for its lack of direct contact by writing around the subject and running an old photograph of Brooke hugging the tiger along with some vague shots of Gothic buildings and portraits of former Princeton luminaries such as F. Scott Fitzgerald, James Stewart, and Ralph Nader. The *National Lampoon* fell just short of the *Tiger* when it ran a cartoon cover of Brooke in panties, pondering a lesson in physics at her desk with a picture of a popeyed Einstein leering down from the wall.

This was backed up inside by a purportedly handwritten letter from Brooke to her mother in which, for instance, she says of her adviser: "He's got a really neat place (he said his office burned down, so I had to go to his apartment) and he invited me to come over whenever I needed help. I have my next appointment Thursday at midnight, 'cause he's real busy during the day." Even less subtle, and stretching journalism to its outer limits, was an article in a national sheet called *Globe* that led off with: "Brooke Shields, who has just started her first semester at Princeton University, could be walking into a scandalous pit of booze, drugs and sex, claim students and graduates of the upper crust college. Insiders say freshman girls, like Brooke, are the target of seduction attempts by upperclassmen who don't hesitate to use alcohol and narcotics to get their way." From there the piece descends to: "Carla Prager, another senior, adds: 'I'd give her less than a year —she's a classic ingenue thrown to the wolves here—and for a cute little virgin from a Catholic high school, that's a tough one.' " Though she may be a senior *somewhere,* Prager and the other "students" quoted by *Globe* have never set foot on the Princeton campus, according to the university records. Nor, in fact, was her school a "Catholic high school." What seems likely is that Brooke Shields's self-prophecy to Andy Warhol will prove to be blessedly correct: "They'll get used to me in college, and I won't be any big deal."

Because of her high visibility, however, she has aroused curiosity about the Princeton she chose to enter, and her very presence is symbolic of the rapid changes that have been taking place in one of America's oldest institutions during the past fifteen years. Although it is possible to stroll the Gothic-arched walks of Princeton for a month without getting a glimpse of Brooke Shields, it is impossible not to get an impression of a fresh variety and vitality in the people who inhabit the old place, including, of course, young women who in astonishing numbers are as attractive in their own way as Shields. More fascinating to a long-gone alumnus than the beguiling females was the sprinkling of black and Asian faces wherever one looked—and the look of serious purpose on all the young faces. The Princeton that was once considered the country club of the Ivy League, where a "gentleman's C" was a laudable goal, the place that once was called "the most northern of the southern colleges," was either gone or rapidly going.

There remains, however, a sturdy bridge between Princeton past and Princeton present—the mesmerizing beauty of the place. It seems now a bit of historical serendipity that the word *campus,* the Latin word for field, was first used to describe the grounds of a college by a Princetonian of the class of 1775, Charles C. Beatty, in a letter home; nowhere else is there a more elegant example of what the word connotes. All six thousand students live, work, and play in an area of some two hundred wooded, grassy acres. The buildings, from colonial to Romanesque to collegiate Gothic to modern, are a standing lesson in architectural history, and the lushly planted grounds—ivy, elm, English yew—are like a giant arboretum. Though surrounded by the borough and township of Princeton, and little more than an hour away from New York and Philadelphia, the campus is, in fact, a self-contained world in which the eye takes delight at every twist and turn, whether it lights on a weird-eyed Picasso statue in front of the art museum, or the stained-glass magnificence of the chapel, or the purity of the Woodrow Wilson School floating like an Oriental temple down its reflecting pool.

The beauty of Princeton transcends particular detail—some of the buildings are actually hideous—as a symphony transcends its individual notes. It gets under the skin and lingers. Fifty years after he graduated, Norman Thomas, the perennial Socialist candidate for president, wrote: "Princeton's beauty, present before our eyes or in memory, has been a part of life's wealth that cannot be taken away." In his first novel, *This Side of Paradise,* F. Scott Fitzgerald served up little slices of it: "The great tapestries of trees had darkened to ghosts back at the last edge of twilight. The early moon had drenched the arches with pale blue . . . through the shadowy scented lanes, where Witherspoon brooded like a dark mother over Whig and Clio, her Attic children, where the black Gothic snake of Little curled down to Cuyler and Patton, these in turn flinging the mystery out over the placid slope rolling to the lake." He tried to catch the essence of the place in a single line: "I think of Princeton as being lazy and good-looking and aristocratic—you know, like a spring day." You don't have to be a Princetonian to appreciate the place. The rather prosaic entry in *The Insider's Guide to Colleges* represents independent judgment: "Princeton boasts one of the nation's most attractive campuses; the atmosphere remains peaceful yet invigorating with plenty of land for the nature lover."

The beauty of Princeton is obvious, but the atmosphere of peace it conveys is more apparent than real. The reason the walks and lawns of the campus seem uncrowded is that students are in classes or labs; or self-chained to a desk in the enormous Gothic Firestone Library hard by the chapel (the paved courtyard in front looks like a wholesale lot for bicycles); or running their legs off on the playing fields and tennis courts; or out on the artificial lake Andrew Carnegie funded to encourage rowing instead of football; or, at night, whooping it up in the Pub in one of the stately campus buildings; or in the clubs on Prospect Street that look like something straight out of a *Previews* offering of America's most expensive homes; or jampacking the almost nightly symposia and lectures on both current and esoteric subjects by "visiting firemen" of considerable international reputation and/ or faculty members. Princeton seethes with an extravagant expenditure of physical and mental energy that is exhausting to contemplate but might reasonably be expected from thousands of overachievers who are determined to get the most out of an expensive—$12,900 a year—undergraduate experience.

For such new members of the community as Brooke Shields and her fellow freshmen, all this activity may be bewildering or challenging, depending upon their stamina. "I came to Princeton because I thought that it was more relaxed than most Ivy League schools," *Daily Princetonian* chairman Waechter confesses, "but it has been a very intense experience. It is so much more than academics—the people you meet and the pressures you're exposed to, the constant learning and pushing from other people who are so talented, who have so many different points of view." As to the last, though it may be physically isolated and committed to the arts and sciences, Princeton reacts to current issues as fast as any television network. Within days of the Korean airline tragedy and the invasion of Grenada, professorial panels were speaking out—generally in opposition to Reagan administration policies—to standing-room-only audiences. Reverend Jerry Falwell, the Moral Majority leader and presumably anathema to what is perceived as a liberal campus, packed Alexander Hall despite several bomb threats. ("I get them everywhere I speak," he said.) About forty members of the audience stood and turned their backs to him when he started to talk about the need of adhering to America's Judaeo-Christian heritage.

The students that night weren't only listening to one man's opinion. A group named the Princeton Alliance to Reverse the Arms Race managed to persuade the Undergraduate Student Government to stage a referendum on their call upon the university to endorse a bilateral nuclear freeze and use its stock holdings in defense-related corporations to encourage an end to the production of first-strike nuclear weapons. More than a quarter of the undergraduates turned out, voting 1276 to 705 in favor of the freeze, but the administration remained silent. Another long-standing issue between students and administration resurfaced when a group of seniors formed a group called Endowment for Divestiture as an alternative to Project '84, the undergraduate version of alumni giving. The idea was for seniors to put their gifts to Princeton into the endowment, which would be turned over to the university when, and if, it divests itself of stock in companies doing business in South Africa; or, if there is no divestiture in twenty years, would be given to organizations working for improved race relations.

More than their exposure to the political winds of Princeton, which, Falwell excepted, blow mostly from somewhere left of center, new freshmen like "the cute little virgin from a Catholic high school" may have been amazed by the speaking of what was probably unspeakable in the upper-middle-class homes from which most of them came. Homosexuality, for instance. There is on campus a Gay Alliance of Princeton (GAP), composed of both men and women, and the *Daily Princetonian,* conservative on the Shields admission, was full of GAP's activities. It ran an article by Frederick C. Foote, a former editor of *Prospect,* a magazine put out by intensely conservative alumni who call themselves Concerned Alumni of Princeton, which began: "How does Anita Bryant spell relief? 'A-I-D-S.' So the joke goes: funny, yet aggressive. It represents hostility to the homosexual community expressed by reference to Acquired Immune Deficiency Syndrome (AIDS), that new and deadly epidemic ravaging the homosexual bars, all-male bathhouses and social science faculties of America." Then the newspaper ran a rebuttal by Marc Wiener, '86, an admitted homosexual, who wrote in part: "For Foote to use AIDS as ammunition against homosexuals and homosexuality is unwarranted and disgusting. It is like labeling heterosexuality as immoral, anti-social and unhealthy because of the high incidence of herpes and venereal disease among heterosexuals." The extent and strength of the homosexual community at Princeton might be judged by the fact that Terrace Club, which had vigorously advertised for new members, threatened to cancel a scheduled GAP dance at the club because, in the words of Dan Daley, '84, house manager: "Terrace has an image problem, and people are reluctant to join." To which Sara Atatimur, '84, who belongs to both Terrace Club and GAP, responded: "It's a sign that we're being pushed back in the closet." In a display of considerable courage, Terrace okayed the GAP dance.

If the homosexuals of Princeton are being driven back into closets, so are a lot of the drinkers. What has to be historically called a hard-drinking institution—a Princeton song with the words "situated and celebrated in New Jersey" has always been amended in the singing to "situated and *saturated* in New Jersey" to reflect both the abominable winter weather and the customs of its adherents—was suddenly confronted with a law raising the legal drinking age in New Jersey to twenty-one. This, officially and legally, wipes out half of the campus contenders for any chug-a-lug contest, and has turned underclass gatherings that would a year ago have been beer busts into ice cream parties. Yet there is no problem getting alcohol on campus. The new law has, however, made life better for at least one segment of the Princeton community, the security forces. As Jerrold Witsil, director of security, explains: "What has changed with the new liquor law is open parties. As far as a student's room is concerned, we view it as we would your home. We never go into one unless invited, or in an emergency, or with a search warrant. But as to the big parties, frankly it's been a pleasant experience. I had about five proctors working the student government's welcome-back event, and there were a couple of thousand students through there in the course of a weekend. The proctors told me how nice it was this year in terms of not having to break up fights or provide transport for students who couldn't make it back to the dormitory or had to be taken to the infirmary because they were so intoxicated that they were ill."

Is life fun in a drier Princeton? The truth may be glimpsed from two freshman girls who reported they got their kicks from suppressing giggling fits in the library. Still, boys and girls do live together in the same dormitories, and the innuendoes that Princeton is a sinkhole of unbridled sex keep coming from the likes of *Globe* and the Concerned Alumni of Princeton, who give evidence of having been born fifty years too soon. The real truth about sex on campus can be read into the *Tiger*'s admission that "it's relatively difficult to get good ass at Princeton" and Waechter's straightforward statement that "this is a very moral place. I do think of lot of parents worry—gee, coed dorms! My parents lived in fraternity and sorority houses that were across the campus from each other, but this is so natural to us that it seems very normal." The morality, if any, is the students' own because, according to Eugene Lowe, the dean of students and an Episcopal clergyman, there are no parietal rules, and the administration takes the same view of private sexual conduct as it does of private drinking—a student's room is his or her castle. Nearly everybody agrees that there probably is no more sexual activity in coed Princeton than in the former monastic Princeton when busloads of girls were imported on weekends.

More visible—or audible—forms of fun are to be found in the eating clubs on Prospect Street. Not as wild as the Animal House of movie fame, nevertheless, beginning about Thursday each week, they try to outdo each other with loud music, aided and abetted by alcohol (ID cards required). Not long ago, Ivy Club, long the most prestigious and exclusive (still all-male) of these social entities, achieved a new distinction when its president, senior Jeb Burchenal, was issued a summons by police at 2:00 A.M. on Sunday for violation of the Princeton borough's noise ordinance. Another fun-loving club, Tiger Inn, more innocently ran afoul of the law when it was ordered to divest itself of its mascot, a pig named Smeggy that was being fattened on table scraps to provide members with a year-end feast to remember.

During football home games, a large representation of the student body, including the otherwise invisible Brooke Shields, could still be seen in Palmer Stadium. In a half-empty arena built for Princeton's days of gridiron glory, they seemed lost as they tried to cheer on a football team that repeatedly dropped heart-breakers by one or two points and laugh at a band determinedly trying to clean up its act, if not discipline its march, after being banned by West Point the year before. At the opening game with Bucknell the band, mindful that the swimming pool in Dillon Gymnasium had been drained for repairs, saluted what promised to be a more sober Princeton season with the crack "This year even the pool is dry for freshmen."

It can be doubted that the freshmen cared, for the heart of today's Princeton is the classroom. Academic achievement for the entering class of 1987—only 1,168 of the 11,007 who applied—was the highest in Princeton's history, and it was only after they passed their first midterms that most of the freshmen could relax and even laugh a little. "A lot of people here are worried about practical things like getting a job. It's the economic reality of the times, and it lends itself to study. The gentleman's C is no longer acceptable," says Waechter, the man with his finger on the student pulse. Little wonder the young faces hurrying to class bear such a look of seriousness. Going to Princeton these days is, in fact, a more serious business than it has ever been, and you don't have to be on campus long to appreciate why Brooke Shields is getting her wish to be "no big deal."

# Chapter Two

# "FIRE" ON THE CAMPUS

$\mathbf{B}$ack in what some of its alumni still regard as the good old days, there was a ritual at Princeton that said a lot about the campus attitude toward sex. Whenever a female would venture into one of the grassy quadrangles surrounded by the ivied walls of collegiate Gothic dormitories, a casement window would be flung open and a male voice would cry: "Fire! Fire!" The cry would be taken up and echoed from window to window until the female retreated in a state of confusion, embarrassment, or just possibly pride.

Such a thing could never happen in the Princeton of today. In what is the most revolutionary change in its 238-year history, Princeton has transformed itself into an alma mater for women as well as men and, depending on one's view, it has either put out the fire or set the whole place ablaze. Though only one of the all-male Ivy League schools to adopt coeducation in recent years

—the last, Columbia, admitted women in the fall of 1983—the Princeton experience in this, as in other respects, is more intense because of its isolation and size. It is like a small stage on which the great national and even international drama of the sexes in change and conflict can be seen in sharp focus.

For Robin Herman, one of the most articulate actors in this drama, it began in her Long Island home in the middle of a spring night in 1969. "My Dad came charging up to my room, woke me out of a sound sleep, and said, 'I just heard on the radio that Princeton's admitting women. You've got to apply.' I rolled over and said, 'Sure, Dad, in the morning.' " When she was fully awake the next day Robin Herman did apply, because there was no time to lose: Princeton had reached its decision late in terms of the national scramble among high school seniors for college admission. With applications already out to Harvard, Yale, Cornell, Penn, and Brown, Robin Herman was still hedging her bets. "I think I'd have gone to Harvard or Yale if they'd accepted me, because I didn't know as much about Princeton," she says, "but when they didn't I decided that Princeton would be better than the others because it would be the place to participate in social change, to have more than an educational experience."

By contrast, Dr. Susan Georgia Nugent, assistant professor of classics and the first Princeton alumna to return as a member of the faculty, responded to that 1969 announcement as something of a fling. Dutifully, because as an only child she was expected to stay near home, she had applied only to the University of Miami. When Princeton opened its doors after all other admissions were closed, it looked to Susan Nugent like a long shot, a last-chance opportunity to have the experience of getting out on her own. "When they let me in, I came with glee," she says now, "but I never thought of myself as being a social pioneer."

Nevertheless, these and the hundred or so other women Princeton managed to fish out of the pool of high academic achievers for its first coed class have gone down in the university's annals as "the pioneers." And no wonder. They were walking into a fenced-off area that for two centuries had been a masculine enclave, a retreat from feminine influence in thought and behavior. Princeton's character was overwhelmingly what today might be called macho. Muscles earned more accolades than minds, however high the academic hurdles were set; rough and tumble, often in the form of hazing, hard drinking, strong language—all the things little boys do behind mother's back—were, if not expected, tolerated. Songs and cheers were peppered with such words as *sons* and *men* and, of course, that mauling beast, the tiger. Such details as furnishings (athletic banners on the walls, bruised and battered leather chairs) and sanitary facilities (communal, open-stalled showers and toilets) were geared to men. True, women were often on Princeton men's minds but mostly as playmates for football weekends, proms, house parties. When these galas were over, a kind of collective sigh of relief went up as the last high-heeled visitor clicked her way up the steps of the departing "dinky" at the Princeton station. Though Princetonians have a remarkable record for marrying and staying married, the macho attitude tended to linger on and is, in fact, engraved forever on a cement slab that was sunk without much foresight into the floor at the entrance to the bar of New York's Princeton Club: "Where women cease from troubling and the wicked are at rest."

That slab is always covered with a rug these days, but the sentiment still burns bright in many alumni minds. Indeed, the announcement that Princeton would accept women set up a howl across the land. It was bad enough that Princeton's WASPish male blood was beginning to be diluted by the admission of blacks, Hispanics, and other minorities; women undergraduates were the last straw for many distinguished alumni. Two of them —Shelby Cullom Davis, '30, who was Nixon's ambassador to Switzerland and had shown his love for Princeton by giving $5 million to the history department, and Asa S. Bushnell, '21, a former Princeton manager of athletics and leading light of both the Ivy League and the Olympics—organized something called Concerned Alumni of Princeton (CAP) and began mailing to all alumni a tartly written, expensively printed magazine called *Prospect*. Although women weren't CAP's only concern about a changing Princeton, articles speculating on the sins into which pure young Princeton men would be led by "cohabitation" have been a staple of *Prospect* for more than ten years now. Its continuing snobbish attitude about the student body can be gathered from a picture in a recent issue, which showed a girl standing in the Admission Office and was captioned: "Sorry, my dear, but there's nothing we can do for you. You're white." Nor have carping asides on the subject been limited to CAP. For instance, in a 1979 issue of *Sports Illustrated,* writer Frank Deford, '61, lamented: "Ever since they let girls in the school, the football team has gone all to hell." With ill-concealed fury, CAP has accused the administration of "stonewalling" on every issue they raise, including that of women.

Stonewalling may, in fact, be all the administration can do. With eyes focused forward instead of backward and sweeping across the American educational scene as well as the campus, the administration, then under the leadership of President Robert F. Goheen, '40, later U.S. ambassador to India, felt that it had little choice. Competition was fierce, and would grow fiercer as the college-age population declined, between top institutions to recruit a student body capable of meeting the demands of excellence in education and at the same time cover the rising cost. Clearly the pool of such prospective students contained as many women as men, and an institution that failed to recognize this was simply cutting in half its chances of getting a fair share of the best people. Moreover, most of the males matriculating at Princeton by then came from public high schools, where coeducation had been the norm, and were clamoring, through the *Daily Princetonian* and other outlets for student expression, for the same normality on campus. In society as a whole both the sexual revolution and the female revolution were tearing down barriers higher than Princeton's fences, and an institution given to the study of society could hardly ignore this sweeping movement. But any college administration is charged, above all, with making the organization under its control viable, and the proof that Princeton's was looking through clear eyes in the right direction is evident in a quotation from Carl Schafer, vice president and treasurer, in the March 31, 1980, issue of *Forbes:* "Actually the smartest thing Princeton has done from a budgeting standpoint was ... coeducation. You talk about economics of scale—pardon the industrial terminology, but that's what it is. Where we had excess capacity was in the humanities and the social sciences, which are the areas that women are still disproportionately going to take. Coeducation was a superbly timed financial bargain."

Not all alumni were against the young women, of course. Many of them had daughters who soon began to apply to Princeton in droves as the sons of alumni had always done. Many were the equal of Davis, Bushnell, and company in terms of wealth and prestige. One active proponent for the administration's proposal on the Board of Trustees, for instance, was Laurance S. Rockefeller, '32, who has also given millions to his alma mater. Another overjoyed alumnus greeted the first contingent of women at an early freshman gathering with a gift of chrysanthemums to each one. Still, it wasn't going to be an entirely flower-strewn path that the 102 freshmen women and sixty-nine transfer students would walk in that fateful September of 1969.

When they talk about their experience, even years later, the image of living in a goldfish bowl keeps surfacing. On the short end of a twenty-to-one sexual ratio, each woman was nearly as unusual and visible on campus as the occasional visitor who once evoked the old cry of "Fire!" A woman was likely to find herself the only one of her sex in a precept, or class; and walking alone into the huge, echoing, Gothic-vaulted Commons, where all freshmen and sophomores ate, was "like a stroll along death row." Still uncertain about living arrangements, Princeton put all the women into one dormitory, Pyne Hall. "It was awkward really because we were separated, we were special, as if we were in a castle," Robin Herman recalls. "They prettied up our rooms a bit—new desks, dressers, plain white curtains. Some of the men resented that. And this is sort of famous in the lore of co-education: the story of the locks. Originally, the entryways to Pyne had locks for the security of women. So they installed a buzzer system, and if somebody wanted to see you, you had to let them in. We didn't like that at all and kept disengaging it until after a while they took it away. We did not want to be closed off or protected. It was a silly notion in 1970." Security for the women might not have seemed so silly to the administration, however. Dr. Marvin Geller, director of Princeton's counseling center, also used the fishbowl image with reference to Pyne Hall and remembers that "there were always men milling around it."

Having at least a shot at some twenty overachieving young men might appear to be heavenly hunting to any girl, but it wasn't in fact. Princetonians went right on importing armies of women for social events, often leaving the local girls out. Robin Herman now concedes that she couldn't blame them: "Who wants to be number twenty on somebody's list?" But it hurt then: "This annoyed me a lot freshman year. I would have these people in lab or class who seemed to be friends of mine and then on the weekend they'd turn around and bring down these girls they didn't even know to spend the weekend with. I used to make a point of doing my laundry on Friday nights. I'd get in coveralls with my laundry bag over my shoulder. It was my way of saying to the women who were on campus: 'You know, you may be here this weekend, but I live here.' I even wrote a song about it called 'The Friday Woman.' "

Robin Herman was also disturbed by the way Princeton men treated their weekend women: "I didn't feel that the respect was there that should have been there." In our discussion of this, I fell right into the yawning generation gap. In my day, as I told her, if the girl you brought down to Princeton was the kind you might marry—and many were, including my own wife—the tendency was to put them on a pedestal. Robin Herman was nice enough not to laugh, but she did say: "You have to remember there was a sexual revolution between your memories and our time. The girls came down and stayed with these guys in their rooms and there may or may not have been some intention to marry."

Confirmation of what she said leaps glaringly to the eye when one reads *Fatal Vision,* the horrifying and tragic story of Jeffrey MacDonald, '65, the Green Beret physician who was convicted of murdering his pregnant wife and two young daughters. Through the book runs a tape of recollections MacDonald cut for author Joe McGinnis in which he gives this glimpse of Princeton weekends—at least MacDonald style—not so long before Robin Herman's time. The Witherspoon Hall to which he refers is a towering Victorian horror in which I once occupied the same room that Woodrow Wilson had lived in and from which women were then banned, except for a few daylight hours on weekends, under risk of expulsion. In MacDonald's voice is heard not only the trumpet of the sexual revolution but the crashing symbols of the disrespect Robin Herman detected:

> In the fall, Penny came down to Princeton for two weekends, but it became clear that something was missing in the relationship. Penny seemed out of place at Princeton. I know that—I don't mean to sound snobby, it's just that things didn't fit. She seemed ill at ease, she was a little uncomfortable with my friends. . . . She seemed to come from working class Patchogue [Long Island] and not to be changing at all. And the fact that she was studying to be a dental technician—it just seemed like such a different world. . . .
>
> We did make love. We made love endlessly. I remember one weekend when she arrived we had a particularly tumultuous episode on the, ah, on my bed in my little room up on the fifth floor of Witherspoon Hall. And, as a matter of fact, Penny came down for weekends, I believe, all the way into the spring of that year.

Though admittedly falling in love at that time with a Skidmore girl named Colette, whom he was eventually convicted of killing, MacDonald goes on: "With Penny, though we made love extremely vigorously and openly and passionately many, many times, sometimes in succession—we had the strength and vigor of incredibly sexed seventeen-year-olds—there just wasn't any of the mental meeting of the minds that Colette and I always had."

Even in the meeting of minds the early Princeton women had problems. In Robin Herman's recollection: "I found that the private school boys who had never been to a school that was coed had a difficult time relating to women on a day-to-day basis as friends. It was just an unusual thing for them. I could tell whether somebody had gone to public school or not by a certain ease of discussion and relationships, where a woman was not made aware of the fact that she was a woman, where you could sit down and talk about something without having that thing sort of hanging there between you." Not knowing quite what to do with women could take a fairly serious turn, as it did with Robin Herman when she became the first woman to join the editorial staff of the *Daily Princetonian* in 1969.

"It was the practice for each *'Prince'* reporter to have a news beat and sports beat. When I'd completed my term as a candidate and went to the bulletin board to see my assignments under news, it said I was to cover the faculty and for sports it was blank," she recalls. "Everybody else, all the men, had a sport. I turned to the sports editor and said, 'Why didn't you give me an assignment?' I remember him still. He had his feet up on the table and had all this wild hair and he said, 'Well, we didn't think you'd want to cover one.' And I said, 'Why should I do half the work of everybody else?' He saw the logic of that and so he said, 'What do you think you can cover?' I remember thinking during that instant that I'd better suggest a sport nobody else would want to cover or maybe he wouldn't assign it. Mind you, I wasn't that interested in sports; I just wanted to do what everybody else was doing. So I suggested rugby because I knew that was early Saturday morning—ten o'clock I think the games were—and also I'd gone out with a couple of rugby players, so I knew the songs at least if I didn't know the game. So he gave me rugby. It's funny in retrospect because it's about the most brutal team sport with macho laid over it."

Robin Herman went from rugby to squash to men's tennis to women's tennis to field hockey to swimming. Finally, in her sophomore year, she got a crack at football. "It was a pretty big deal," she says, "and I remember going to the Yale game and walking up the steep steps to the press box, and some old guy said, 'Good thing you didn't come last year, because we didn't let women in then.' Here it was—a press box, not a locker room—at a public football game. I kept thinking it *was* good I hadn't come last year or I would have had the urge to punch somebody."

She could easily have yielded to that urge. Darkly handsome, direct in manner, she is admittedly "sort of aggressive. My girl friend and I in high school were the first two girls to wear pants to school instead of skirts. It was a cold winter day, and she called me in the morning, and we decided enough was enough. We weren't going to wear little skirts with high socks and have our knees get cold. So we wore slacks—not blue jeans even." Robin

Herman thinks her aggressive spirit was shared by her female classmates. "Even to have applied to Princeton, not knowing whether we'd be admitted, not having been recruited and given only the slimmest encouragement, said something about us," she argues. "Most of the other women had the same orientation."

Susan Nugent, a softer personality who is given to quick laughter, apparently never equated going to Princeton with aggression. "I loved it from the moment I came," she says. "I never had any trouble here. There were positive aspects to being so visible and that's been confirmed a lot. I came back in 1979, and I found in advising freshmen that the typical problem they now have, which we didn't have then, is a sense of being lost. So many of the kids who come lose their self-confidence because they were brilliant where they were and come here and are average or below average. They disappear in the crowd. But for our group it was impossible to disappear."

Professor Nugent's feelings are almost identical to those of another professor, Dr. Nancy Joan Weiss, professor of history and master of Mathey College, who experienced the other side of feminizing Princeton. With female students it was necessary to have female faculty, and Dr. Weiss was brought to Princeton in that same fall of 1969 directly from Harvard, where she earned her Ph.D. "That year there were only three women in the professorial ranks," she says, "and my students were kind of intrigued by the phenomenon. They'd do funny things like pull out my chair when I came to class, and some of them even brought me apples during my office hours. They would say things like, 'You teach from a female point of view,' but when I asked a student what he meant by that he couldn't explain it. I would be invited to a club for dinner—I was only twenty-five then—and there'd be conversation about women faculty and what was it like to have one as a teacher, and the student who brought me would be embarrassed because the others didn't realize that there was one right there. But they got over that quickly.

"In terms of faculty, they were as curious as the students. I always regarded that as a big advantage. Colleagues would invite me to lunch or to dinner, but I found that the common pattern for new male assistants was to feel ignored. Because people were so curious about the beast, I felt a very welcoming atmosphere—to walk into a faculty meeting and have the university's president know you immediately by name is not a usual experience for a new assistant professor. There was also a lot of interest in having one of us women participate in all sorts of things. I always regarded that as much more of an opportunity than an imposition. I figured I'd get a lot of interesting things to do and learn more."

By the second year, with more women coming on campus, the university got its act together—that is, restructured the sanitary facilities—and broke the goldfish bowl. Women were scattered around in entryways of the various dormitories, thus giving rise to CAP's fears about "cohabitation." But it wouldn't be until 1974, when the university instituted a totally open admission policy under which applicants would be chosen on their merits regardless of sex, that the male-female ratio began to even up. As late as 1979, Emily Buchanan, '81, could write this report for the *Princeton Alumni Weekly:*

On a hot and starry night in 1977, I took a long walk with a woman who had been at Princeton for a year. I was anxious to find out as much as I could; in less than a month I, too, would become a Princeton student. . . . I asked her, "Doesn't it ever bother you, having all those males around?"

"No," she said.

"But isn't the ratio something like three to one?" I pressed.

"Yes," she affirmed, "but I figure that out of every three males, one is a nerd who spends his life in the library, and one is in love with a girl back home . . . and that leaves one for each of us."

Nevertheless, I spent Freshman Week cowering, inevitably finding myself—in one line or another—standing behind, in front of, or between two or three male students. It was only when I took a job serving beer at the Pub that I believed myself to be rid of my feminine self-consciousness. The first night I worked, a male junior danced on a table, stripped down, and threw his underwear onto the balcony, and I did not even blush. There were several other women in the Pub that night, equally unperturbed by this somewhat unusual display, and our presence did not inhibit the dancer in the least; after all, we'd been around for quite a while.

By now women have been around quite a while longer and the ratio has reached a fairly livable 1.8 to 1. Arriving female fresh-men who were only four years old when the great event took place don't even know that Princeton wasn't always coed until they start hearing the legends. Robin Herman, a free-lance writer who later settled in Princeton with her husband (she still uses her maiden name), was startled in the fall of 1983 when one of the female seniors said to her: "Oh, when I was growing up, I always wanted to go to Princeton." Dr. Weiss, whose position as master of a college brings her into close and constant contact with under-graduates, says: "I think for most women students this is now the most normal kind of place in the world."

As a result social life has settled down into a pattern much like any other coed school. The importing of women has dropped to a trickle, and weekends are more likely to be spent in fun and games at the eating clubs on Prospect Street just off the central campus than in junkets to other colleges or the fleshpots of New York. Inter-Princeton marriages began with the first graduating class with women, and are on the increase, though nobody has bothered to count them. This is not to say that the situation is without strain, attributable to the classic pangs of late adoles-cence and the still unbalanced male-female ratio. Although one handsome male sophomore claimed he wouldn't know there weren't as many women as men on campus without reading the statistics, the fact is that freshmen and sophomore males can have a thin time of it as upperclassmen date younger women.

Indeed, the problems Dr. Geller faces have taken an interest-ing twist: "At first the women had a good deal of trouble. Many of them had not been popular in high school, and now they'd have seven or eight guys interested in them. They were overwhelmed by it, and they'd come for help. But as the women grew in population, it became clearer that there would be guys who would get the girls and guys who wouldn't. It was a new kind of competi-tion that hadn't existed in an all-male Princeton. Perhaps it was there, but failure could be masked by having 'a girl back home.' "

It isn't this phase of relationships between the sexes that continues to disturb CAP and other conservative Princeton watchers. They pounce on every shred of evidence that there is free and easy physical contact, whether the fact that official advice on contraception is made available to female students or an unofficial estimate Susan Williams, '74, made in a *Princeton Alumni Weekly* column: that 30 percent of Princeton girls live with Princeton boys. In a 1973 issue of the conservative *National Review*, William F. Buckley, Jr., a Yale graduate, cleverly put the above two facts together to give Princeton a double sting. Perhaps feeling its way then, the university had made an unfortunate mistake by authorizing distribution of a birth control handbook that also contained an introduction advocating Maoism. After citing Williams, Buckley wrote: "So why don't Princeton Maoists begin their revolution by cleaning up sexual immorality at Princeton?"

But the critics of coeducation are, as discovered, simply whistling in the wind. Like a chorus in unison, everybody—chaplains, doctors, administrators, trustees, teachers, students—chant: "Coeducation is a good thing." Dr. Geller: "Overall, the place is healthier—a more interesting place and a more complex society." The dean of the chapel, Frederick H. Borsch, '57: "The admittance of women opened floodgates to more sensibility, if you will." President William G. Bowen: "The women among us have now added their gifts of fallibility to our own, and I think we are a far better university—and a far richer community of people—for them."

In the minds of today's students Princeton is, above all, a dead-serious educational enterprise, and the feminine enrichment most prized is in the province of the mind. Nearly everybody talks about the input and fresh point of view women bring to Princeton's small classes, now that they are enrolled in large enough numbers to have the courage to talk. Rather fittingly, since he recently retired as a lecturer in drama, William McCleery furnished the most dramatic examples of the changing dynamics that women bring to class. McCleery, also a playwright, would often seek from his students criticism of his plays in progress, and would often get more than he was looking for.

"My basic theme is the new woman and the old man. I was always writing plays with female leads, and I would think that I'd given the woman the principal role," he recalls. "Well, I read one of these to my class one day, and one of my girls said: 'Yes, but you gave the man all the funny lines.' In a comedy, never mind whether you're preaching women's liberation or what, if you give the man the funny lines, he wins. It was fascinating. This was a gut thing with her that I hadn't realized. She was right. I learned the meaning of consciousness raising. It's not just an empty cliché.

"And then I remember I had a wild, prolific male student. No student in those days would think of writing a play that didn't have a four-letter word on every page. This particular fellow was full of them, and he was reading along and he stopped and turned to this girl, and said: 'Am I shocking you?' She said: 'No, are you trying to?' A nice putdown."

Not only the dynamics but the contents of classes are changing, although Princeton women are still somewhat impatient. "If you look at the curriculum—and this isn't confined to Princeton —it has been slow to change to the reality that the world is made up of experiences of women as well as of men," says Dr. Weiss. "We did succeed two years ago in instituting a program of women's studies, and that's making an important difference. We have encouraged a number of departments to establish courses in the issues of gender or to think about the way they teach existing courses to take cognizance of the fact that the world is made up of women as well as men; that there are texts written by women worth looking at and that there are problems raised when one thinks about gender that reshape the way we conceptualize issues in the various disciplines. In some departments we've made real headway; in others less. You have students, for example, who look at a reading list and say: 'Didn't any woman ever write a good short story?' Or tell a faculty member that they want to write a paper on an issue relating to gender and are told: 'Oh, I don't think that's worth writing about.' I don't know how many such experiences there are quantitatively, but when there are some, if there's a group of students who have particular sensitivity to these issues, they expand sometimes out of proportion and say to those students that this place doesn't take adequate regard for the kinds of issues that are really important to us."

The people with particular sensitivity to gender issues may well be the ones who hole up in something called the Women's Center, which is significantly lodged just off campus in a fortress-like structure called Burr Hall. The center tries to keep alive such issues as sexual harassment, but the evidence that feminism is not rife on the Princeton campus comes from a recent student poll that showed only 17 percent of undergraduate women had ever attended an event at the Women's Center. Indeed, there is a widespread belief that Princeton's current women students are showing more interest in traditional love and marriage than their career-minded forerunners.

Whether true or not, a vivid picture of today's Princeton woman comes from a vivacious sophomore from the Chicago area named Valentina Vavasis: "The girls here are just as girlish as anyone their age in the country, but they are also so intelligent and so ambitious and so competent. I was impressed with the girls because I'd never known anything quite like it. When people talk about their lives after college, it seems to me that the Princeton men are very interested in getting married and having families— much more than the guys I know at home. But the girls here, they never, ever talk . . . Like, you ask them what they'll be doing and they might mention that they'll be married, but to the girls here, and to me, too, marriage is something you do after twenty-five."

Whatever may be happening to the curriculum, the presence of women at Princeton has given rise to an unofficial study that has almost reached the level of sport—an analysis of what is going on between men and women. In the fall of 1983 the *Weekly Nassau* conducted a poll on the general subject that included the provocative question, put to both men and women: "What do you feel are the advantages of being a woman?" The answers were equally provocative.

From men: "They can have multiple orgasms. . . . With the reverse of discrimination, women are likely to receive opportunities because employers do not want to seem sexist. . . . Women also have the advantage of making themselves look pretty by the use of makeup and such. If you're a guy you have no choice but to comb your hair. If the guy's ugly, he's ugly."

From women: "I just love being a woman. I see my opportunities as infinite—career, maternity. . . . Women may cry without being looked upon as weak. . . . I thought about this for half an hour and I can't think of any inherent advantages of being a woman."

This last statement as well as the rest of the survey, indicates that the apparently independent and spirited young Princeton woman still has image problems. Women often described themselves in relation to men—"I don't have to wear a tie"—and only 53 percent of them said that their role models were most often women. Interestingly, *no* man selected a woman as a role model. Forty-three percent of the women said that their sex was a hindrance to them, while only 5 percent of the men took the same position. Among the hindrances: sexual harassment. Some 27 percent of Princeton women felt that they had been sexually harassed (compared to 34 percent in a recent Harvard survey), but a compelling difference between the male and female view of the world emerged in a subquestion: 48 percent of the females considered "verbal remarks, whistles, jeers" as harassment, compared to only 32 percent of the males; 67 percent of the females rated obscene phone calls as harassment, compared to 57 percent of the males.

However Princeton women view themselves, a Princeton man, George Borden, writing for the *Daily Princetonian* about the same time the *Weekly Nassau*'s survey was published, must have given them some heart. He said, in part:

Men come to Princeton accustomed to being the big fish in the pond, and to having the little fish gather around them deferentially. For too many of these people, women have always been small fish. Confronted for the first time at Princeton with women who are independent and successful in their own right, who do not coo and pander, they conclude that there is something wrong with these women. These chicks just ain't like them good ol' girls at home, they think. They miss the cooing and pandering.

Yes, it's true that Princeton women are more intellectual and ambitious than many women elsewhere, that they have goals and opinions of their own, that they want to be respected. But this is missing the point. Princeton *men* are also more competitive and ambitious than most *men* elsewhere. It is unfair to judge Princeton women only against women in other places—as if all of them had to hew to some great social standard which applies only to women, regardless of setting, background and native intelligence—and not against Princeton men. Because when it comes right down to it, Princeton men and Princeton women are remarkably similar. They are successful, competitive, ambitious, intelligent people. If Princeton men see only competitiveness and ambition in Princeton women, it is because women remind them that they possess the very same unseemly qualities.

"Princeton men and Princeton women are remarkably similar." I wandered down to the playing fields one afternoon to watch the women's soccer team in action, and even before I could see them, the sounds I heard—cries, in the treble to be sure, of "Go, Tiger, go. . . . Get in there, Tiger . . ." amid the thudding of bodies in contact—were so like what I had experienced in my all-male Princeton days as to be almost shocking. Fiercely competitive these girls indeed were, and they beat George Washington in the final seconds, 3–1, in a pouring rain. They weren't women who worried about their hair, shredded and pasted to their heads by falling water, and I could appreciate Dean Borsch's comment: "Instead of seeing someone who comes in primped up for a weekend, Princeton men are seeing someone in class or with their hair down in grungy clothes or maybe playing field hockey. You're talking then about a human being versus somebody brought in here to socialize, with sexual possibilities."

In truth, the athletic drive of Princeton women has come as somewhat of a surprise to the "pioneers." Dr. Nugent says: "When I came back I was struck by how similar the female undergraduates are to the male in all their interests. One aspect that especially struck me, which I think is something of a national trend, was the athletic aspect. A lot of my female students are very interested, active athletes, which is fairly typical of any

Princeton undergraduate. I think in my class they had probably gone for the academic record on admissions, and there weren't all the facilities."

A question was put to Dr. Weiss, who had done her undergraduate work at all-female Smith: "Wasn't it difficult for women at Princeton, because of male traditions and competition, to get the experience of real success that they could at a woman's college?" Her answer was a lilting litany of female triumph—and only a little downbeat at the end: "If you look now at the campus, you see that the chairman of the Undergraduate Student Government is a woman, the chairman of the Undergraduate Life Committee is a woman; the valedictorian and salutatorian of last year's [1983] graduating class were women; there have been women editors of the *Prince*, there are women in everything from the Triangle [a dramatic group] to sports teams to whatever. Do women take full advantage of activities here and rise to the top? Yes. Is it easier here to rise to the top? No, because all of the positions aren't reserved for women. Thirty-eight percent of the chairmen of the *Prince* have not been women; 38 percent of the chairmen of the USG have not been women, nor 38 percent of the class presidents. Are we yet to the point where women are represented in top jobs in student activities in proportion to their representation on campus? No. In that sense, we have some distance to go."

That Princeton women will eventually go this distance can hardly be doubted. The strongest evidence that Princeton women are similar to Princeton men came in 1983 when Robin Herman and her classmate Sharon Naeole completed a survey of those pioneers of the class of 1973 ten years later. "At first we looked at the results and thought that they were boring because the results said that the women had done almost exactly what the men had done, and felt the same way about it," she said. "We said, 'Oh, look at this: it's all the same.' But then we said, 'The same—oh, my God, that's incredible!' The women had become true Princetonians."

There was one difference. Although both men and women had entered roughly the same professions—banking, teaching, law, medicine, business, advertising—the median salary for Princeton women was $33,000 and for men nearly $46,000. At that, Princeton women came in 85 percent above the national average for women college graduates; the men were only 63 percent above the average. Since both men and women rated their compensation and opportunities for advancement as equal to that of coworkers of the opposite sex, Robin Herman explained away this discrepancy in income in a report to the *Princeton Alumni Weekly* by the fact that family duties—about 33 percent of the women had borne children and 38 percent had moved domiciles to accommodate a husband's career—had interrupted the women's climb up the career ladder. The extent to which these women are career minded is underlined by one statistic—only six of the mothers were full-time homemakers—and a rather sad letter from one of them: "Somewhat shameful for having let the group down, I avoided our tenth reunion. It was my way of bowing out gracefully."

The women were almost unanimously grateful for their experience at Princeton (86 percent of them *liked* being pioneers), because they are so obviously pioneering in life too. Sixty-three percent do work that was "traditionally male," and 43 percent are the first of their sex to hold their present responsible positions. They aren't finding it easy to get the necessary respect. "The men are 'Professor' this and 'Doctor' that, but the secretaries call me by my first name," complained a female educator; and Hava Lynn Pell, who became one of the country's few female rabbis, wrote: "Some people cannot listen to a woman in authority, especially when they believe God is an old man."

The biggest problem Princeton women face is a problem they share with women everywhere—trying to be Superwoman by combining motherhood and career. Any number of them referred to the struggle, but Laurie Watson Raymond, a psychiatric resident at Massachusetts General Hospital, spelled it out. Although she has worked out a way of leaving her four-year-old daughter in a nursery school or with a couple who rents rooms from the Raymonds, she says: "It is hard. I really do get tired out. And in psychiatry, as part of the training, I'm also undergoing analysis, and that takes up a lot of emotional energy. The thing I would like is less conflict between being at home with my child and being at work and feeling responsibility for my patients. I love both aspects of my life, but sometimes it's hard to integrate."

In another way, of which even CAP might approve, Princeton women are similar to Princeton men. They not only give generously to the old school but volunteer to take positions of responsibility in alumni affairs, including positions on the august Board of Trustees. "I give more to Princeton than my husband gives to Harvard," Robin Herman confided. Now that is a form of fire nobody ever had in mind in the good old Princeton days.

# Chapter Three

# FROM WITHERSPOON TO WU

Some thirty years ago a young Chinese man from Hong Kong, new to the country, new to the campus, wandered around Princeton University trying to get his bearings. He took note of the names of the buildings—Pyne, Blair, Edwards, Firestone, Cuyler, Dod, McCosh, Witherspoon. As a Confucian, a circumstance that would later serve him well, he was probably unaware of the solid Presbyterian ring to those names. What did impress him, however, was that those buildings memorialized in an enduring fashion men who had somehow served Princeton, either with their lives or their money. It did not take long before Gordon Y. S. Wu developed an ambition to someday be part of that pantheon.

The sentiment of a foreigner who says he was made to feel welcome in the Princeton community may have had something to do with Wu's determination. He likes to recall with a smile, for instance, the sympathy that the then very Scotch Presbyterian dean of the chapel showed for his faith. In those days attendance at chapel, or at another religious service of one's choice, was compulsory for underclassmen; but young Wu, with a 7:30 A.M. class every morning of the week, wanted to sleep late on Sundays. Thus, with motives not entirely religious, Wu went to Dean Ernest Gordon, explained that he had been reared as a disciple of Confucius and would prefer to attend Confucian lectures. "I had checked and there was nothing like that within fifty miles of Princeton," he told *Princeton Alumni Weekly* writer Leslie Aldridge Westoff. "I won my argument. I got out of chapel, and I could sleep as late as I wanted."

It is hard not to like a place where one can find such tolerance. But the real understanding was on Wu's side. Evidently gifted with the innate shrewdness that later made him a business success, Wu was aware as an undergraduate of the economics of operating a private institution on Princeton's scale. "I wasn't on financial aid, but my tuition was only $850. I looked around and noticed there were only thirteen students in my civil engineering class: not enough to pay for one professor," he says. "I knew then that I was a taker, not a giver."

It took a while for Gordon Wu to turn the tables, but when he did he put himself into the same league with the Rockefellers and Firestones, the Pynes and Palmers. A few years ago, with his business—Hopewell Holdings, a high-rise construction firm now branching out to build mainland China's first turnpike, from Hong Kong to Canton—well in hand, Wu put up $1 million to endow the Gordon Wu Professorship in Chinese Studies. Then, to mark his twenty-fifth reunion in 1983, he gave the sum of twenty-five million Hong Kong dollars (about $4 million) for the construction of a brand new building, Wu Hall.

Whether from deliberate intention or happy accident, Wu Hall, both in name and design, is a fitting symbol of what is emerging as a brand new Princeton. Wu Hall serves as the core —dining facility, library, offices, mail drop—for one of the residential colleges that have recently begun housing all freshmen and sophomores and that will transform undergraduate social life, which has been in a state of ferment for more than a century.

With Wu's blessing, architect Robert Venturi, '47, eschewed the prevalent collegiate Gothic look and created a functional, brick-and-glass contemporary building. Its large bay windows and decorative touches echo English country houses and thus harmonize with the surrounding Gothic; but what may be its most arresting decoration is the group of Chinese characters near the door that bear Wu's name and almost shout the tidings that today's Princeton is no longer an exclusive enclave for WASPs or, for that matter, even Americans.

Wu Hall was erected in the middle of a group of dormitories on the southeast corner of the campus next to the playing fields. They are mostly named for the classes that provided funds for their building, and are now known as the New New Quad. The college Wu Hall serves is called Butler in consequence of the gift of the late Lee D. Butler, '22, and uses all or part of seven dormitories to house its five hundred members. At the farthest possible remove, on the northwest corner, are two other new colleges—Rockefeller (John D. Rockefeller III, '29) and Mathey (Dean Mathey, '12). Using, as does Butler, the existing dormitories, these colleges have their central facilities in the remodeled Gothic Commons along Nassau Street and University Place, which for long served as the principal dining facility of all freshmen and sophomores. Rockefeller and Mathey colleges are storybook Princeton with pointed arches, ivied stone walls, casement windows, and turreted towers. Even Witherspoon, a huge Victorian mass that looks as if it had been built with a child's set of blocks and is now part of Rockefeller College, has been in place so long that it seems to belong. The other two colleges—Wilson, next to Butler, and Forbes (formerly Princeton Inn College), across the railroad tracks from the campus to the west—were started in the late 1960s in an effort to manage a student body swollen by the admission of women and, it would now seem, in a spirit of cautious experimentation with contemporary living arrangements.

Whether because of Princeton's prominence as a pace-setting educational institution that predates the Republic, or whether because of the social and political eminence of individual Princetonians in later life, the undergraduate social system has received

an inordinate amount of public attention. This is surprising because, unlike fraternities and sororities, which provide the clichéd
version of American "college life" and which were officially
banned from Princeton in 1855, the upperclass eating clubs that
are an integral part of Princeton's system are unique and have
never been imitated. Perhaps they are unusual *because* they are
upperclass in the general rather than technical sense of the word.
For much of this century at least, the popular vision of a Princetonian was that of a wealthy young man dressed in blazer and
white flannels, lolling on the pillared porch of an outsize southern
plantation mansion. At one time the description was not wholly
inaccurate. There *is* such a clubhouse on Princeton's Prospect
Street (or Avenue, as it is officially designated) across Washington
Road on the east side of the campus, and there are fifteen other
equally elegant structures nearby in a profusion of styles, from
timbered Tudor to brick Georgian. It was the existence of these
clubs, unimaginably more luxurious than any but the richest
homes in the land, that caused Princeton to be called a "country
club," with all the connotations of that label in an era when golf,
too, was distinctly an uppercrust pursuit for such multimil-
lionaires as John D. Rockefeller and Andrew Carnegie.

How the clubs came into being in the first place had very little
to do with intimations of glamorous living. It was more a matter
of survival. In the late eighteenth and early nineteenth centuries
feeding students was a problem with which residential colleges
such as Princeton either couldn't or wouldn't cope satisfactorily.
In *The American College and University,* Frederick Rudolph tells
of a Harvard student who wrote in his diary in 1822, "Goose for
dinner—said to have migrated to this country with our ances-
tors," and relates how students at South Carolina College in 1811
seized an old bull intended to be slaughtered for their commons
and drove it into the river, where it drowned. At Princeton,
according to *A Princeton Companion,* students launched an
unusual protest against refectory food in the 1840s: "At a given
signal, up would go the windows and out would fly the tablecloths
and all that was on them." Unable to find a solution to the feeding
problem, Princeton first permitted, then forced students to eat in
boardinghouses around town, which later became informal clubs.

That they weren't much of a gustatory improvement and were far from elegant can be judged from some of the names—"Hollow Inn," "Numquam Plenus" (Never Full), and "More."

These "clubs" were temporary affairs, mostly for the convenience of undergraduates, until in 1879 a group of congenial upperclassmen organized Ivy Club and eventually received permission to incorporate and build on Prospect Street. Others followed quickly, and it became a convenience and financial saving to the university, which, when it decided to return to the feeding business, limited its efforts to a commons for freshmen and sophomores. The legal status of the clubs was thus private, with financial support coming from student food fees and alumni contributions, and the university's authority over their operations was limited. People who didn't join clubs—a large majority—could still seek solace in town; it was a fairly equable arrangement until the early 1900s, when there were enough clubs to choose from that only a small minority of upperclassmen were left to fend for themselves.

It is not hard to comprehend how and why clubs soon became a form of social selection at Princeton. Starting with Ivy (still the most prestigious club) at the top, the clubs formed a social hierarchy almost in the order of their founding—Cottage, Tiger, Cap and Gown, and so on, on a descending scale. The selection of members from second-year classes had to be formalized, and some malign genius invented what came to be called "bicker week," during which sophomores desiring to join clubs would sit in their rooms, sometimes in groups, sometimes alone, while upperclass members of the various clubs would call and look them over as prospective companions. After this ordeal was over, those sophomores held to be "clubable" would receive bids. An unfortunate few, including most Jewish students prior to World War II, received no bids at all; and many prospects didn't get bids to the club of their choice. It is not difficult to imagine the anguish this system caused for a significant number of Princetonians for many years.

A poet laureate of the clubs, as of everything else Princetonian in his day, was F. Scott Fitzgerald, '17. In his thinly disguised autobiographical first novel, *This Side of Paradise*, Fitz-

gerald made the Princeton club system part of the mental furniture of most literate Americans. Here is his lyric characterization
of the clubs: "Ivy, detached and breathlessly aristocratic; Cottage, an impressive melange of brilliant adventurers and well-
dressed philanderers; Tiger Inn, broad-shouldered and athletic,
vitalized by an honest elaboration of the prep school standards;
Cap and Gown, anti-alcoholic, faintly religious and politically
powerful; flamboyant Colonial; literary Quadrangle; and the
dozen others varying in age and position." And here is his picture
of "bicker" through the eyes of his hero, Amory Blaine:

Amory by way of the *Princetonian* had arrived. The minor snobs,
finely balanced thermometers of success, warmed to him as the
club elections drew nigh, and he and Tom were visited by groups
of upperclassmen who arrived awkwardly, balanced on the edge
of the furniture and talked of all subjects except the one of absorb-
ing interest. Amory was amused at the intent eyes upon him, and,
in case the visitors represented some club in which he was not
interested, took great pleasure in shocking them with unorthodox
remarks.

"Oh, let me see—" he said one night to a flabbergasted delega-
tion, "what club do you represent?"

With visitors from Ivy and Cottage and Tiger Inn he played
the "nice, unspoilt, ingenuous boy" very much at ease and quite
unaware of the object of the call.

When the fatal morning arrived, early in March, and the
campus became a document in hysteria, he slid smoothly into
Cottage with Alex Connage and watched his suddenly neurotic
class with much wonder.

There were fickle groups that jumped from club to club; there
were friends of two or three days who announced tearfully and
wildly that they must join the same club, nothing should separate
them; there were snarling disclosures of long-hidden grudges as the
Suddenly Prominent remembered snubs of freshman year. Unknown men were elevated into importance when they received
certain coveted bids; others who were considered "all set" found
that they had made unexpected enemies, felt themselves stranded
and deserted, talked wildly of leaving college.

In his own crowd Amory saw men kept out for wearing green
hats, for being "a damn tailor's dummy," for having "too much
pull in heaven," for getting drunk one night "not like a gentleman,

by God," or for unfathomable secret reasons known to no one but the wielders of the black balls.

Although the changes in the social atmosphere of Princeton have been nothing short of sensational in the more than sixty years since Fitzgerald wrote his novel, the echo of the novelist's evocation in Paul Chamberlain's front-page story from the *Daily Princetonian* of September 29, 1983, is almost eerie:

> Andrew '85 was numbed by the reality before him. Perched on the Ivy Club's staircase Saturday night, he watched below as four new members—successful candidates in last week's Fall Bicker—downed the initiation drink with religious zeal.
>
> "I would have done anything to drink that, and I hate both oysters and vodka," he said with a frustrated look.
>
> Andrew couldn't understand why, but he had been denied an Ivy bid for a second time. It hurt. His eyes were cast downward, and he shook his head in disbelief. . . .
>
> Post-bicker depression, while not among the entries in any standard medical handbook, afflicts a good number of students at Princeton. Candidates seeking selective club membership place themselves at the mercy of their interviewer's whims, and many consider it to be a very personal statement when they're denied a bid. . . .
>
> "Maybe I shouldn't read too much into this whole episode, but I can't stop myself," said David '85, a two-time bickeree at Cottage Club.
>
> "I feel abused, and it's hard to stop my mind from dwelling on what's so repulsive about me that some people wouldn't want to eat dinner with me," he said.

It is a good question, one that has been at the bottom of almost ceaseless turmoil about the clubs. Social selection at Princeton is a deeper mystery, if not a more significant one, than at other schools because *all* Princeton students have already passed through a narrow gate defined by evidence of academic achievement and "personality" that would not admit the vast majority of their peers. That preferred bids have tended to go to winners either on the athletic field or, as with Fitzgerald's hero, in other admired activities is easily understandable; any group of people wants to have winners among them. But, until recently at least, there were many factors at Princeton over which the individual had no control. One was economic, since some clubs cost more than others, and all clubs cost more than alternative eating arrangements. Another was the "legacy." With Princeton's student body tending strongly toward a generational drift of son following father following grandfather, clubs out of need often felt obliged to accept the progeny of their own alumni givers whether they were, in today's parlance, "nerds" or not. Closely related to this specific legacy was a vaguer one: young men from preparatory schools tended to cling together and follow their forerunners into clubs—St. Paul's to Ivy, for instance. All in all, there was a distinct implication in the selective process that some people are simply "born better" than others.

It is a notion as old as mankind and still certified to some extent by what passes for royalty in other parts of the world. But it is officially, at least, anathema in democratic America, and many a sensitive Princetonian has tried to change or abolish the club system, usually on egalitarian grounds. Ironically, reformers have often sprung from the very high-born class that might be expected most to enjoy club privileges. One was Richard F. Cleveland, '19, son of President Grover Cleveland, who persuaded ninety sophomores to pledge that they would continue eating in Commons rather than join clubs, but the Cleveland revolt was buried in the greater concerns of World War I. Nearly every decade since there has been some similar undergraduate revolt, many of which have been led by favored "winners." One was Paul Spyros Sarbanes, '54, now senator from Maryland, who was a varsity basketball player, Phi Beta Kappa, winner of a Rhodes Scholarship, and a member of Cannon Club. Looking back twenty-five years after graduation, he cited his greatest growth experience at Princeton as this: "The fight I got into trying to get the clubs to take one hundred percent of those sophomores who wanted entrance was important, something I felt very strongly about and got very much into." But by far the most resounding battle fought over the clubs took place long before Senator Sarbanes's foray. It was waged—and lost—by none other than the president of Princeton, Woodrow Wilson, and it was one of the factors that eventually caused him to be elected president of the United States.

When Wilson took office in 1902 the clubs were becoming such an important part of undergraduate life that the university was, in his words, "only an artistic setting and background for life on Prospect Avenue." Bicker week was described in those days as an "annual frenzy" and "a blight destroying sleep and friendships." What was even worse, a violation of all agreements that club selection would be limited to that one week was that sophomores and then freshmen were forming shadow clubs as feeders to the real thing on Prospect Street; some young men were even being proselytized in the more famous prep schools. Traditionally, about a quarter of the class was left out of the selection process. Since the clubs were off campus and divorced from official connection with the university, Wilson saw all this as a case of the "side show running the circus," and in 1907 his answer to the problem was to come up with something known as the Quad Plan.

His idea was to split the student body into quadrangles where they would take their meals, enjoy recreational facilities, and, above all, be exposed to resident faculty members. Wilson suggested that the existing clubs become part of his prospective quadrangles. His aim, he said, was educational—to stimulate interaction between members of all the classes and between students and faculty. Important alumni, many of whom were trustees and loyal to their clubs, vigorously opposed the plan. The university's chief fund raiser reported that he had not been able to collect $300 since the plan was proposed; other alumni expressed shock at what they perceived as a "democratizing" effect on the school. Typical was an alumni committee of Ivy Club, which, after pointing out that Princeton freshmen often came from prep schools where groups of boys were formed by "natural selection," went on to say: "The work that Princeton should do for our country cannot be fully accomplished unless she attracts all grades of boys, including the wealthier and more socially desirable boys." But, as Wilson biographer Henry Wilkinson Bragdon says: "The attitude was put in a nutshell remark attributed to a

Philadelphia matron: 'No one is going to make my boy eat with muckers.' "

Nobody did. Wilson's position was complicated by the fact that he was also waging a battle with such powerful trustees as ex-President Grover Cleveland over the location of a proposed new graduate college, and his Quad Plan was voted down by the board. As would be the case later with the League of Nations, the longer Wilson fought for his Quad Plan, the more convinced he became that he was right, that his idea was Princeton's salvation. He viewed the people who opposed him as stupid or selfishly motivated, and he lost many friends by airing his strong feelings. Outside the university's inner circle Wilson was viewed as a courageous champion of the undergraduates who were left out of the clubs, as a proponent of the people against the privileged; thus the seeds of a political career that was to flower only a few years later were planted. Ironically, Wilson proved as farsighted in advocating the Quad Plan as he had in pushing for the League. Just as the United Nations finally came into being, a version of the Quad Plan—the new residential colleges—is now a functioning reality.

If it took inspiration from history, the present Princeton administration quite evidently learned a lesson from it, too. What Wilson envisaged was a complete revolution; what is now happening is, to some, more like creeping socialism. One could say that earlier administration decisions such as the recruitment of minorities; the admission of women, leading to an increase of the student body from 3200 to 4400; and the establishment of experimental Wilson and Princeton Inn colleges forced upon the university a major revamping of the system rather than the other way around. Moreover, in the radical social atmosphere of the late 1960s the clubs suffered other reverses. Several went under financially, were taken over by the university and combined into a nonselective eating facility called Stevenson Hall (named after Adlai E. Stevenson, class of 1922), which, among other things, has what is reported to be the only kosher dining room in the Ivy League. In the scramble to stay solvent, all but five became nonselective—that is, took members on a more or less first come, first served basis. Only recently clubs that once broke young men's hearts by denying them bids were frantically advertising for members as would night clubs or hotels. (What would Scott Fitzgerald think?) Evidently, then, the situation had changed to the point where any upperclassman who wanted to join *a* club could do so. The problem for the administration to solve rested in the freshmen and sophomore years; in classes of more than a thousand students with little social organization to speak of, people have a tendency to get lost. It was here, in what Churchill might have called the "soft underbelly" of Princeton, that the administration struck.

Except for being limited to the first two undergraduate years, the new plan now in effect is so similar to Wilson's as to be startling. Incoming freshmen are assigned by lot to one of five residential colleges. With sophomores, each college population is about five hundred students, a manageable number and one small enough for students to get to know each other. Wilson would probably spin in his grave with delight if he knew that each college also has a faculty master, live-in faculty members, and up to fifty faculty "fellows" who pledge themselves to drop in regularly for meals and informal fraternizing with students. Each college has its own student council, which looks after social events, intramural sports, and such other activities as, for instance, the *Wu Review,* a Butler College literary magazine. The residential colleges are truly a microcosm of the larger entity that is Princeton University, and there is even a director of studies who acts as dean in each college.

Enthusiasm for the colleges is extremely high—partly stemming from the excitement of something new—but for people who have been around Princeton a while it may be a recovery of something firm and traditional. The student body that Wilson wanted to organize into quads was only a little larger than one undergraduate class today, and even as recently as twelve years ago, when Emory Elliott, professor of English and master of Butler College, arrived at Princeton, there was, he says, "an intimate feel to the place." In Elliott's recollection: "Though the student body had already expanded, the place felt smaller psychologically than today. I lived in apartments just off campus and students would drop by and I'd hold my last classes in the living room. Then the economics changed, and a lot of junior faculty had to live out in Lawrenceville or Kingston. So I think that the reason the college system came into being now is the sense of separation that the freshmen and sophomores began to express, especially the freshmen, that they came to Princeton for its reputation of intimacy and didn't find it. What I think we're achieving in the residential colleges is to reestablish this sense of closeness between students and assistant masters who live in dormitories and the faculty who come to visit."

How close and enduring that intimacy will be is too early to predict. Apart from resident faculty, there was a sprinkling of professors and even their spouses and children throughout the dining room at every meal I enjoyed not long ago at Butler College. For personal reasons I predict success. In my time I was a member of Gateway Club, a university-owned club that was an early experiment in this area; like Cleveland's revolt before an earlier war, it went under in World War II. We not only had a member of the faculty in residence, but other professors who felt free to drop by for lunch or dinner, and among my best memories of Princeton are the stimulating talks with these men. One, named Walter Lincoln Whittlesey, deserves to be briefly memorialized. One of the young preceptors Wilson recruited for Princeton after he successfully restructured the faculty, Whittlesey carried an unusual distinction: he was a tenured professor who held only an A.B. degree; never mind, he was a great teacher. When Wilson was running for president, Whittlesey went out on the stump for him. One day Whittlesey was speaking in a barnyard and a heckler climbed up on a manure pile to see over other heads. "What's Wilson's platform?" he shouted. Whittlesey snapped back: "I'm not sure of his, but I know you're standing on yours." He was just as sharp across a dining table, and the same can be said of many faculty members today.

The Butler students seem uniformly high on their undergraduate experience to date, but few have known any other way of life at Princeton. One exception is a sophomore who dropped out for a year and returned. By comparison, he said, his freshman year was a lonely one; he was tucked away in a dormitory filled with upperclassmen who paid little attention to him. There is occasional criticism that colleges cut off contact with the upperclassmen and curtail campuswide activity. Master Elliott views this as more of an unfounded fear than a real problem. There are some upperclassmen in each college as resident advisers—there are twelve in Butler, for example—and, of course, academic activities are not segregated as to colleges or even classes. Extracurricular activities on a college level are something like a feeder system for the entire university. "For example," says Elliott, "we had a terrific six-man touch football team at Butler last year that beat some of the upperclass clubs, and most of them as sophomores have joined the Princeton lightweight football team, just as our kids who publish the *Wu Review* will want to go on to the *Nassau Lit.*"

Most of the fuss, actually, has been made by blacks in the junior and senior classes. Before there were residential colleges at Princeton, blacks rather naturally tended to stick together and almost made Princeton Inn College their own habitat. Now they are distributed evenly throughout the colleges in what some observers see as a form of forced integration. The black students at Butler, having experienced no other system, seem not to be distressed, at least upon informal observation. So perhaps the administration's hope that this problem will eventually go away by 1985, when the precollege classes leave, is not a vain one.

A Third World Center for minorities thrives on Prospect Street, and minorities are members of most of the clubs as well. There were always blacks in the Prospect Street clubs—whitejacketed and deferential servants to be sure—and it is a heady feeling to walk into one of the clubs now and find white student employees serving black members. Although the clubs with their loud music and drinking parties (ID's required) remain *the* social centers of Princeton life, the democracy Wilson is accused of legislating for Princeton now seems close at hand. As might be expected, it isn't close enough for some Princetonians and altogether too close for others.

A number of years ago a young lady named Sally Frank, class of 1980, filed suit against the university and the three all-male clubs—Ivy, Cottage, and Tiger—on the grounds that she was not able to join them due to sexual discrimination. Perhaps it is just as well that she went on to law school, because her cause has been dragging through state boards and the courts for five years. Thomas H. Wright, '62, Princeton's general counsel and himself a member of Ivy Club, expects it will be another few years before any resolution is reached. Wright argues that the university should not be a part of the suit since the clubs are private; the New Jersey Division on Civil Rights agrees; its opinion was that the clubs were excluded from its jurisdiction. The Appellate Division of the New Jersey Superior Court, to which Ms. Frank brought her case, apparently has mixed feelings. It ordered the Civil Rights Division to hold fact-finding hearings and opined that "the furnishing of meals and food by way of the exchanging of gratuities, if no way else, suggests a nexus which may well constitute a challenge to the claim of the clubs to an individual private status."

While the case drags through the courts, the argument within the Princeton community—whether clubs should exist at all—continues with a familiar threnody. Nowhere is it as well summarized as in this self-explanatory letter to the *Princeton Alumni Weekly* from Dudley E. Woodbridge, '44:

I read with amazement former Dean of Admission James W. Wickenden, Jr., '61's parting shot at the eating clubs implying that admissions had suffered as a result of their presence. I find it difficult to believe that this excuse would be considered at all when it is well known that admissions turns away many hundreds of fully qualified applicants including sons and daughters of alumni. Could it be that the clubs were again being unjustly used as a whipping boy?

Then there appears Congressman James A. Leach '64 addressing the incoming freshmen with the statement: "This university has some faults. After all, we still tolerate the bicker system. We still allow some clubs—including the one I belonged to—to discriminate against women." I find it incredible that Mr. Leach would pick out such a "fault" and feel it was of such significance to be worthy of mention.

Having been involved with the clubs for many years, I find it hard to believe that the university and many of our alumni still make Prospect Street their favorite target. It seems to me that some of those institutions now spanning almost half the life of the university . . . might just have something to offer undergraduates which is good, and just possibly they should be worthy of commendation rather than bad-mouthing. . . . We have nothing of which we should be ashamed except for the bad P.R. . . . The clubs offer a great deal of diversity themselves which, when added to other options available to upperclassmen, provides a great number of opportunities.

It is conceivable, when all is said about the clubs, that both Ms. Frank and Mr. Woodbridge are looking in the wrong direction. While nobody would admit it openly, or for the record, nobody would flatly deny the possibility that new generations of Princeton students will so accept the colleges that they will be reluctant to leave them in their junior year. If that is to be the case, Wilson's grand plan will come to full fruition, and the university will have to take over the clubs, as he proposed, and somehow work them into an extension of the college system. Whether that happens or not, a place with a building called Wu Hall has a very different feeling from a place with only names like Witherspoon, and more in the way of change can easily be anticipated on the anciently ivied campus.

# Chapter Four

# THE VIEW FROM NASSAU HALL

From the windows of his office in Nassau Hall, President William G. Bowen can, on a clear day and figuratively speaking, look north and east right over the tops of the turrets at Yale University in New Haven, Connecticut, and catch a glimpse of the colonial cupolas of Harvard University in Cambridge, Massachusetts. The view was not always as far nor as fair for Princeton presidents. As the last of the three colleges to be founded, Princeton was often left in the dust of its front-running competitors. Whatever Princeton did, Harvard and Yale seemed to do it bigger and better, with the result that Princetonians developed either a resigned sense of inferiority or an unseemly belligerence toward their ancient rivals. Now, after a century or so of running on a different track, Princeton is catching up to Yale and gaining on Harvard.

Athletic metaphors seem appropriate in relation to the competition between educational institutions, since so much of it in the public mind is on the playing fields, particularly the gridiron. So it is not surprising to find Princeton attitudes reflected in specific writings on sports. Not long ago, Frank Deford, Princeton '61, writing in *Sports Illustrated,* sang the inferiority blues: "Whenever anybody refers to Harvard, Yale and Princeton, they always do it in that order. We Princetonians know in our hearts that the rest of the world thinks of us as number three, and that has always provided us with a greater incentive to try to show up the Harvards and Yales between the sideline stripes." The belligerency was acknowledged in the fall of 1983 in a Philadelphia *Inquirer* article about the Harvard-Yale game that became the "quote of the year" in the *Daily Princetonian:*

> The general feeling among many Ivy Leaguers is that Harvard and Yale coexist nicely because Yale doesn't push the issue. In both money and tradition, Harvard is older and richer and that is that. However, Princeton which was, after all, founded and presided over by six Yale graduates (and one Harvard man) when it was known as "the infant college of New Jersey," has never acknowledged its third-class citizenship in the Big Three.
>
> As one Harvard athlete put it, "We get along with Yale because they understand the order of things. What annoys Yale, even more than Harvard, is the fact that Princeton still won't acknowledge that order. Imagine, after all these years, Princeton still hasn't figured out the pecking order."

Those stubborn Princetonians who wouldn't acknowledge *any* inferior status had abiding faith in a particular philosophy of education and, it would seem, foresight. In recent years the winds that are clearing the view from Nassau Hall have been blowing harder and from every quarter. Even in athletics, football excepted, Princeton has been leading the Ivy League. In other less visible but more important forms of competition, Princeton has been setting a strong pace. One of these that can be measured in absolute terms is endowment. As of the spring of 1983, Princeton's portfolio, with a market value of $1.253 billion, was the third highest in the nation behind Harvard ($2.3 billion) and the University of Texas ($2 billion). The significance of these figures in terms of educational enrichment for the individual—Princeton's philosophy in a phrase—can be judged by a comparison of combined undergraduate-graduate student populations: Princeton, 6,000; Harvard, 15,611; Texas, 48,145.

The overall quality of any institution's performance is more difficult to measure. Yet people are always trying to do so. One organization devoted to evaluating the effectiveness and quality of undergraduate education is National Education Standards in Los Angeles, which periodically publishes "The Gourman Report," a study of "1,845 colleges and universities in terms of objectives, curriculum, faculty, faculty research and honors, administration, library, budget, resources, student scores on standardized tests, admissions policy, other desiderata" by Dr. Jack Gourman, professor of Political Science at California State University, Northridge. Dr. Gourman assigns evaluations in a range of scores up to five. His fall 1983 report shows that, in the administrative areas, for instance, Princeton's alumni associations came in a close second to Harvard's (4.93–4.94) out of forty-nine ranked institutions with scores over 4; Princeton's athletic-academic balance at 4.91 was again just short of Harvard's winning 4.92 out of 121 ranked institutions. But in the overall ranking of forty-seven institutions with scores in the 4.41–4.99 range, Princeton University was first.

Princeton didn't fare quite as well in a more popular survey taken at the same time to rate the quality of undergraduate education in American colleges and universities. In a poll by *U.S. News and World Report* of 1,308 presidents of four-year colleges, the 660 heads who responded voted Princeton fourth among "major" national universities. Although Princeton was put back to third place in the Big Three pecking order, the surprise of the poll was that Stanford University edged out Harvard for the number-one spot, proving that myths can die. The good news for the university office in Nassau Hall was that for the first time since records of such matters have been kept the numbers of accepted applicants declining Yale to enter Princeton and vice versa drew so even as to be called a tie: 141 to Princeton, 146 to Yale. It must be admitted that Harvard was still nearly out of sight in this race with 281 declining Princeton to enter Harvard and only 96 going the other way.

If it seems overly "collegiate" to talk in terms of competition in relation to the highest of the higher educational institutions, the facts of life on the academic scene suggest otherwise. Especially in the private sector, America's colleges and universities *are* in fierce competition, in some cases for mere survival and in all cases for maintaining the quality of educational life. The goals of roughly equal value that they must score are getting students, getting faculty, getting money. It is obvious that the glamor of being in the winner's circle will make all three easier, and it is obvious, too (the ascent of Stanford and descent of Yale), that it has become a precarious place to be.

Although historically the educational game has always been tough, it was a fairly free-scoring contest in the first decades after World War II. Government support, from the G.I. bill through the research grants panic-inspired by Sputnik, grew steadily; a boom in babies in families made middle class by inflationary incomes created a vast market. There arose a great American expectation of more education for more people, and institutions proliferated to meet it. Then, rather suddenly, the game got tight again. With all the piping in place to handle a large flow of scholars, educational institutions began to hear echoes from an empty well. There were fewer people of any kind in the right age group, let alone people qualified for college, and the well is getting drier all the time. "The college-age population is going to decrease dramatically into the mid-1990s, when it will be 15 percent less than now (30 percent in the Northeast)," says Robert K. Durkee, Princeton's vice president for public affairs. Somebody is bound to lose in the scramble for students. In addition, the economic-political scene shifted drastically with ever-rising inflation giving way to recession. The cost of labor and energy-intensive educational operations went right on up, but Reaganomics, with evidently widespread public approval, began cutting back on educational support systems other than military research. Even so, Princeton, according to Durkee, is likely to stay in the winner's circle through the next troublesome decade, as it has through many similar periods in the past two centuries, and the administrative thinking that makes this probable should have impact on the whole educational enterprise in America.

The single most important factor in Princeton's durability and resiliency is the philosophy of education in which Princetonians rest their faith. Although it has evolved over the years and through many administrations, it remains curiously the same: creating an institution in which students can learn, as its second president, the Reverend Aaron Burr, said in 1748, "the manifold Advantages of the liberal Arts and Sciences in exalting and dignifying the humane Nature, enlarging the Soul, improving its Faculties, civilizing Mankind, qualifying them for the important Offices of Life, and rendering them useful members of Church and State." Ever since then, Princeton has been cautious in not trimming its sails to any winds of change that do not blow in that direction.

There is an echo of Burr in the way Princeton's president, William G. Bowen, describes how Princeton differs from other institutions of higher learning: "First, Princeton is very much arts and sciences. What I mean by that is that our strength, our efforts, are very much in the basic arts and sciences. We do not have here a range of professional schools. Those schools are very valuable and very necessary, but the absence of that set of professional schools and professional activities allows us to focus our energies, including our emotional energies, on the arts and sciences. The whole feeling of the university is a sense of the fundamental importance of learning, and I think it is very important that there be at least one university of world-class standing which really is an arts and sciences university.

"Second, we emphasize an unswerving commitment to work of the highest quality. We are not alone in that, but I think we take it especially seriously. So we try not to become so large as to threaten quality at the graduate level, or the undergraduate level. We see our goals in qualitative not in quantitative terms.

"Third, the connection between research and graduate teaching and undergraduate teaching is especially close. We have no separate faculty for graduate and undergraduate instruction. The leading scholars in their field teach beginning courses here; freshmen ask the most basic questions, and that's valuable.

"Fourth, we have a distinctive way of teaching. Teaching is very much in the active mode with a lot of emphasis on the student's own response. There is more paper writing done here than in any comparable university, for instance. I see all that as essential in giving people the capacity lifelong to think their way through problems.

"Other factors are the physical beauty and residential character of the place in which we're all thrown together so that there is a lot of growing outside the classroom. Then there's also a tradition of service which has expanded from Woodrow Wilson's 'in the nation's service' to include service on all levels of society. All these things somehow coalesce into a special feeling, a quality of experience, that causes people to leave Princeton feeling good about their education and wanting to help, as our generous alumni giving demonstrates."

A specific illustration of the difference the Princeton philosophy makes in the administration and direction of an educational institution is the nature of two large projects underway at Princeton and at Hofstra University on Long Island. President Bowen admits that the emotional energy that he doesn't have to give to overseeing the sprawl and diversity of another kind of institution is going into the $46 million development of a faculty and building to study molecular biology, one of the most exciting frontiers in basic science. At Hofstra $4 million is being spent for a center that "will surpass many of the cable and public service television facilities in the nation" for the teaching of video skills in which the university grants a bachelor's degree. Although it is right, and probably necessary, for somebody to meet the demand for such instruction—there are four hundred undergraduates enrolled in the Hofstra courses—it may be one secret of Princeton's success, one element of its elitism, that it leaves the often expensive following of fashion to others.

Nor does Princeton follow fashion in the matter of faculty. Princeton makes life difficult for itself by holding to a historical emphasis on teaching. It probably began with Burr, who was for a time a one-man faculty as well as the president; it continues with Bowen, who teaches a class section in beginning economics twice a week. "I do it for the most selfish reason—it's fun," he says. But he adds: "It keeps me in touch with the fundamental purposes of Princeton; I don't see administration as an end in itself." Bowen's personal performance may well be by way of example, since *all* faculty hired by Princeton are required to teach on all levels at a time when, elsewhere, prize faculty members are lured with offers of freedom from the classroom to pursue lucrative research and consulting projects or with presumed status as graduate-only instructors. Since Princeton is only "competitive but not ahead" in faculty salaries, according to Dr. Aaron Lemonick, dean of the faculty, this can create problems.

"When we recruit faculty what, in fact, we recruit is the very best scholars we can find with the complete understanding that they will teach," Dr. Lemonick says. "We recently had the case of an eminent scholar whose home institution offered him one semester off from teaching every year, and he asked if we would do the same. We said no. It was unthinkable that we would offer a contract which had the stipulation of one semester off every year. What do I do about all the other faculty for whom this would begin to be a pattern? That's not the pattern we're willing to follow, so some faculty select themselves out. Most faculty who come here, even if they come from a place where they didn't do a lot of teaching, become engaged, because the student body is very good. I think places that don't have teaching deprive the faculty of a certain stimulus, a certain excitement, a certain effervescence."

This effervescence comes out of what President Bowen called the way of teaching at Princeton. Although there are the customary lectures to large groups, labs, classes of twenty-five or so in some courses, what is called the preceptorial method sets the style of Princeton teaching. It was Woodrow Wilson's greatest educational gift to the university. In an adaptation of the Oxford tutorial system, Wilson proposed regular meetings of small groups of students—usually less than ten—with a professor in courses in the humanities, social sciences, and mathematics. The idea was that the precept would be a free-wheeling discussion, guided by the preceptor, of the students' independent reading on a subject, and it may have come to Wilson because the wide reading he did rather than the lectures and texts of any course was the substance of his own undergraduate education. In 1905 Wilson startled the academic world by recruiting and importing a group of thirty-two promising young teachers from other institutions to get the system underway. Among them was Robert K. Root of Yale, who later became dean of the faculty. As related in Alexander Leitch's *A Princeton Companion,* Root recalled having doubts about this "new-fangled method of teaching" until he met Wilson; but, as he said, "before five minutes had passed, I knew that I never before talked face to face with so compelling a person. Had Woodrow Wilson asked me to go with him and work under him while he inaugurated a new university in Kamchatka or Senegambia I would have said 'yes' without further questions."

Wilson's desire to "import into the great university the methods and personal contact between teacher and pupil which are characteristic of the small college and so gain the advantages of both" worked so well that it is still in operation today. Good preceptors use the Socratic method of instruction by questioning, and students are encouraged to think rather than recite and thus achieve, as Wilson said, "their proper release from being schoolboys." Depending on a professor's style, precepts have been held out of doors, in taprooms, in living rooms, as well as in classrooms. It is possible to sit silent through them, but silence is so obvious that most students eventually develop some adeptness at intellectual discussion. It is impossible to meet with a professor in this informal, intimate fashion without getting to know him or her quite well. Not only do students feel free to challenge the preceptor's opinions, but familiarity has caused generations of Princetonians to treat faculty as fallible human beings. This attitude is almost institutionalized in a faculty song, amended and updated and sung from the steps of Nassau Hall on spring evenings by seniors who have nothing to fear in the way of reprisal. The fixed refrain is:

> *Away, away with rum by gum!*
> *See them come with a rub-by-dum-dum,*
> *Looking as if they'd been off on a bum,*
> *The faculty of Princeton College, oh!*

Wilson, much admired as both teacher and president was not exempt:

> *Here's to Woodrow King Divine,*
> *He rules this place along with Fine,\**
> *We fear that soon he'll leave this town*
> *To try for Teddy Roosevelt's crown.*

Nor was the greatest mind ever to grace Princeton exempt:

> *The bright boys here all study math*
> *And Albie Einstein points the path.*
> *Although he seldom takes the air,*
> *We wish to God he'd cut his hair.*

Nor was the dean of the chapel:

> *Here's to Reverend Bobby Wicks*
> *Who knows the soul's most inward tricks;*
> *He gives out socialistic knowledge*
> *In this most capitalistic college*

That Princeton students nevertheless appreciate the wit and wisdom of their professors is evidenced by a recurring feature in the *Weekly Nassau,* an undergraduate publication. Called "Verbatim," it quotes off-the-cuff professorial remarks from lectures or precepts. A sampling follows.

Professor Louis Menand, English 313—History of Literary Criticism: "Stupid questions are the sort you feel comfortable asking a candidate for Miss America."

Professor Arthur Hanson, Humanistic Studies 205—Classical Roots of Western Literature, on the Book of Revelations: "The first time I read this, I thought it was Saint John describing an acid trip."

Professor Froma Zeitlin, Classics 323—Greek Drama: "The great discovery of the 'sexual revolution' was that women had sexual desires. In the Victorian age, women had been divided into two groups: good and bad. The good women closed their eyes, opened their legs and thought of England."

---

\* Henry Burchard Fine, then dean of the faculty.

Professor Malcolm Diamond, Religion 333—Psychology and Religion: "Don't be so open-minded that your brains fall out."

Despite the hard work and hazards of teaching the Princeton way, its 819 teachers—328 professors, 64 associate professors, 196 assistant professors, 16 instructors, 122 lecturers, and 93 visiting lecturers—compose a distinguished company by any academic standards. Their awards are too numerous to list, but since 1977 there have been four Nobel Prize winners. Significantly, one of them, Val L. Fitch, Cyrus Fogg Brackett Professor of Physics, teaches a freshman course. The overall quality of the faculty can be judged from the results of a recent study by the Conference Board of Associated Research Councils of the effectiveness of graduate programs in America. Since Princeton's faculty teaches on both graduate and undergraduate levels, the study is reflective of the whole university. Princeton was ranked first in the United States in mathematics, music, and German; second in philosophy and French; third in physics and history. Of twenty-six Princeton departments rated in the survey, ten were in the top five in the country, and all but three were in the top sixteen.

Just as Princeton's singular philosophy of education attracts an outstanding faculty, it also seems to exert sufficient pull on prospective students to justify Vice President Durkee's confidence that unfavorable demographic projections will not be a problem at Princeton. The 1983 entering class of 1,168 was culled from 11,007 applicants, and even a 30 percent drop in that "pool" would leave the university with a good margin of safety in numbers. Although he acknowledges that Princeton may get by, President Bowen is not complacent about the demographic situation. "The smaller private colleges will be very hard pressed, and some of the state institutions, too," he admits. "I worry about the divisive effects on higher education. There's nothing wrong with competition, but it can obviously take forms that are destructive of educational values. You can imagine an institution that would allow people to come who are not qualified or allow them to stay, and we already have situations where people are trying to attract students by fair means or foul, by blatant advertisements that aren't really appropriate."

Although Dr. Bowen intends to keep Princeton out of this

unseemly scramble, the university will be taking no chances on losing its share of the shrinking pool of qualified applicants. Indeed, Princeton mounts one of the most intensive recruiting efforts in the country. The key to this is a 2,500-strong, coed army of alumni who so prized their Princeton experiences that they are willing to volunteer considerable time and effort to give others the same opportunity. Conveniently scattered through the fifty states and in strategic places elsewhere in the world, the Alumni Schools Committee supplements the dean of admission's staff in singing Princeton's praises in secondary schools and in interviewing applicants. The sales pitch that they and the more official Princeton recruiters use is, according to Dean of Admission Anthony M. Cummings, almost precisely what Dr. Bowen has outlined—a beautiful campus, small size, a single faculty, no professional schools, the challenge of independent work. The campaign has been effective so far, but it is a hard sell in a vocationally minded society and at a time when the price tag for the product is fearsome.

For the 1983–84 school year, the cost of a Princeton education is a staggering $12,900 a year, and costs continue to mount. Even at that price tag the cost of providing a Princeton student with reasonably comfortable living, with enough professors to maintain the preceptorial system, with forty-six departments and programs for academic concentration, with labs and classrooms, with gyms and playing fields, with a library of 3.5 million volumes, with a computer center and chapel, with everything that goes into the nature of an elite institution, is at least twice what the student pays. Herein lies the rub for Princeton and all private institutions of similar standing where the discrepancy between costs and income from students is roughly the same. They play a form of Russian roulette known as "need blind" admission, which means that students are accepted without reference to their family's ability to pay, that in some cases the entire $14,500 must be conjured out of thin air of student employment, loans, and scholarships. Fortunately the laws of chance are among the more reliable forces operating in the universe, and only about 50 percent of each admitted class seems to need financial assistance. Still, the difference between the amount of required aid that needed to be raised from outside sources and what Princeton had to take out of its own pocket in 1983 was about $12 million.

Despite this considerable "gift" to its students, the university has been under heavy fire from undergraduates for its continuing policy of raising fees at a rate faster than inflation. After pointing out that total fees now represent 49 percent of the median U.S. family income, the *Daily Princetonian* quoted senior Tom Bartel, an undergraduate member of the Priorities Committee, which sets the university's budget and fees, as warning: "Princeton must be careful or it could price itself out of the college market." Princeton *is* careful, preferring to take that risk instead of losing out in the quality market. As Christopher McCrudden, the associate controller, explained, the things that make for quality like the purchase of library books rise higher than inflation. Moreover, the basic nature of a quality educational operation, which boils down to the labor-intensive practice of providing enough good faculty for the Princeton way of teaching, makes it impossible to take advantage of inflation-beating technological improvements.

Indeed, *care* would be the operative word for describing Princeton's financial administration. For example, Princeton's spectacular performance in the endowment sweepstakes is due in large part to its outside money managers' ability to increase the yield on investments 142 percent in the last five and a half years —compared to a Dow Jones Industrial Average rise of 101 percent—and to its discipline in spending only a designated percentage of that yield to make up about a quarter of the costs not otherwise covered. In another way Princeton is showing a form of care for quality that makes its costs rise higher than inflation —continual maintenance of a plant that includes many buildings a century or more old. Although maintenance costs are rising at a rate of 20 percent a year, Princeton doesn't want to slip into the perilous position of other educational institutions that have let large maintenance backlogs accumulate to meet more pressing needs, according to McCrudden. One result of this is savings of 25 percent in energy, another inflation-stopping cost. "Ten years ago, for example, our steam lines were leaking, not as badly, but nobody cared then how much they leaked," McCrudden says.

"Now we can't afford to let a steam line leak because of the cost of energy."

All in all, Princeton is in sound financial shape, and the only real disaster McCrudden can foresee would be a sharp decline in alumni loyalty, which provides, aside from endowment grants, an annual spendable income in the range of $12 million. The alumni annual giving has increased as federal aid has decreased in proportion to costs. "The problem here is in aid to students," says Vice President Durkee. "The year before last [1982] we had a total scholarship budget of roughly $10 million, out of which federal scholarship dollars were $1.5 million. For this year [1983] that will stay at $1.5 million—though it would have gone down to about $300,000 if administration proposals had been accepted— but our total will go to $11.5 million. So the funding of these programs has not kept pace with rising costs, and the irony is that this hurts private institutions even though the administration favors them. There's a misconception when students are forced into the public sector: it doesn't cost the society any less; it may even cost society more because so much of the cost of those institutions is paid by the taxpayer. With state and local participation, there's more public money by far going into supporting students in public institutions even though there may be a decline in federal dollars. Our argument to Washington is that by clamping down on these programs they make it more difficult at the margins for people to elect private education."

Clearly it is the issue of choice in education, that there *be* a Princeton that any qualified person can choose, that concerns Dr. Bowen, whose view of the costs may reflect his specialty as an economist. "It's important to see the cost of education in the right perspective," he says. "Education is an investment, an investment that will yield lifelong benefits. It should be thought of as other investments of value over a long period of time and not as something to be paid out of current income. If you look at it that way and look at the trend of the cost of education compared to other things like automobiles or houses or whatever, it does not appear that the cost of education is as great as most people think after making those corrections and in relation to money income. It hasn't gone up as fast as the general income of the population.

You are driven back to the test of evidence, and so far we have been able to enroll people of all economic backgrounds who have been willing to make the sacrifice because they value the result. We've been able to do what we've done because we have had very significant increases in financial aid to accompany increases in charges. Over half of our students work, and I think that's very appropriate."

When it comes to soliciting financial support, critics claim that Princeton may eventually drop behind in the race, particularly in soliciting corporate gifts, by clinging to its tradition of basic research in the arts and sciences. Stanford, for instance, with its satellite Silicon Valley full of high-tech companies, is way ahead in getting private money. But Nassau Hall doesn't seem to be worried. Plums keep dropping—a recent $1 million grant from IBM for research in the sciences and engineering, a $700,000 unrestricted gift from five Bell companies late in 1983, a $1.25 million donation from nearby Squibb for Princeton's molecular biology program—and Princeton's alumni keep coming through with gifts and contributions. A $330 million Campaign for Princeton is currently underway and going well. Aside from a grant of $125 million a year from the Department of Energy to run the Plasma Physics Laboratory, Princeton gets about $27 million in federal and state research funds, and this amount may increase, because, as Durkee says: "The National Science Foundation— very much a basic research mission—was proposed for increases this year [1983] in excess of 10 percent out of a conviction that basic scientific research has to be strong if you're going to do applied research in the long run. This is important to Princeton because we do so little applied research."

In effect, Princeton's income structure means that it stands on four sturdy legs—30 percent from student fees, 20 percent from the government, 24 percent from investments, and 26 percent from gifts and grants and auxiliary activities. This is not only an insurance against catastrophe in any single sector but a guarantee of independence. It enables Dr. Bowen to say flatly: "We are not for sale, we are not for sale." And as in the recruitment of students and faculty Princeton seems to be passing "the test of evidence" in financing: not long ago Dr. Bowen was able to announce that the university closed its books on fiscal 1983—a $275 million budget with 14,000 separate accounts—with a surplus of $277,000.

Not surprisingly, President Bowen is widely credited with running a tight financial ship, which is not to say that he is always sailing calm seas. Recurrently, students and/or faculty have raised ruckuses about the university buying products from or investing in companies such as those operating in South Africa, with whose policies they disagree, or have submitted earnest pleas for the university to take a stand for what they see as a "good cause," such as support of a nuclear freeze that was endorsed by a campus referendum. Buoyed by the concept of what Princeton is and should be—an educational institution—Dr. Bowen has for the most part let these waves wash over him, but he has been patient in articulating his position. When in 1978 he was petitioned to have the university join in a national boycott of the products of J. P. Stevens Company, he wrote a closely reasoned nine-page response, the gist of which is in the following paragraph:

> What is right and proper for individuals may be wrong and damaging for the institution. If the university is to serve well the purposes for which it exists, there must be a continuing commitment to the freedom of each individual to think freshly and independently, to be as free as possible of every form of coercion, of every pressure to join a position because others—even a substantial majority—happen to hold it. Required too is a large measure of forbearance on the part of students, faculty and alumni, who will naturally and properly feel strongly about a great many causes which are extremely significant to them. The university itself advances important causes by assuring that both their champions *and* their opponents have a full opportunity to argue their cases. This requires institutional restraint and a willingness to differentiate between the right of the individual to argue vigorously for what he or she believes and the obligation of the institution to remain open in fact and in appearance to different points of view.

That Dr. Bowen continues to hold a steady helm is evident from his comments on the nuclear freeze question. "The issue isn't whether we're for or against the nuclear freeze—we're neither. The issue is whether it fits in with our purpose as an educational institution to be involved in that particular dispute. It does not. I feel strongly that the openness of Princeton to all controversial points of view is an essential part of our character, and the first instance that I declare that Princeton believes this, that, or the other thing about the nuclear freeze, that openness is called into question. I would feel that way if 99 percent of the people were on one side of the issue and 1 percent was on the other side. We have an obligation to the 1 percent. We just do not believe in stating that that position is wrong. Who knows, in ten years it might prove to be right, whatever it happens to be. We are determined to provide a forum for individuals to argue, and I'm certain that we provide a better forum if the university isn't leaning in on the argument."

So far President Bowen's policies and positions have had the support of the university's ultimate seat of power, the self-perpetuating Board of Trustees, which has been in existence since colonial times. Never a rubber stamp, the thirty-seven-member board has fired outright a number of Princeton presidents and, in effect, caused the most illustrious of them all, Woodrow Wilson, to seek employment as governor of New Jersey by rejecting two of his most passionately proposed plans: the Quad Plan for undergraduate living and the location of the graduate college at the center of campus. It is not surprising that the trustees accept the Bowen concept of "institutional restraint." As one of them, Nicholas deB. Katzenbach, says: "You probably couldn't find a subject on which our Board of Trustees would agree other than Princeton. But they are really, really very much dedicated to doing what they think is right for the university even if that is not something their friends think is right for the university. This is true of the young ones, too, who are impressed very quickly that the trustees are sincere and serious in what they're trying to do."

To that end each trustee must attend at least twelve days of meetings throughout the year, not to mention doing rigorous homework. This can be considerable because on any issue "you get more information out of the administration, pro and con, than you probably contemplated," according to Katzenbach, Princeton '43. As a former U.S. attorney general and now general counsel for IBM, Katzenbach has a good basis for comparison when he adds: "The staff work they do there is superb. It's as good as any company I've ever seen and better than most." The board exercises its own kind of restraint in refusing to invade the area of academic appointments, although it has the power to do so, because, as Katzenbach says: "If the trustees really began to pass judgment on who they thought ought to be appointed to tenure in the English or the engineering department, there would be a mass exodus of faculty from Princeton. The principal problem we face is to attract and to hold the best kind of faculty." What the trustees do get involved in are broader policy matters such as the decision to go coeducational and, most recently, to approve the creation of the costly Department of Molecular Biology to strengthen Princeton's position in basic scientific research.

It is apparent that Princeton's trustees and administration are hand in glove in holding the institution on its historic course of adhering to learning for learning's sake. Since it is hard to lose if you concentrate on doing better whatever you already do well, it is easy to predict that the view across the educational landscape from Nassau Hall will continue to brighten. There are, of course, critics of this "institutional restraint," both within and without the university. Their argument might be summed up in an undergraduate anecdote about a professor who often returns student papers with the comment "This is all right, but it's too Princeton." Pressed for an explanation, the professor will add: "Well, you know, too cautious and conservative." But, as the saying goes, you can't argue with success, and barring overwhelming catastrophe, Princeton seems destined to stand almost alone for an academic elitism that is fortunately held in high value by a society badly in need of its services.

# Chapter Five

# PRINCETON'S PRESSURE COOKER

A few years ago a distraught female sophomore at Princeton sought out the highest place she could find on campus—a twelfth-story room in the tower of Fine Hall, the ultramodern mathematics facility—opened a window, and jumped to her death. The incident is still talked about on the campus because of its freakish nature. Hers was the more recent of only two successful suicides at Princeton in the last fifteen years, and because Fine Hall is built on a line between two communities the young woman departed this life from Princeton Township and entered the next in Princeton Borough, causing a ticklish jurisdictional legal problem. It is astonishing that suicide remains a rare phenomenon at Princeton at a time when it seems to be approaching almost epidemic proportions in the national college-age group, since the single word young people most often use to describe supposedly carefree college life is *pressure.*

Unfortunately, Princeton's remarkably low suicide rate among its 6,000 strong student body—on an average, there is one suicide per year for every ten thousand college students—is not a matter for boasting. It is, in fact, a form of failure. In 1983 there were nine cases of attempted suicide or suicide gestures. There are, of course, less obviously self-destructive students who starve or stuff themselves, and it may not be without significance that one of the recognized student organizations on campus is called POWER—Princeton Organization for Women Eating Right. Nor does anybody know for sure how many off-campus deaths are suicidal. Single-car accidents in that age group, for instance, are now widely viewed as possible suicides by psychiatric experts.

Although it would be irresponsible to emphasize suicide in relation to specifically Princeton pressure, the fact that it happens at all in a group of mostly healthy, highly motivated, comparatively successful, and certainly fortunate young people is the most dramatic evidence of the existence of that pressure. This is not, however, a negative factor. Despite the occasional tragedy it may cause, the pressure of Princeton can be the most positive and important element in the mysterious process of creating an elite, which is the university's real business. It does, nevertheless, come as a surprise and shock to the kind of people who manage to make it into Princeton at all. Like their peers in the Ivy League and such institutions as Stanford and MIT, fledgling Princetonians have *already* undergone the most rigorous selection process in American society with the possible exception of the astronaut program, and the mere fact of admission—a sweating pressure in itself—might reasonably be looked upon as the ultimate achievement.

Consider what it takes even to get the opportunity to become a Princetonian. Among the factors that would give an applicant a chance of being one of the 19 percent of some twelve thousand applicants who are accepted, the most measurable are one's scores on the College Board Scholastic Aptitude and Achievement Tests. Whereas the mean SAT score for all college-bound students is in the mid-400 range (against a perfect 800), the average of those accepted for Princeton's class of 1987 was 649 verbal and 695 mathematical, the highest in history.

Although a high SAT score may indicate something academically positive, it is not enough for the Princeton admission people, who lean more heavily on the secondary school record. They *know* the kind of pressure a student is going to face, as indicated by Dean of Admission Anthony M. Cummings: "The quality of the high school program is the most important factor. We'd look with more favor on someone who is number five in the class and has taken a harder program than a valedictorian who's taken a softer program. *So the extent to which a student has put himself in situations where he will be stressed is probably the single most important factor.* That always has to be judged in the context of the opportunities available to the student. The second most important factor is performance; then, I guess, teacher recommendations."

There is no handy computer formula for judging academic potential, and each person has to be considered individually. Dean Cummings recalls the case of a young man whose grades were good and whose SATs approached the maximum score of 1600, but who was rejected because his teacher wrote: "While he's bright and well organized and a competent student, he lacks the intellectual hunger that is found in the best students. Intellectual issues do not move him though he does understand them. His orientation is to the practical, the pragmatic, and stays at a middlebrow level that is neither superficial nor deep." Another young man with 250 points lower on his SATs was accepted on this recommendation: "He's brilliant, original and intense. The range of his reading, the depth of his perceptions and his writing mark him as so far superior to his classmates as to be in a class by himself. There is always respectful silence when he speaks on a subject; his peers recognize brilliance when they hear it. I've met only one other student in my career who could possibly equal him at this age. He is now a college professor with many undergraduate and graduate honors."

Even harder to judge are the personal factors that are given equal weight because, as Cummings says, "Princeton feels that part of its mission is to educate students who are going to make a contribution to their communities when they leave the university, and that depends as much on values and qualities of character as it does on qualities of the mind." Although participation in various extracurricular activities often indicates a well-rounded personality, the admission office relies more heavily on a sixth sense about a person that shines through in personal interviews or personal essays. This may be why, for a recent Princeton class, only 457 out of 1,115 secondary school valedictorians, only 30 percent of 624 student council presidents, only 31 percent of 1,107 editors-in-chief of high school newspapers, and only 28 percent of 1,604 team captains who applied were accepted.

Some personal characteristics receive *no* consideration: among them, sex, religion, and the ability to pay. But when it becomes a toss-up between two seemingly qualified individuals, the university will give preference to the one who fits its needs. One of these needs is to acquire a fairly representative geographical and social distribution on the grounds that a Princeton education includes rubbing elbows with people of mixed backgrounds. There is no fixed formula for this, according to Cummings. As to geography, the country is divided into six regions, each covered by a representative of the Admission Office as well as by resident alumni who volunteer for the Schools Committee; there is a fairly equal number of applicants from each region. As to the social mix, there is little doubt that a qualified member of a minority group seeking Princeton admission will get a break. Indeed, the Admission Office purchases a list from the Educational Testing Service of those minority students who have done well on *pre*-SATs and seeks them out. "We just try for a sensible figure," says Cummings. In the 1987 class, it was 6 percent black, and another 11 percent that included native Americans, Asians, Puerto Ricans, Chicanos.

Others who are favored for the contribution they might make to the university are athletes. All other things being equal, the Admission Office will follow the recommendation of coaches who spend time and money seeking out good athletes who can also meet tough academic standards. And, for contributions their families *have* made to Princeton, sons and daughters of alumni are more likely to get the nod than those of non-Princeton families. Many alumni have children who unfortunately can't clear the higher academic hurdle and who therefore may find this hard to believe. Hardly an issue of the *Princeton Alumni Weekly* appears without a letter from an enraged old grad threatening to cut off his giving because his offspring was denied admission. The facts are that 47 percent of alumni children applying to the class of 1987 were admitted compared to 35 percent of the next most favored group—blacks; that 17 percent of the total class were alumni children, compared to a not much larger 19 percent of my own class more than forty years ago, in a time that some alumni now recall as the golden age of Princeton purity. In actual numbers, 195 alumni children entered Princeton in the fall of 1983, compared to 134 in 1938. There would have been a lot fewer than 134 if the academic gate had been as narrow then as it is today.

Under these circumstances it might be suspected that every student walking onto campus for the first time through the gates in front of Nassau Hall or up the back way from the dinky train that brought him or her from Princeton Junction, is a little cocky inside, however shy on the outside. After all, just being there is irrefutable proof of some overachievement even in a young life. But disillusion is likely to set in even before the bell atop Nassau Hall rings out the first classes. What happens is that you start meeting your classmates and . . . well, listen to some student voices, male and female, from recent interviews.

"By the time you go through freshman orientation your ego is gone. You realize that you're in the fast lane, that all of a sudden you're one of a thousand—or four thousand—stars in some particular aspect of life. In the first few weeks it cuts you down to size and after that gives you a chance to grow up. . . ."

"It is a very competitive place—the people you meet, and the pressures you're exposed to, the constant learning and pushing from people who are so talented, who have so many different points of view. . . ."

"The pressure here? Well, it's not cutthroat. I have never seen or heard of anybody who did something to knock somebody else. But there is a lot of pressure that is entirely from yourself. A lot of people who come here were top in high school. They're used to being big fish. They're very successful people. They're ambitious. They come here and are given very challenging work, and they dive in. You can't get through Princeton taking 'guts' because there aren't that many and they aren't that easy. You definitely can't party for four years. You definitely have to work if you want to pass. If you want to do well, you *really* have to work. . . ."

More than in the recent past, today's Princeton student feels a compulsion to do well, especially in academics. What they see ahead is an uncertain financial future, an economic and social climate in which having made it through Princeton is no guarantee of survival. The same higher hurdles that they had to leap to get into Princeton are being set up at the other end by the graduate professional schools. Not long ago the *Daily Princetonian* lamented that the days are gone when an Adlai Stevenson could get into Harvard Law School with a C average at Princeton and lay the foundation for a career that almost put him into the White House. This lament reflects the opinion of the *Princetonian* chairman, T. Richard Waechter, Jr.: "The gentleman's C is no longer acceptable. There's a real pregrad school and preprofessional mentality. By statistics, some 80 percent of each class goes on. You kind of come here with the knowledge that this is not the end of your education."

The awesome tasks as well as the infinite opportunities before them are implicit to freshmen in the thick "Undergraduate Announcement" they receive before matriculation. There are some 250 pages listing courses and programs, but the choice among them is not entirely free—Princeton has definite demands for its degrees. Bachelor of Arts candidates, for instance, *must* establish competence in writing and take courses to that end in freshman and sophomore years; they must also demonstrate through tests or by taking courses proficiency in a foreign language; then they "must successfully complete two one-term courses in each of four general areas: science (laboratory courses); social science; arts and letters; and history. Beyond that, each A.B. candidate must choose a department in which to major during junior and senior years with a program including at least eight departmental courses and independent study which "usually consists of the writing of essays or reports junior year and a thesis senior year." Candidates for the degree of Bachelor of Science in Engineering hardly get by by playing with a calculator or computer. In italics they are informed that their thirty-six courses *will include not less than seven courses in humanities and social sciences.* Princeton is not alone in requiring science and engineering majors to take such courses, but it does make life tougher for the engineer because, instead of sitting in on what would be a "service" course in a more specialized institution, the Princeton engineer is subject to the professorial discipline of the best scholars in the field and is in competition with fellow students who are majoring in the specialty.

The wonder is not that a few students confronting this formidable program and keen competition crack, but that more don't. What they say about the pressures they feel is amply confirmed by the observations of their guides and counselors.

Dr. Marvin Geller, director of the Counseling Center, sometimes has to pick up the pieces: "There's a very strong feeling of competition. What you have here is a collection of able people from very success-oriented families. You see kids who can't tolerate less than A's and B's. Their self-esteem is based on their achievement. I saw a student who was falling apart because she got a B on her junior paper. That's the epitome of the hard-driving Princeton student. Many of these kids, deep down, don't feel they are worthy as they are. There was another case of a girl with crying jags whose father said, 'I want to see you make all A's this year.' Her father is very successful and critical of her mother. She wants to be like him. She's terrified of being like her mother, who can't balance a checkbook. She wonders why she's crying and full of tension. She's a sophomore and has to select a major, and she's terrified of picking one that won't lead to success. She's so dependent that she wants me or somebody to get her on the right track. People like that suffer a lot."

Dr. Geller and others observe an extra measure of pressure on those groups most favored at admission time—athletes, alumni children, minorities. "A lot of black students don't feel historically affirmed by this institution," Dr. Geller said. "A lot of them feel that they're here because they are black and not because they are able. We see this, too, with children of alumni and also with athletes. I made it a point to follow a black girl, an athlete, and an alumni son. The first two made it with lots of trouble, but the alumni son transferred out after sophomore year."

Another keen observer of the Princeton psyche is Rabbi Edward Feld of the Hillel Foundation. Not an alumnus (he graduated from Brooklyn College) and not officially associated with the university even in his role as an authorized outside chaplain, Rabbi Feld views the undergraduate scene with wise detachment. In the decade since his appointment the Jewish student population has grown to the point where his services are in considerable demand, yet he still feels a strong sense of "Waspness—not inculcated by any official or other action but just here in the architecture."

He also feels a powerful sense of competitiveness: "A colleague of mine calls the competitiveness 'the Calvinist ghost of Princeton.' You know, you have to prove that you're saved. The proof is only through visible success in the world, and Princeton challenges you to do that. I've never seen such a thing. At Harvard the assumption is that, if you're accepted, you've made it, and you are already saved. But here there is a feeling communicated that you must prove you are worthy of Princeton. Even *I* feel it. Every time I come back to Princeton from somewhere else, there's a knot in my stomach. The first two years I was here nobody came to talk to me, nobody on the faculty called me for lunch. I felt it was this kind of thing—prove you are deserving of our attention. One way or another, I've gotten over it, but I also must tell you that I grew in Princeton. It stretched me in a way I wouldn't have been stretched anywhere else, and I think that happens to most students. Test yourself to see what you can produce at your limit. Some people are stretched in ways they didn't know they had, and they get a lot out of Princeton; and some people are broken, and I see both. I don't know how much the statistics tell us, but I know a lot of people who got through here with good grades, won awards, but were scarred for the next five or ten years of their lives. These were not people who were tops, but good middlings. But there was nothing the place gave them that told them they were really good—on the contrary, it told them they never quite made it."

Although it may be more intense than ever, there's nothing new about Princeton competitiveness. Almost every alum—a word preferred to avoid distinguishing between an alumn*us* and alumn*a*—is willing to talk about the competitiveness, usually in a positive way. As Arthur Collins, '52, who is engaged, among other projects, in a multimillion-dollar revamping of Palmer Square, Princeton's commercial heart, says: "I thought it was competitive in everything. But I think having gone through four years of that at a very formative time of life and being with your peers, who are going through the same thing, is a help in later life. For instance, a lot of my friends have done very well, and so it gives me some confidence, too." A Princetonian who preceded Collins by thirty-five years, F. Scott Fitzgerald, '17, put the matter thus in the mouth of a fictional character: "From the first he loved Princeton—its lazy beauty, its half-grasped significance, the wild moonlight revel of the rushes, the handsome, prosperous big-game crowds, and *under it all the air of struggle that pervaded his class*" (author's italics). A Princetonian who followed Collins twenty-seven years later, John Aristotle Phillips, '79, says: "To me what Princeton meant was more than the classes, more than the professors, more than the prestige; it was the exposure to all these brilliant kids, all these aces walking around. You try to excel, but even when you do nobody is particularly impressed. But when you get out in life and spot a Princetonian in some endeavor you're pretty sure that he or she is going to be good at it."

What happened to Phillips as an undergraduate when, by designing an atomic bomb, he became the most famous Princeton student in recent history, is illustrative of the safety valve on the Princeton pressure cooker—the value placed on original and independent work. As recounted in *Mushroom,* the book he coauthored with his roommate, David Michaelis, Phillips arrived at Princeton in the fall of his junior year, a transfer from Berkeley, where "things were too comfortable. I wanted to work. I wanted to be challenged. My brain was slowly turning to oatmeal and I had to break out. I wanted to go back east. Harvard was too snooty. Yale was too close to home. I decided on Princeton. Princeton was a new start and a fresh challenge. I would have to test myself against the ivy wall." Actually, as Phillips recently admitted, his father, a Yale professor, had proposed Princeton because his son, a physics major, was also interested in politics, and the crossover possibilities presented by Princeton's Woodrow Wilson School of Public and International Affairs are unusual, if not unique. (A young woman engineer I met, for instance, is also earning a certificate from the Woodrow Wilson School to accompany her B.S. degree.)

Phillips's first challenge seems to have been getting the most out of a collegiate life he had missed at Berkeley. He applied himself diligently to getting accepted as a member of prestigious Ivy Club, to prancing around in a tiger suit at football games, to dancing in the Triangle Club musical show, to chasing girls, which he confesses had been his real major at Berkeley. Naturally, by the end of his first term he was on academic probation. His assertion that he had below-average grades was thus substantiated, but in the light of future events one had to doubt his claim to a below-average IQ. There was also evident seriousness beneath Phillips's collegiate surface, and it was lifted into view when he attended a crossover course, Arms Control and Disarmament 452, in the Woodrow Wilson School.

During a class discussion, a student brought up the fact that a terrorist could make an A-bomb from about fifteen pounds of lost or stolen plutonium. "An idea suddenly comes to mind," writes Phillips. "It is at once ridiculous and brilliant. (I've found that these two things often go together.) Suppose an average— or below-average in my case—physics student at a university could design a workable atomic bomb on paper. That would prove the point dramatically and show the federal government that stronger safeguards have to be placed on the manufacturing and use of plutonium." Phillips put his brilliant idea together with a pressing personal need—to write a junior paper that would save his academic skin—and went to work.

Because he had come late to the idea and had little time to make the deadline for submission of his paper, Phillips had to perform a feat of scholarly heroics that may yet become the stuff of a movie. He had to virtually give up sleep, subsist on coffee and sandwiches, barricade himself in a room at Ivy Club where he could achieve absolute concentration. To learn the "secrets" of the A-bomb he had to pore through mountains of unclassified documents—one of his purposes was to prove that *anybody* could have access to the necessary information—and then put the bits and pieces together into a workable design. Phillips needed brass as well as brains. When, at the eleventh hour, he couldn't find one vital bit of information, he simply phoned the manufacturer of the item in question and, to his surprise, got what he wanted. Literally huffing and puffing from running, he dropped his completed thirty-five-page paper in the office of the physics department almost on the stroke of the twelfth hour.

Phillips got an A on the paper, which, because of its workable design of an A-bomb that would fit in the trunk of a car, was almost too hot for the physics department to handle. With the heavy weight given to independent work, he cleared his probation by that one effort. He also received more notoriety than any other Princeton student until the advent of Brooke Shields. He was featured in publications not only in this country but in Europe, Latin America, Australia; he appeared on major network TV shows. As the *Princeton Weekly Bulletin* described it: "The TV camera crews seemed as ubiquitous on campus as blue jeans and copies of Samuelson's *Economics.*" More sinister attention came from a representative of the Pakistani government, who sought to get a copy of his paper, and Phillips had the FBI as well as cameramen on his heels. No shy physicist, Phillips enjoyed his starring role, partly because all the notoriety helped him put across the real point he wanted to make: "The only way to stop proliferation of nuclear weapons now is to restrict the distribution of plutonium and uranium."

For the purposes of a look at the Princeton academic scene, the Phillips story would have little meaning if it were an isolated feat. In fact, it is a more vivid illustration than most of Princeton's historic stress on the value of innovative, independent work. The Phillips story in some ways paralleled my own experience of forty years earlier with respect to "working" the Princeton system. Like Phillips, I got more interested toward senior year in extracurricular matters, including catching every movie that came to town, and found my grades slipping into the danger zone.

But, as a major in the School of Public and International Affairs
(now the Woodrow Wilson School), I came into daily contact
with high-powered researchers in the social sciences. One of them
was Hadley Cantril, professor of psychology, who had started the
Office of Opinion Research; another was Melville Branch, who
ran the Bureau of Urban Research. Mildly taken with both pursuits, I had a Phillips-like flash and proposed that for my senior
thesis I put them both together and originate and conduct a
public opinion poll on urban planning. Both Professors Cantril
and Branch were enthusiastic, and I was off and running.

I can't say that I made the papers, but the results of that
project were more astonishing than I could have imagined. One
happy circumstance was that, because there had never been a poll
on urban planning and because public opinion polling itself was
a technique still in its infancy, I had only *one* relevant volume to
footnote in my thesis and never had to enter the library, where
most Princeton seniors toil, and thus didn't miss a single movie.
I did tramp the slushy streets of Canonsburg, a small town near
my home in Pittsburgh, during Christmas vacation to take the
poll, but it was actually fun. I was a little worried that, without
a bibliography, my work might be considered *too* independent for
academic consideration, but the Bureau of Urban Research decided to publish the results, and I was able to submit a nicely
printed volume as my thesis. By then war was upon us and, thesis
done, I arranged to sit alone for my comprehensive examinations
before departing for Washington to join the Office of Strategic
Services. Months later an incredible telegram arrived from
Princeton informing me that I would graduate Phi Beta Kappa
and *summa cum laude.*

What I took away from that experience, as I believe Phillips
did from his, is a good part of what Princeton tries to teach: that
independent thought can be more valued than rote learning. But
not everyone can be lucky enough to find the academic escape
valve to the pressure cooker, which is one reason why extracurricular activities have always loomed so large at Princeton. Particularly now that each of the five freshman-sophomore colleges
has its own drama groups, publications, musical ensembles, athletic teams, and government councils, the possibilities for a

Princeton student to exercise a talent and let off a little attention-getting steam are boundless. One student, when asked whether Rabbi Feld's "Calvinist ghost" was real, replied: "I guess I'd have to agree. People around here don't have to be good in school, but they have to be good in *something.*"

Fortunately, that "something" doesn't require organizational success any more than academic achievement requires class recitation. One gets a feeling of how pressure can be handled by listening to Valentina Vavasis, a sophomore who came to Princeton from Arlington High School in suburban Chicago: "When I first got here I definitely felt the shock of being surrounded by people who were equal to me or better in many ways. I wasn't really that used to it in high school. I thought, 'Gee, I've really got to find something I can feel confident about around here.' It started out being my friends because I was confident about my personality. [With good reason—author's note]. Then I started getting satisfaction out of smaller things like going to a precept and saying something brilliant and the teacher was impressed because I thought of it. And you see this happen all the time. Someone gets a challenge in a paper, a project they think they can never do. And they dive in, call everyone in the U.S. who knows anything about the subject and write this brilliant, too long, too good, overly wonderful project, and they turn it in and their teacher is ecstatic and the whole world is in love with them and they think how greater this is than high school. Things like this happen, and you don't have to be president of every group on campus. You can do small things that you really feel good about. It doesn't always have to have anything to do with school. There was this girl I know who always had a lot of sharp pencils around and was always bending over her desk doing something she'd never let anybody see. One day when she was out, her roommate took a peek and found these incredibly good fashion designs."

That girl belonged to another Princeton tradition. Since there is almost nothing vocational to a Princeton education, students have to pick up this experience on the side. The incentive to do so is another element of Princeton pressure—cost. Princeton has been a pricey place from the beginning, with the result that those students whose parents can't afford to pick up the tab are under double pressure. The annals of the university are full of stories of promising, and later prominent, people who couldn't quite make it. None is more sadly illustrative of what has often happened, and still does, under these circumstances than that of Leonard Jerome, Winston Churchill's grandfather and a match for Jay Gould as one of the truly high rollers on the wild American stock markets of the mid-nineteenth century.

A poor boy from upstate New York, Jerome entered Princeton in 1836 with the assistance of an older brother who had grown rich in speculation on silkworms. Sensing that this money could vanish as fast as it had come, Jerome took advantage of a freshman average of 83.6 to skip a year and jump into the junior class in order to cut down on the overall cost. It was a mistake. The junior year was then known as "the mathematical year" at Princeton, and Jerome, as might be expected in a man who was to win and lose fortunes in speculation, was weak in math. His average slipped to 69, and he had to hit the books so hard that he gave up his outside jobs. When his brother's support dried up, he moved off campus to a cheaper lodging and, according to his biographer, Anita Leslie, "wore his clothes until they were transparent and tried to eat very little and very cheap." But he still couldn't meet the tuition fees of $40 a year, the room rent of $12, and the board of $77, and "in August, 1838, withdrew from Princeton and entered Union College in Schenectady where living expenses were lower."

Today, even with total costs running at about $12,900 a year, Jerome's story would probably have a happier ending, although he would have to work just as hard. For one thing, he would have a lot more company since fully half of every Princeton class *has* to work in order to qualify for something that hardly existed in Jerome's time—loan and scholarship aid. In terms of making it possible for anybody with a will to get an education, the aid picture at Princeton today is very bright, but in terms of what it means in the way of standing up to pressure it takes on darker hues.

Here's how Don Betterton, director of Undergraduate Financial Aid, outlines it: "I never encourage people to pass off financial aid as 'don't worry about it, they'll make up the difference.' It's far more complicated than that. The way we put it here is that, if you're seeking financial aid, be prepared for sacrifice. Parents are still going to have to give some money according to their ability to pay. If you write down on a piece of paper what you think they can afford, the system will probably ask them for a lot more than that. So the chances are that the family is going to have to sacrifice to meet that contribution, whatever it happens to be. Then the student should be fully prepared to work and to borrow and to bring outside awards to the university and to use savings. It's not an easy street at all."

Indeed not. Before a student can qualify for unrepayable scholarships or grants, he or she is expected to work during the school year at a rate of about nine hours a week in underclass years, ten in upperclass years, for an average earnings of $1,200 to $1,450; is also expected to contribute from a low of $950 to a high of about $1,450 from summer earnings off campus, depending on the year in school; then is expected to borrow to create a package of about $4,000 in personal contribution on top of whatever the family contribution might be. The university will make up the difference with a scholarship that can run from as little as a few hundred dollars to as much as $10,000 annually per individual and, in total, amounted to $11.5 million in 1983. The kind of pressure this can exert was dramatized in a *Daily Princetonian* feature in which several students bared their financial souls. One, Stephanie Thornton, '86, was in trouble because her parents had divorced, and her father had failed to submit the proper financial forms. "It leaves a lot of stress on me. You're not expected to be your parent's parent," she said. Another, Maria Valentin, '85, had earned only $1,250 working for the Urban Corps in New York as a summer placement counselor and, after deducting living costs, had to apply for additional loans to make up her $1,200 compulsory contribution. "I think the university should go easier on summer earnings," she said. "That's the only time you have to relax. You need a couple of months to recuperate."

However hard it may be on some students, working at Princeton has acquired a kind of cachet comparable to being on the *Daily Princetonian* (for which a reporter does earn money in the junior-

senior years) or the tennis team (no money). Self-contained small
universe that it is, Princeton is able to reserve jobs mostly in the
areas of food, library, and computer services. The first of the
twenty-five hundred or so available jobs go to students in need, but
the seven hundred or eight hundred additional jobs are always
seized by students who simply want to work. Beyond that are the
lucrative arrangements invented by students themselves, whether
or not they are in need, and these entrepreneurs become a form of
campus hero. It is probable that John Aristotle Phillips had a
higher standing on campus as the "pizza czar"—his agency served
pizza at a profit to students in their rooms—than he did as the
A-bomb kid. Recently the *Daily Princetonian* ran a feature on
Douglas Eberhart, '85, whose enterprises include renting tuxedos
and furnishing corsages and boutonnieres for parties and importing Taiwanese products for resale to American firms; James La-
velle, '85, whose Pin Stripe Investments, Inc., registered with the
Securities and Exchange Commission, invests some $140,000 of
other people's money in the market; and Robert Jeffries, '85, who
runs out of his dormitory rooms, aglow with computer screens, a
consulting business called SIFT INC., which brings him $100 an
hour in fees for the kind of advice that saved an Arkansas store
owner $30,000 in purchasing a computer system.

If the Princeton experience is clearly competitive, it has another dimension implicit in the student's statement that it's "not
cutthroat," which in itself is a kind of pressure. This is the university's ninety-one-year-old honor system. Although limited, in
fact, to signing a pledge on every examination paper that "I have
neither given nor received assistance," the effect of the honor
system is better described by Jeremiah S. Finch, a former dean
of the college, in *A Princeton Companion:* "The honor system is
less a set of rules than a state of mind—that honesty in examinations is assumed—and is a common bond among Princetonians."
There are no proctors or faculty members present during examinations, and every Princeton student is under obligation to report
any cheating that he or she witnesses; discipline under the code
is administered by an undergraduate honor committee.

Over the years it has been a heavy burden to bear for seven-
teen- to twenty-one-year-olds driven by personal and family sac-

rifices to make a go of Princeton, and there have been a number of heartbreaking incidents where a violation ruined a life. I am personally grateful that I never had to confront the anguish of reporting a fellow student and equally grateful for having witnessed the gallantry of men who failed rather than compromise their honor. In my day, grades on exams were always posted in Nassau Hall for everybody to see. A "gentleman's C" was then honorable enough, but open failure was something else. Not infrequently, a student confronted with the damning grade would write cheerfully opposite his grade: "Off to Virginia!" (At that time the University of Virginia was even more famous as a gentleman's country club than Princeton and, ironically, it had originated the honor system before it migrated north to Princeton.) It is not that there wasn't pressure to cheat. In his collection of short stories *In Princeton Town,* published in 1939, Day Edgar devotes one of them to the drama of a young man who, under heavy parental pressure to graduate and enraged by a professor who was picking on him, goes back to his room during an exam, copies perfect answers out of his books, and then at the last moment can't bring himself to turn in the exam paper because "no one, in the years that lay ahead, could remember whether or not he had received his diploma, but he himself could never entirely forget this examination. Every time he came back to reunions, every time he met a classmate—every time he saw the university's name in the sporting page—he would remember the morning he had sat in this room and broken the honor pledge."

As can be imagined, this system has not been above criticism by students boiling inside Princeton's pressure cooker. Scott Fitzgerald, who created an idealized Princeton, once called it in a *College Humor* article "Princeton's sacred tradition . . . something humanly precious," and added, "I have never seen or heard of a Princeton man cheating in an examination, though I am told a few such cases have been mercilessly and summarily dealt with." But when in 1928 he encountered some Princeton students on a train who cynically gave him chapter and verse about violations that had not been reported, he wrote Christian Gauss, then dean of the college, and was told in response that the honor system was completely in student hands—a response that moved Fitzgerald to comment: "Here is probably the greatest educator in the country. Nevertheless he is pulling a Pontius Pilate here—not deliberately but waiting for a cue."

The cue never came to Gauss, but it did not long ago to President Bowen, who gave a similar response when he had to testify in court on the first suit ever brought against the honor system by a student convicted of cheating. The suit, heard in the First Federal District Court by Judge Harold A. Ackerman, was filed by Robert A. Clayton, '82, who was charged with conferring with another student, consulting a lab manual, and changing an answer on a biology test in 1978. Following a year's suspension, Clayton returned to Princeton, graduated, and was admitted to the University of Maryland Medical School; yet he asked $500,000 in damages on the grounds that the honor committee had not informed him of his rights, given him adequate notice of a hearing, or provided competent counsel, and he argued that his conviction was an unwarranted effort on the part of the honor committee to prove its effectiveness in the wake of a campus poll that purportedly showed that some 17 percent of the student body had cheated at some time in their college career. Dr. Bowen countered that he had reviewed the proceedings and was satisfied that "fairness had been done" and argued that "we are not a court of law and don't intend to be one."

Regardless of its specific merits, the fact of a suit suggests that the heat is being turned up under the Princeton pressure cooker because of the outside academic atmosphere, where cheating is widely accepted as part of the game to get the high grades required by employers and graduate schools. The honor system will probably continue at Princeton, however, because it *is* a "bond among Princetonians" who are otherwise closely bonded by living together in relative isolation from the outside world. Not to be able to trust one's fellows in that most vital concern of college existence, academic achievement, would destroy the ambience of a place where the grosser forms of crime are virtually unknown and where the pilferage that causes students now to lock their doors is, according to the security service, the work of disadvantaged townies. Pressure or no, Princeton is fundamentally a place of peace because it is a place of trust. There are many Princetonians who would testify that having learned to live by the honor system was in the long run more important than any other aspect of the Princeton experience, the very essence of Princeton's special elitism (it is the only Ivy League university with an honor system).

If there aren't more pressured kids jumping out of windows at Princeton, one good reason might be that they can quickly appreciate that they belong to a do-as-I-do and not a do-as-I-say place. The pressures their elders and instructors accept may be even greater than their own. The elite cadre of graduate students (some fifteen hundred) who are struggling toward a master's or doctor's degree in some fifty-two disciplines are for the most part sequestered like medieval monks (nuns, too, now) in a Gothic quadrangle off campus where uninterrupted study is the order of the day, and night—that is, when they are not assisting in undergraduate instruction or helping a professor with his research. Observing them, one brilliant senior—perhaps the most brilliant, Valentina Vavasis's brother, Stephen, a mathematics major who won the Princeton Scholar Award—confessed that he would never attend graduate school at Princeton. "The life of graduate students here is pretty miserable," he said. "They're off by themselves and they never even get to meet each other and certainly not undergraduates. They're supposed to be scholars and not have social lives. I don't know if that's such a hot idea." If Woodrow Wilson, who lost the second most important battle of his life, when his desire to put the Graduate College in the center of campus was thwarted, could hear Steve Vavasis, he would undoubtedly rise from his grave and embrace him.

But more important by way of example of grace under pressure is the faculty. A group of people doesn't earn four Nobel prizes, nine MacArthur fellowships, and countless other awards and honors in the course of their undergraduate college careers while also publishing books and papers, giving lectures, and holding classes by sitting around on their duffs. Princeton's may be the only major university faculty where all members are required to teach, but that doesn't let them off the scholarly hook. "Publish or perish is too glib a phrase," says Dean Lemonick, "but, yes, it really is publish or perish in the sense that you have to expose your ideas to other people." Being awarded a tenured position on the Princeton faculty is a far longer, harder grind than getting into the college as a student. "The life of an assistant professor is tough, and many question whether it is worth it," says Dr. Emory Elliott, professor of English and master of Butler College. "Only one out of six in my department managed to get tenure. Nobody I came with stayed, so you really have to prepare yourself to leave in the first five years." What happened in Elliott's department is, according to Dean Lemonick, par for the course throughout the university.

Years ago a colleague of mine, Dan O'Keefe, described life at the *Reader's Digest,* where we both worked, as "a pie eating contest in which the prize is more pie to eat." The same might be said of Princeton. Consider, for instance, the load that tenured Professor Elliott carries. The effort he puts into teaching can be imagined from a report in the *Daily Princetonian* that his course, Literature 133—"Major American Writers"—was for the second consecutive year rated the most popular in the university by a student evaluation. In addition, as master of Butler College, Elliott oversees the administration of a facility feeding and housing five hundred freshmen and sophomores. More important to the Princeton tradition, Dr. Elliott feels obliged to get to know all the young people by name at least (250 fresh faces each year) and must therefore spend a good deal of time eating or otherwise socializing at the college. To that end, and because he wanted to entertain at home small groups of students and the faculty fellows of the college, Dr. Elliott sold his house, uprooted his family, and moved into a faculty rental housing only a few minutes' walk from Butler. And since Dr. Elliott doesn't intend to perish, he is also working on a book.

What one brings away after a spell at Princeton is that the myth of its tranquility is real. In *Humboldt's Gift,* a novel that includes a fictionalized account of his brief experience teaching creative writing at Princeton, Nobel Prize winner Saul Bellow writes: "And I couldn't see that Princeton was such a big deal as Humboldt made out. Between noisy Newark and squalid Trenton it was a sanctuary, a zoo, a spa, with its own choochoo and elms and lovely green cages." A novelist who knew Princeton better as a member of the class of 1947, Frederick Buechner, pictured in *A Long Day's Dying* a young instructor enjoying cocktails with friends on the terrace of the then Princeton Inn and saying, as the bells started to ring from the Graduate College's Cleveland Tower: "A Gothic music box, and such is college." Although taken out of context and possibly in violation of the author's intent, such comments still create a hazy, lazy public image of Princeton. But it can be said, and fervently, that people do not jump out of "Gothic music boxes" or swallow pills in "lovely green cages"—or find out in such circumscribed places that they can go out and lick the world.

# Chapter Six

# DID YOU PACK MY COMPUTER, MOM?

In the matter of educational philosophy, Princeton University is not what one would call trendy. When it was founded in 1746 in the colony of New Jersey for the purpose of producing Presbyterian ministers, the sole requirement for entrance and exit was competence in Latin, Greek, and Hebrew. As other courses were gradually introduced, Princeton resisted the great American movement toward practical education that flourished in the mid-nineteenth century. While other institutions constructed an inverted pyramid of professional schools—medicine, law, agriculture, dentistry, business—above the undergraduate level, Princeton stubbornly stuck to basic learning in the arts and sciences out of a still-current conviction. As President Bowen affirms: "We think it's very important that there be at least one university of world-class standing which really is an arts and sciences university." In view of his judgment, it is surprising to discover the extent to which the latest trend in education—the computerization of learning—is making a creeping conquest of Princeton's ivied campus.

The fact that the computer is not so gradually overtaking the leatherbound volume and the quill pen as the educational tool of choice in a conservative institution largely dominated by the liberal arts may be the surest sign yet that the computer, like sex, is here to stay and of great excitement to young minds. Some seats of higher learning, such as Carnegie-Mellon and Drexel universities, where within a few years every student will be *required* to have a personal computer, have gone much farther down the electronic road than Princeton. But this could be expected with the heavy tilt toward technical instruction in those places. What made a throwback to the precomputer age feel fossilized in the Princeton of today was to find that computer use is being demanded in some courses in the major I survived with a portable typewriter—public and international affairs—and that the electronic wonder is serving scholarship in the even more humanistic pursuits of classics, music, psychology, and art history—every course one can name.

If a visitor never entered the campus or talked to students or professors but simply walked up University Place from the railroad station and ducked into the Princeton University Store in search of a sweater or socks, he would literally bump into concrete evidence of the computer's presence and appeal. A whole section of the store not far from the entrance is devoted to display cases of hardware, shelves of books, and racks of magazines under an overarching sign: THE ELECTRONIC CANDY STORE. The profusion, not to say confusion, of material related to computers is incredible. I counted at least thirty magazines dealing with software, the stuff that makes computers talk. Many of them are put out by manufacturers, and the Apple people, for instance, carry the overly cute metaphor of their name into publications entitled *Peelings* and *In Cider.* Considering my personal awe in relation to the mysteries of the computer, I preferred a magazine with the incomprehensible title *80 Micro,* which featured an article on "Demystifying Bar Codes." Computers are serious business and nothing underscored this lesson more effectively than the store's willingness to surrender so much valuable commercial space to vending these products.

In getting with computers, as in so many other aspects of a changing Princeton, the university is recognizing some of the rather startling facts of contemporary American life. Nowhere are these facts set forth more fully than in *Focus 1983,* a publication of the Educational Testing Service, coincidentally headquartered in the Princeton vicinity. Says the ETS report: "The April 25, 1982, *New York Times* reports IBM has predicted that, before long, 75 percent of the work force will need some computer skills to do their jobs. By the end of the current millennium, it is entirely possible that computers will be so pervasive in every aspect of business that only those who can use them with facility will survive in the marketplace. The pace of this transition into the computer age has caught educators largely unprepared, and experts at every level are now struggling with the difficult problem of how best to prepare children for life in the future."

In these days when the commercialization of the personal computer, with its associated "games," has almost made it the Christmas toy of choice for any reasonably affluent American child, it is hard to believe that the first large-scale electronic computer was, as *Focus* reminds us, built as late as 1946 by J. Presper Eckert and John W. Mauchly at the University of Pennsylvania. But if Princeton does succeed in coping well with the computer, it will be historically fitting, since much of the heavy thinking about computers was done by mathematician John von Neumann, who taught at the university in the early 1930s, then joined the faculty of the nearby Institute for Advanced Study. Among other accomplishments, von Neumann computers assisted in the construction of the hydrogen bomb and provided the Navy with a twenty-four-hour weather watch. It was not until computers started shrinking dramatically, both in size and cost, over the last ten years that they became a feasible tool for the average citizen, and now students. The University of Pennsylvania machine ENIAC (the Electronic Numerical Integrator and Calculator) required a thirty- to fifty-foot room to contain it and used eighteen thousand vacuum tubes and many miles of wire; today a more powerful computer than ENIAC can be created on a chip of silicon less than a quarter inch in size and costing only a few dollars. Nor is the shrinking at an end, as *Focus* suggests: "According to Harold G. Shane in a January 1982 *Phi Delta Kappan* article . . . by 1980 it was possible to etch the equivalent of 60,000 to 70,000 vacuum tubes on a microchip; by the spring of 1981, in a U.S. laboratory, 750,000 equivalents were squeezed onto a chip."

As rapidly as they are shrinking, computers are proliferating. The National Center for Education Statistics estimated that elementary and secondary students had access to 96,000 microcomputers and 24,000 terminals in 1982–83, compared to 31,000 and 22,000 only two years before; and the industry foresees 300,000 to 650,000 being available on that level of education by 1985. "In many places," says *Focus,* "educators are torn between their fear of being left in the dust by the new technology and their uncertainty about how best to use it." It is this dilemma as to use that makes fascinating, and possibly instructive, an examination of how Princeton, by any measure one of the world's most prestigious educational institutions, is accommodating itself to their instrument, which, proponents claim, is revolutionizing the knowledge industry more radically than Gutenberg's printing press ever did.

Princeton, in fact, came to grips with the computer, per se, rather early in the game. Since it does have an Engineering School —which, along with architecture, is its only concession to "professionalism"—that includes a department in electrical engineering and computer science, the university installed one of the earlier generations of computers, an IBM 7090, in a computer center within its Engineering Quadrangle in 1962. It was viewed at the time primarily as an instrument for mathematical and scientific research and training. But as demand for its services increased and new generations of computers appeared, expansion was clearly in order, and a separate building was erected a few blocks away from the E-Quad to house the computer center. As of now, it is equipped with a $4.5 million IBM 3081, current with the state of the art, and its associated machinery—terminals, printers, card readers, tape drives, storage banks, and the like. In addition to the terminals in the computer center, more than a hundred others are scattered around the campus—in the E-Quad, the mathematics department in Fine Hall, the Firestone Library, a few residential colleges, and at least one eating club—through which students, or professors, can gain access by phone to the 3081 and, through that, to outside systems like the cross-country network of universities from Berkeley to Orono, Maine.

The Princeton Computer Center is a little world of its own within the larger world of the university. Architecturally, it is a functional, three-story brick building that actually looks like some sort of machine and, whether intentionally or not, hides shyly behind the row of elegant eating clubs on Prospect Street just east of the main campus that still evokes the rich boys' Princeton of Scott Fitzgerald's time. Inside the center, however, it is definitely present, or even future, time. Fitzgerald could not have imagined as Princetonians the jeaned and earnest young people of both sexes whose shaggy heads nod to smooth electronic heads as they struggle to tap out on the keyboards messages that the machine will turn into answers to their problems or convert into neatly printed papers. Open around the clock, weekends and holidays included, the place is as full of life at 4:00 A.M., particularly when senior theses are due, as at noon. There is a lounge for smoking and naps, vending machines that provide instant energy. It is possible to live there, and it is even possible for a computer aficionado to get his kicks there. The people who do this by playing a far-out exploration program called "Adventure" are known as hackers and looked upon by their fellows almost as creatures from another planet.

Although too much hacking would undoubtedly be discouraged by the operators of an already overloaded system, a little of it is probably a welcome sign to the staff of the computer center that their message is getting through. They are like advance-guard missionaries for a new religion, and they want *everybody* in the Princeton community to be converted, to experience the joy of salvation. During freshman week of 1983, the computer center sent out among the new arrivals some four hundred upperclass apostles for the computer creed. Their mission: to get the freshman to sign up for, and use, the $250 worth of computer time included in each student's tuition. "We really believe that the computer is a useful tool that will benefit the student in terms of getting a good education," says Howard Strauss, associate director of the center. "We're evangelical about it. We go out there believing we're doing this wonderful thing for people. I think we are, and we should eventually get eight or nine hundred of those eleven hundred freshmen in here."

Strauss is perfectly cast as the computer supermissionary. Young, bearded, bespectacled, articulate, he holds a master's degree in electrical engineering from the leader in the field, Carnegie-Mellon University. As manager of the computer center's user services—unlike much that has to do with computers this is plain English, which means getting and helping people to use the tool —his emphasis is on making the whole operation what he calls "friendly." To begin with, he tries to cut the computer itself down to size, as it were. As he told Robert H. White in the *Princeton Alumni Weekly:*

> People's images of computers tend to be grandiose. Some television station did a news segment on Princeton's computer a few years ago. They brought all of their camera equipment into the machine room and the producer said, "All right, where's the computer?" I pointed to the central processing unit, or CPU, the computer's "brain" which looks like nothing more than two medium-sized filing cabinets, and he said, "Sorry, that doesn't look enough like a computer. What else you got?" He spied a very impressive looking piece of equipment that was actually our air conditioner, and they ended up filming the reporter standing in front of it saying, "Here I am with the Princeton University computer."

The user, of course, doesn't have to understand the complicated electronic functioning of a computer any more than he or she probably understands the mechanics of an automobile or TV set. It is not even necessary ever to *see* the computer; all one needs is a terminal, which generally consists of a typewriterlike keyboard and a screen, and a telephone line to call in. "When our director fell out of an apple tree and was hospitalized, we wheeled a terminal into his room, and he could work when he couldn't even stand or turn," Strauss recalls. "Then we had a systems programmer who stayed home to take care of the baby while his wife went to work, but he had a terminal and could do everything at home that he could here. He was in such close and constant contact that I'd be surprised when I'd forget and go down to his office and find he wasn't there."

If most people can safely ignore the hardware except for learning to type a bit, the software upon which the computer feeds remains a formidable stumbling block to the uninitiated. For one thing, there are the many computer "languages," which appear even less comprehensible than Greek, that Princeton students were once forced to learn; for another, there's something called programming, which is the art (or science?) of instructing the computer what you want it to do, usually in a meaningless mixture of numbers and letters that constitutes a "language." For most of the potential users in a liberal arts university like Princeton, Strauss dismisses programming out of hand. Their objective is usually to use the computer for word processing or the retrieval of information already computerized, and for these purposes there are enough existing programs that can be adapted to their needs.

"The big misconception is that people who use computers have to be good programmers. About half the people who use the computer here don't do any programming at all," Strauss says, "and one of our functions is to run around trying to make it easier for people *not* to program. So to use the computer you don't have to be a mathematical wizard or a logician. All you have to do is understand what you are using the computer for. Let's say you are in psychology or sociology and have gathered a lot of data. You can use the computer for complex statistical analysis. You can find a program already written, feed in your data, and it will do the analysis for you."

As to language, Strauss's User Services—there are three full-time staff members and more than forty computer-wise students doing part-time work—is making an extraordinary effort to bridge the gap between plain English and the electronic tongues in the interest of making the computer "friendly." One example is to tell it how to use the machine that prints with a laser beam. "The laser printer is relatively new, and internally it's a difficult machine to use," Strauss explains. "It has a very complex command structure, and when we first saw it, we said no student will ever be able to use this. We wrote all kinds of programs that would make it so simple to use that no student would have to know about the command structure. Now, to use this, the student only has to learn one new word—*laser.* As a result, the very first week we announced it, there were twenty thousand sheets of paper printed on it. I've talked to people at places where they've had the thing a couple of years and people weren't printing that much. We chose to tie three or four people up for four months to make this printer easy to use; at Princeton we think that's a good way to spend our time. And when it comes to printing, you can print with different typefaces—italics, boldface, elite, and so on. To do this at a dozen other schools I can name, you use the IBM number, which it is impossible to remember. Here you just say you want italics or whatever. It's a lot of work to get a machine to know the word *italics,* but if that word is something you already know, it's far better than the best documentation or providing the best courses to teach something new."

The computer center does, however, provide free, noncredit courses ranging from elementary explanations for people new to computers to advanced instruction in programming. In the past academic year there were seventy-five such courses, many of them held between 12:30 P.M. and 2:30 P.M., when students were encouraged to bring sandwiches for a "lunch and learn" session. Since they are open to anyone in the larger Princeton community, these courses attract an audience salted with gray heads and even an occasional bright, wriggling ten-year-old. During the one I dropped in on, Strauss was offering an introduction to programming. "A program takes some data and converts it into answers," he was saying. "It consists of a series of instructions, written by a person and very detailed, that go from data to answer. It's like a recipe to take a lot of separate ingredients and turn them into a delicious cake." Bouncing around in front of a blackboard, Strauss chalked a series of boxes, each of which would contain a command, and connected them with lines "like beads on a string" to illustrate a structural program. I felt that even I, who had never had any hands-on experience with a computer, was beginning to grasp the concept. If I couldn't, I already knew that I could wander into the center's ever-open clinic, manned by staff or student assistants, for an answer to any question, ranging from what a symbol in Fortran means to where to find the coffee machine.

This helpful, open atmosphere at the computer center is luring ever more Princetonians of every stripe into giving electronics a try. Several upperclassmen reported that at least 60 percent of their classmates were using the computer, mostly for word processing junior papers and senior theses. Solider evidence of increasing computer use comes from the center's dollar figures. Total computing charges (the IBM 3081 also services the university's administration) in 1975–76 were $3 million, with student use accounting for about $600,000, or 20 percent; in 1982–83, the total had risen to $5 million, $2 million (nearly 40 percent) of which was attributed to student use. Nevertheless, missionary Strauss sees a long way to go, particularly in converting the faculty. "It's not enough to have computers or learn about them if the faculty is not brought up to date," he says. "We're seeing the beginnings of that in Princeton, but it's really got to spread before we're going to see any widespread computer literacy."

Among the early enthusiastic faculty members is Dr. Lynn Townsend White III, associate professor of politics and international affairs at the Woodrow Wilson School. White, a specialist in Chinese politics, got hooked on the computer for a very practical reason: he thought that he could save a lot of time by word processing a book he was writing about China. The computer can, in fact, do marvelous things when it comes to writing and editing. It can check the writer's copy against a thirty-thousand-word dictionary in its memory, and when a word is misspelled or a word used that is not in its lexicon, it will stop and flash a possible alternative. One can also type footnotes to a word or sentence as one writes, and the computer will automatically number and print them out at the bottom of the page; or one can note items to be indexed, which the computer will automatically rearrange in alphabetical order at the end of the text. But more important, in White's view, is the aid the computer gives to thinking.

"Computers are thought of as big calculators, but they are not that any more than they are obviously typewriters," White says. "They're really symbol manipulators, and symbols can be anything—numbers or words or paragraphs. They're marvelous because they can move these symbols around so easily and quickly. So when you write with the computer you can improve the flexibility of your thinking and especially your writing, because you can put things on a screen and change them around into the order that is most logical."

It was a short step for a humanist like White ("you don't study China unless you're a humanistic type") from fiddling with the computer to becoming a missionary within the Woodrow Wilson School. Among other things, he wrote his own "Script Guide" for humanists. More practically, he preached the gospel to fourteen students in a task force that he was conducting on U.S. policy toward Taiwan. The task force is one of the teaching devices in the Woodrow Wilson School in which students research various aspects of a subject, write papers on their findings, and meet in committee to prepare an overall report.

The advantages offered by the computer to students in the course were immediately apparent to White: "People write first drafts of their papers and then do revisions and then a final. The computer is very useful because it saves a lot of typing and encourages people to make revisions, sometimes stylistic and sometimes substantive. Changes come up in the course of debating, and the computer makes it easy to take out a section and put in a new one. It's a tool. Then when you've finished you can print a report."

Despite his enthusiasm, White did not press computer use on his class; only four of his students had computer experience. "One of the advantages of this kind of course is that the students run it," he says. "There was one meeting when I was half an hour late, and the student chairman led a discussion on procedure in which the leading question was whether they wanted to use the computer. If so, they'd all be forced to learn. By the time I got there, they'd voted to use it." Thus, in one stroke, ten more Princetonians joined the ranks of those who will have some familiarity with the computer when they enter the business world, and it seems likely that computer use will spread like an infection throughout the humanistic Woodrow Wilson School. "You have to remember," says White "that that class contrasted sharply with the present incoming classes who have had computer experience in high school."

Much farther away from the computer center both physically and philosophically than the Woodrow Wilson School—which, in fact, is at the campus end of club row on Prospect Street—is McCormick Hall in the center of the campus proper, where Dr. Marilyn Aronberg Lavin, visiting lecturer with the rank of professor in art and archaeology, has her office. Moreover, Dr. Lavin, trim, energetic and of precomputer age, is a specialist in a field of art centuries removed from the electronic age—the Italian Renaissance. Yet today Dr. Lavin is one of the most active users of the computer center, and she uses it specifically to organize research and generate new ideas about "the history of the disposition of fresco cycles in the thirteenth, fourteenth, and fifteenth centuries in Italy."

Dr. Lavin began to think about the computer while engaged in research in Italy. During the Italian Renaissance there was a large-scale revival in painting scenes of Christ, Mary, Saint John the Baptist, and a host of saints on the walls of public places. "These are the most famous paintings of the Renaissance, and they have been studied every which way from the point of view of style, chronology, iconography, attribution, and so on," says Dr. Lavin. "But what I am studying has not been studied. The artist was told what to paint—the contract might call for something like depicting the life of Saint Stephen—but he was not told where to put the scenes or in what order. So in studying how and where the artist chose to position things, I think I have found a new way of tapping into the creative side of the paintings." Dr. Lavin visited churches and chapels and took notes on such details as the size and shape of walls, the number and location of windows, the placement of figures and natural features in the paintings, whether the design ran from left to right or right to left.

Her notes quickly accumulated, and soon she had eight thousand items to cover. She had once undertaken a similar project and found that it took as much time to organize her shoeboxes full of note cards as it did to undertake the research. "So I thought, 'Let the machine do it.' I'd never been near a computer, but when I got back I just walked into the computer center like an idiot and said, 'I want to use the computer. What do I do?' They have been very intelligent and patient with me and taught me how to teach myself, so to speak. I've been working over two years now, and I have a data bank more than twenty-five hundred lines long," Dr. Lavin says.

What can she do with it? "Well, I can use it as a teaching tool, or even a guide book. For example, if I say, 'Give me Santa Maria Novella,' the machine goes directly to that entry. I can get the artist, date, city, church on any item without going through a file; I don't even have to enter material in alphabetical or chronological order. Or I can do an analysis. If I want to know when the devotion to the Virgin Mary became manifest in the visual arts, I could ask the computer what is the earliest representation of the life of the Virgin, where is it, how many are there from that era. I'd immediately get a graph showing me that, say, there's one in the thirteenth century, seven in the fourteenth century, perhaps fifteen in the first half of the fifteenth century, but then they disappear."

Dr. Lavin did not have to program to create her data bank. She was able to use an existing program called SAS (statistics analysis systems) on lease to Princeton. But she does have to write what she calls a "tiny program" every time she wants to ask a question. "It took me three months to program one question, and it took the machine twenty seconds to answer it," she recalls. Like Dr. White, she finds working with the machine an aid to thinking: "You have to be very systematic, and you have to mean what you say. I have, for instance, to think exactly what I mean when I say something is on the left—on the left of what, what's my point of departure?" Like Dr. White, too, Dr. Lavin has become something of a lay missionary to her department. Not only is she teaching students how to put information into the computer, break it down and retrieve it, but she is also encouraging art history scholars in the periods before and after her own to add to her data bank.

Although computerizing art history is relatively new at Princeton, composing music on the computer is old hat, thanks to years of experimentation by Professor Paul Lansky. The way it's done is the composer works out an exact description of each note in a digital code of binary numbers, which when fed through a DAC (digital to analog converter) are turned into electrical impulses that come out of speakers as sound. "The digital computer is the most powerful musical instrument ever devised—it can create any sound than can be described," according to Lansky. "The main virtue of the computer for an undergraduate interested in composition is that he becomes a performer rather than a person who gives instructions to people. The computer feedback is very helpful from an educational point of view. You hear your music soon after you create it, rather than having to wait until you can round up performers to play what you've written."

Although the computer is now getting fairly heavy use in English and the classics to analyze texts fed into it for, say, stylistic effects—how often is a certain phrase used, how many times is a word repeated, what is the rhyme or meter scheme— it is still getting its hardest workout in the E-Quad. The frontier of computing is in the area of graphics. A young computer whiz, a junior named Rakefet Stier, led me to a room in the E-Quad bristling with the two-headed terminals of the graphics system. Ms. Stier, by the way, epitomized not only the computer generation but also the Princeton overachiever in that she arrived on campus with some computer literacy, is working toward a certificate in the Woodrow Wilson School, in addition to a degree in engineering, and is helping to pay for her education by serving as an adviser and programmer in the computer center. While I watched, she sat at an ordinary terminal, a keyboard topped by a black and white screen, typed in instructions until she called up an image on the other "head," a color screen. Using a small joystick, she began to manipulate and change the image like a three-year-old playing with his magic slate. But there is considerably more magic in this device, since one can not only wipe out and alter what goes into the machine but store it in memory— or translate it into hardware.

The farthest-out experiment with graphics is taking place in the basement of E-Quad, where the terminals are linked to a

Japanese-made microcomputer called a Fanuc, which controls a Tsugami "Mercury"—an automated lathe and milling machine. Using the joystick, the operator draws on the screen a three-dimensional design of a product, such as a metal candlestick, sends it through the computer, and then watches the wheels turn. This is known as computer-assisted design with computer-assisted manufacturing, CAD/CAM for short, and to say that its refinement and development will result in another industrial revolution is probably putting it mildly.

With all this mechanical activity going on, it is obvious that the university has to find a way to live successfully with the computer. As in education generally, Princeton seems to be marching to its own drummer. Whereas other universities are introducing computers and computer training by fiat for students and faculty alike, Strauss doubts that such a policy will, or should, work at Princeton. "The faculty here is too fiercely independent, as they should be," he says. "You've got some top people here, and it isn't a group that can be pushed around easily." As articulated by Vice Provost Richard R. Spies, the overall policy at Princeton is moving in the direction of retaining its character of stubborn, individual scholarship. In sum: help individuals solve their own computer problems. The university is in the process of arranging bargains in personal microcomputers through major manufacturers and encouraging departments to get up their own microcomputer operations. The computer center is establishing programs to teach individuals how to make the best use of their own equipment in conjunction with the main-frame computer. An experiment is underway leading to the possible linkage of all university buildings to the computer center by cables capable of carrying information faster than telephone lines. But the flavor of administration thinking is apparent in Spies's statement: "To the extent that individuals decide to purchase their own computing capability rather than relying solely on university resources, this will allow us to concentrate our resources on supporting *people* and their computing needs, rather than just supplying and maintaining equipment."

The Princeton student of the future probably should ask Mom if she packed the computer along with the hi-fi and tennis racket; he or she will doubtless need it. At one underclass college at least 10 percent of the class of 1987 arrived with a computer.

However widespread computer use does become at Princeton, it is to be hoped that users will take to heart a bit of wisdom with which Professor White concluded his instructions on scripting that neatly puts the computer in its proper place at Princeton: "In Italy during the Renaissance, famous sculptors paid much attention to carving pulpits. They did such a marvelous job that their work is a standing insult to preachers. It is extremely difficult to utter anything from these pulpits that is worthy of the artistry put into them. With the computer you face the same problem. The gadget can help you immensely to compose a well-organized, literate thesis. What is finest about its complexity and elaboration, however, is that it points away from itself: you are the one who must say something."

*Opened in 1756, Nassau Hall housed for almost fifty years all of Princeton University's classrooms and dormitories, its library, chapel, dining room, and kitchen. During the Revolutionary War it sheltered troops of both sides and has been designated as a National Historic Landmark.* PHOTO BY ROBERT P. MATTHEWS

*Closeup of Nassau Hall, showing the famed tigers that guard the entrance to the historic building.* PHOTO BY CLEM FIORI

*A pair of considerably more rampant tigers guard the approach to another part of Nassau Hall.* PHOTO BY CLEM FIORI

*The splendid faculty room in Nassau Hall features, among other portraits, an idealized painting of George Washington by Charles Willson Peale.* PHOTO BY JOHN W. H. SIMPSON

*At 50 McCosh Hall, the main academic building for instruction in the liberal arts, students sit for important lectures.* PHOTO BY JOHN W. H. SIMPSON

*A beloved Princeton landmark is the Mather Sundial in McCosh Court.*
PHOTO BY JOHN W. H. SIMPSON

*The magnificent Harvey S. Firestone Library, built in the prevailing collegiate Gothic style, was dedicated in 1946. The noted industrialist sent five sons to Princeton. The sculpture, "Song of the Vowels," is by Jacques Lipschitz.* PHOTO BY CLEM FIORI

Princeton is a campus of arches: Blair Hall, built in 1897, was the first dormitory to be built in collegiate Gothic style and forms part of Dean Mathey College, where Brooke Shields has her digs. PHOTO BY CLEM FIORI

A student notice board makes this archway a popular gathering place. PHOTO BY CLEM FIORI

The archway entrance to Holder Hall dormitory. PHOTO BY JOHN W. H. SIMPSON

*Student members of Cloister relax in front of the ornate arch that leads to their eating club.* PHOTO BY CLEM FIORI

*Another view of Blair Hall, framed in a typical Princeton archway.* PHOTO BY MAHLON LOVETT

*Even the off-campus McCarter Theatre sustains the collegiate Gothic arch motif.* PHOTO COURTESY OF PRINCETON UNIVERSITY

*Departures from the Gothic style include these handsome contemporary buildings: the Woodrow Wilson School of Public and International Affairs and the Jadwin Gymnasium.* PHOTOS BY CLEM FIORI AND ROBERT P. MATTHEWS

*An aerial view of the entire Plasma Physics Laboratory facility and a
closeup of the futuristic Tokamak Fusion Test Reactor (TFTR).* PHOTOS
COURTESY OF PRINCETON UNIVERSITY COMMUNICATIONS/PUBLICATIONS

*A lot of learning goes on in small classes, called precepts, such as this one.*
PHOTO BY CLEM FIORI

*In an undergraduate biology lab an assignment calls for determined concentration.* PHOTO BY CLEM FIORI

*The arts do not go neglected at Princeton. Here Tina Kachele, '84, and Accra Shepp, '84, install exhibits for the Visual Arts program.* PHOTO COURTESY PRINCETON UNIVERSITY COMMUNICATIONS/PUBLICATIONS

*Informal study sometimes takes place in McCosh Court, especially in springtime.* PHOTO BY CLEM FIORI

*And, when the trees begin to leaf, precepts may be held in front of Nassau Hall.* PHOTO BY CLEM FIORI

*A student finds a quiet spot in the lounge of his eating club to catch up on his reading.* PHOTO BY CLEM FIORI

*A group of students brown bag it in Palmer Square while a prototype (foreground) is forever caught in the act of reading and munching.* PHOTO BY CLEM FIORI

*A group of freshmen take time off to pose for a group portrait in their dormitory suite. The tiger is the work of a contemporary.* PHOTO BY CLEM FIORI

*Members of Elm, one of the luxurious (and still controversial) eating clubs on Prospect, enjoy a postlunch bull session.* PHOTO BY GEORGE EAGER

*A hundred years ago freshman fought sophomore for the right to carry a cane on campus. Although reduced to a symbolic ritual, individual matches still bring out considerable class spirit.* PHOTO BY STEPHEN CASSELL, '85

*However it looks to the fans, Ivy League football is a bruising game as played at Palmer Stadium.* PHOTO BY ACTION SPORTS

*A football victory over arch rival Yale is still celebrated with a bonfire in front of Whig and Clio halls, once the seats of the oldest literary and debating societies in America.*

*Members of the class of 1980 jubilantly take part in a joyful annual event—the "P" Rade.* PHOTO BY CLEM FIORI

*The culmination of it all: Princeton commencement, class of 1982.* PHOTO COURTESY PRINCETON UNIVERSITY, COMMUNICATIONS/PUBLICATIONS

*A member of the class of 1980, on her commencement day, is a study in pride and accomplishment.* PHOTO BY CLEM FIORI

*Two old grads of the class of 1909 return for a June reunion. "Going Back" is a favorite alumni song and, as the sign proclaims, it's "forever."* PHOTO BY CLEM FIORI

JAMES C. CRAMPTON

| BORN | 1909 |
| PRINCETON | 1932 |
| DIED | 1983 |

*A Princeton association lies deep in the heart, even unto the grave.*
Drawing by H. MARTIN; © 1983 The New Yorker Magazine, Inc.

# Chapter Seven

# "TIGER, TIGER, BURNING BRIGHT ..."

In these days when, on a Superbowl Sunday, it is possible to believe that football is the national religion of the United States, a look at where the sport began is both instructive and corrective. If given an associative test, only those with long memories would respond to the word *football* with Princeton instead of Giants, Redskins, Cowboys, or the like. Yet not only was Princeton a participant with nearby Rutgers in the first intercollegiate football contest, but the school, as well as its players and coaches, developed, refined, and nearly dominated the game for generations and were still making headlines as late as the 1960s. Thus, millions of pro-football fanatics owe a debt of gratitude to a place that they probably scorn as an ivy-encrusted retreat for effete eggheads.

That football came out of Princeton is only one bit of historical evidence of the fact that, paradoxically, an institution supposedly devoted to the life of the mind has always been, and remains, one of the most athletically active places in America. Televised collegiate games provide the public image of college sports, yet it is not generally known that Princeton also participated in the first intercollegiate baseball game, held the nation's first collegiate track contest, furnished more than a third of the American team for the first modern Olympics in 1896— or that for the last five years Princeton has been at or near the top of the Ivy League in the composite standing in all sports. Princeton fields thirty-two varsity teams (fourteen composed of women) and twenty-five "club" teams in athletic skills ranging from rugby to sailing to frisbee. "There are no statistics, but I would bet a lot of money that there's no other institution of our size, probably in the world, that has as large a percentage of students participating in intercollegiate athletics," says Robert John Myslik, Princeton's director of athletics. "If you add the intramural sports—six hundred teams playing thirty-six hundred contests in one year—you have something like 60 percent of the student body involved regularly in some athletic activity."

To an unusual degree the athletic spirit of Princeton has tended to be inspired by practice rather than preaching. When he arrived in Princeton in 1869, the year of the first football game, President James McCosh made construction of a gymnasium one of his first priorities; Woodrow Wilson was an undergraduate manager of both football and baseball teams and is credited, as president, with siphoning funds from Andrew Carnegie to build an artificial lake for crew; more recently, President Robert F. Goheen was a varsity soccer player and coach as a graduate student; and President William G. Bowen is athletically active too, according to Myslik: "One of the things I do every once in a while is get beaten in squash by the president. He's about as tough a competitor as I've ever met, and he understands the value of sport. I'm really glad he does. Princeton has always been a school where athletics at the proper level is important."

It took quite a while, though, for athletics to reach any level at all in Princeton. There is no mention of sport in the ten years of the colonial college's existence before the students were finally settled under one roof at Nassau Hall in 1756. Even then they were so steadily on their knees in prayer or had their noses so stuck in books that an after-dinner walk seemed to be the extent of physical activity—only a few of the richer boys kept horses to ride. Around 1761, accounts of handball and shinny, a ball and stick game, creep into students' letters. The handball was played against a wall of the president's house, and so many erring shots sent glass shattering into its rooms that, by 1849, a court was built to contain the game. The first thing resembling a gym—little more than a barn—was erected in 1859; the first baseball game was played in 1864 against Williams, Princeton winning 27 to 16, and the first track meet was held in 1874.

Other sports followed rapidly. In 1874, a crew, practicing at its peril in the Delaware and Raritan Canal, worked up enough steam to enter the intercollegiate races at Saratoga, despite objections from Amherst that "you have to draw the line somewhere." The Princeton freshman crew not only won their race but created an even more enduring legacy in the form of the school colors, which would evolve into that ferocious mascot, the tiger. Orange had already been worn at President McCosh's inaugural at the suggestion of George K. Ward, class of 1869, because it was the color of the House of Nassau, one of his favorite subjects of study. By chalking black numerals on their orange shirts, the Princeton crew unwittingly started a tradition and sportswriters threw in the tiger later when Princeton football players wore socks and sleeves striped in those colors.

Since football, even in its present state, is still the "flagship sport" at Princeton, as it is everywhere else, its beginnings are of more than usual interest. An informal version was actually being played as early as 1844 on the open green behind Nassau Hall. It sounds like formalized riot. Virtually the whole student body would divide itself in half, line up to defend one or the other of the dormitories flanking the green, and go at it with a round rubber ball under rules that were said to be "as elastic as the ball itself." The game hadn't shaken down much by November of 1869, when Rutgers sent a challenge from New Brunswick to which a group of Princetonians eagerly responded.

There is evidence that the Princeton players were as eager for a day on the town as for a game. Coming as they did from a rural crossroads with a handful of college buildings, they spent the morning walking the streets of New Brunswick, "during which stroll billiards received a good deal of attention," as a contemporary report noted. In early afternoon they gathered on the Rutgers commons and prepared for battle by unceremoniously discarding hats, coats and vests. Meanwhile, the two captains—William S. Gummere of Princeton (later Chief Justice of the New Jersey Supreme Court) and William J. Leggett of Rutgers (later a Dutch Reformed clergyman)—got together to hash out the rules.

The game they intended to play was more like rugby than football. There were twenty-five men on each side, two of whom stayed by the opponent's goal and were known as "captains of the enemy's goal"; half of the others were assigned to one section of the field as "fielders," while the other half, called "bulldogs," rushed back and forth with the ball. It is easy to see that the active bulldogs were the foundation of the modern eleven. The roundish ball was moved by kicking, dribbling, and batting, but the bulldogs would protect ball handlers by "massing" around them. To even things up, both captains surrendered favorite tactics. Princeton would yield the right of a player who caught the ball in the air to have a "free kick," and Rutgers would agree to mount the ball and kick off instead of "babying it." The game would end when one team scored six goals.

In view of the fact that the Princeton-Rutgers rivalry would end 111 years later because the Scarlet Knights were going "big time," it is well to recall the description of the teams by an anonymous reporter for the *Rutgers Targum:* "The Princeton men were almost without exception tall and muscular while the majority of our '25' were small and light." Nevertheless, Princeton's kickoff was a dribble to one side, and the light, fast Rutgers men massed around it and moved it within minutes downfield to a point where their "captains of the enemy goal" put it through the Princeton posts. Score: Rutgers 1; Princeton 0. A mortified Princeton captain got hold of the biggest man on the squad—Jacob E. Michael, or "Big Mike"—and instructed him to break up the Rutgers mass. On the next go-around, Big Mike scattered the opposing players "like a burst bundle of sticks," and Princeton scored the tying point.

From then on it was a seesaw into the twilight: "Every goal was like the one before—the same headlong running, wild shouting and frantic kicking." At one point a mercifully unnamed Rutgers man earned another "first" in football by kicking at his own goal and setting up a Princeton score. By far the most exciting action took place when the ball landed beside a fence on which a row of cheering students was perched like crows on a wire. Two behemoths rushing for the ball hit the fence, knocked it over and sent the perchers flying. The final score was Rutgers 6, Princeton 4, and "after the match the players had an amicable 'feed' together and at eight o'clock our guests went home, in high spirits, but thirsting to beat us next time."

Princeton more than slaked that thirst. A week later, using their "free kick" rules on home turf, they beat Rutgers 8-0. In the ensuing sixty-nine contests between the two schools, Princeton racked up a 53-15-1 record, but Princeton lost seven of the last eleven games before the rivalry was ended. The style of football in that first game, called "association football," was continued for a while and used in 1873 when Princeton and Yale began the longest continuous rivalry in American football. But Harvard played a modified British rugby, and in 1875 Columbia, Harvard, Princeton, and Yale got together to agree on using the rougher rugby style for intercollegiate matches. This featured a clash of "flying wedges," "V formations," and other brutal strategies that reportedly caused bare-knuckled prizefighter John L. Sullivan to shudder and declare: "There's murder in *that* game." It wasn't until 1905, when President Theodore Roosevelt intervened to stop the mayhem, that the rules began to change to allow forward passes and other less injurious ways of moving the ball.

Tough as it was, football quickly picked up an enthusiastic following. An account in *Harper's Weekly* of the Princeton-Yale game in New York on Thanksgiving Day, 1893, by famed journalist Richard Harding Davis rings familiar today. "The city surrenders herself to the students and their game as she never welcomes any other event except a Presidential election," Davis wrote. Stores throughout the city were decorated in blue or orange and black, young women paraded Broadway with bows of the colors they favored in their hair, churches scheduled services an hour earlier so that worshippers could make the game on time. Princeton clinched a perfect record for the season with a 6-0 victory over Yale, and Davis, following the Princetonians to their dressing room, was moved to write this purplish passage:

> People who live far away from New York, and who cannot understand from the faint echoes they receive how great is the enthusiasm that this contest arouses, may possibly get some idea of what it means to the contestants themselves through the story of a remarkable incident which occurred after the game in the Princeton dressing room. The team was being rubbed down for the last time after their three months of self-denial, and anxiety, and the hardest and roughest sort of rough work that young men are called upon to do, and outside in the semi-darkness thousands of Princeton followers were jumping up and down and hugging each other, and shrieking themselves hoarse. One of the Princeton coaches came into the room out of this mob, and holding up his arm for silence, said, "Boys, I want you to sing the doxology." And standing as they were naked and covered with mud and blood and perspiration, the eleven men who had won the championship sang the doxology from the beginning to the end as solemnly and as seriously, and, I am sure, as sincerely as they ever did in their lives, while outside the no less thankful fellow students yelled and cheered, and beat at the doors and windows, and howled for them to come out and show themselves.

Ivy League football was at the center of public attention through World War I, which may account for the fact that one of the most untarnished athletic stars of all time belongs as much to America as to Princeton. Much about this everlasting hero would be impossible for the imagination to invent, beginning with his name itself—Hobart Amory Hare Baker. Physically, he was handsome and blessed with a shock of golden hair, which he refused to cover with a helmet. At five feet nine inches, and weighing 165 pounds, Hobey Baker was rock hard and, from iron self-discipline, always ready for action on the hockey rink and football field, and as events would prove, totally without fear. He so dominated his favorite sports that typical headlines during his Princeton years, 1910–13, often read: BAKER DOES IT AGAIN or PLAIN CASE OF TOO MUCH HOBEY BAKER.

Football then was still largely a defensive game, a boring tangle of grunting bodies, but Baker invented a daring way to get around this mess and to star as an individual, according to his biographer John Davies. A lot of punting went on, often on the first down, and Baker was invariably the Princeton safety man. "Hobey worked out [a] most sensational variation on the conventional tactics for a safety man," Davies writes in *The Legend of Hobey Baker*.

> No one who ever saw him use it forgot it, as indeed he should not have, for Baker is the only player in the history of football who was skillful enough to use it. He would deliberately stand about five yards back of the place he calculated the ball would land; while the ball spiraled down the field and the ends converged on him, he would stand like a matador, slowly flexing his legs up and down, and then take off on the dead run. He caught the ball at his stomach by wrapping both arms around it, forming a cradle with his elbows and hands, and then either shot between the ends or cut outside, usually going to his right.

Often he got away for long runs, but as often ended in a crash with an opposing player. It is said that when this happened the wife of Princeton's president would shut her eyes and say, "I just hope that golden-haired boy doesn't get killed." Far from being killed, he became "the most feared open field runner in the game" and, as a drop kicker, set an individual Princeton season scoring record of ninety-two points in 1912 that stood for sixty years.

The son of a Princeton halfback, Hobey seemed to be that rare phenomenon, the "natural" athlete, and yet he never took any chances. His efforts to improve his play were astonishing. After a football victory over Yale, when everybody else was relaxing and rejoicing, Baker took a train to New York, went out to an ice rink and started to work on his hockey game. One of his ice hockey skills came from skating alone for hours in the dark and learning to handle the puck by feel. When Baker appeared on the ice, promoters didn't bother to list the opposing teams. The marquee at Madison Square Garden simply announced: HOBEY BAKER PLAYS HERE TONIGHT. Hobey was the kind of sportsman who would go into the opponents' locker room after the most bruising contest and shake hands all around. Once, in a hockey game against Yale, Davies relates, "he and the opposing captain went down in a heap, and the referee called a charging penalty against Yale. Hobey instantly protested, 'He was playing the puck not me, and that penalty could cost them the game.' The referee shrugged in disbelief, and with a what-next expression reversed himself."

Good as he was, Hobey's feats would inevitably have been eclipsed by those of later generations of athletes, but what happened next turned his life into enduring myth. With war approaching, Baker learned to fly and was one of the first American fighter pilots to reach France. On December 21, 1918, he was captain in command of the 141st Aero Squadron, AEF, at Toul. That morning he received orders to proceed to Paris by night train for demobilization. It was a rainy day, and a repaired Spad was being returned to the squadron's hangar as Baker made his last rounds. He had flown the plane in combat and he insisted, despite protests from his men, on taking it up for a quick test of the repairs. At six hundred feet the engine failed and the plane dropped like a stone. At 11:55 A.M. Hobart Amory Hare Baker died in the ambulance that had picked up his shattered body. It was a front-page shock to the nation, and at Princeton it was quickly decided to raise funds for a most appropriate memorial, a hockey rink bearing his name. No glowing epitaph could more effectively proclaim how much Hobey Baker epitomized athletics as the variety of donors who contributed to the rink—1,537 men from 39 colleges, including 172 from Harvard and 90 from Yale.

After Baker's day Princeton fielded better teams and better players, such as Dick Kazmaier, winner of the 1951 Heisman Trophy, and all-Americans Cosmo Iacavazzi and Charlie Gogolak in the mid-sixties. What is now considered Princeton's "team of destiny" was the undefeated 1922 eleven that went to Chicago for what was the Super Bowl of its time, the first football game in history to be broadcast. Trailing 18-7 with twelve minutes to go, Princeton scored two touchdowns and converted to pull ahead 21-18, then held Chicago inches from the goal line in the last seconds to complete a perfect season. In the mid-thirties, under Fritz Crisler, later coach at Michigan, Princeton again had undefeated teams, and Crisler had some surprising help in his efforts to keep them on top.

One of the reasons that Princeton football is still a concern at an otherwise highbrow institution is that, by its very nature as a spectacle, it serves as a rallying point for Princeton's unusually loyal and incredibly generous alumni. A member of that team of destiny, H. F. "Pink" Baker, for instance, never missed a contest in sixty years, freshman or varsity, except for wartime service. Almost in a class with Baker during his short life was F. Scott Fitzgerald. Fitzgerald, in fact, and like many others, came to Princeton largely because of football. Though an indifferent prep school football player himself—he was once taken out of a game for appearing to be yellow—the budding novelist in Fitzgerald saw the football star as hero writ large. After a Princeton-Harvard game, when Princetonian Sam White ran ninety-five yards for the winning touchdown, Fitzgerald noted on his ticket stub: "Sam White decides me for Princeton." But it wasn't really winning that intrigued Fitzgerald about Princeton football; on another occasion he said: "Yale always seemed to nose them out in the last quarter by superior 'stamina' as the newspapers used to call it. It was to me a repetition of the story of the foxes and the big animals in the child's book. I imagined the Princeton men as slender and keen and romantic, and the Yale men as brawny and brutal and powerful."

By the 1930s, Fitzgerald, like many of his fellow alumni before and since, had developed the kind of keen interest in Princeton gridiron success that has always kept Princeton coaches under considerable pressure. One of his biographers, Andrew Turnbull, '42, who knew Fitzgerald personally and was himself interested in Princeton football, picked up on this aspect of the author's life. An alcoholic, Fitzgerald suffered from insomnia and, as Turnbull tells it, "There were nights when he couldn't write and he couldn't sleep either, and he would reach out desperately for human contact. On such a night Asa Bushnell, Princeton's graduate manager of athletics and a clubmate of Fitzgerald's, was wrenched awake by a phone call at 3:00 A.M.

" 'Get a pencil and paper,' said Fitzgerald. 'I have some suggestions for Fritz Crisler.'

"Bushnell did not stir but let an appropriate time elapse before telling Fitzgerald to proceed.

" 'Yale will be laying for us,' Fitzgerald went on. 'They've had a good chance to scout Crisler's system and he's got to cross them up. Here's how he does it. Princeton must have two teams. One will be big—all men over two hundred. This team will be used to batter them down and wear them out. Then the little team, the pony team, will go in and make the touchdowns.'

"Before Bushnell had a chance to reply, Fitzgerald had hung up, but half an hour later the phone rang again.

" 'I forgot to mention,' said Fitzgerald, 'that the big team will be coached on defense and be given only a few power plays. Little team will be coached on offense, great variety of plays. Substitutions to be made as a unit.'

"Toward dawn came a final call wrapping it up.

" 'Incidentally, my system will do away with all the parental and alumni criticism about playing the wrong men in the games because under this system everybody will play.'

"Informed of Fitzgerald's brainstorm, Crisler wrote him that the plan had many virtues and would be adopted on one condition —that it be called 'the Fitzgerald system' and that he take full responsibility for its success or failure. Fitzgerald wrote back that he guessed they'd better keep the Fitzgerald system 'in reserve.' The idea, however, was less fantastic than it seemed, and when two-platoon football became universal in the forties, Crisler, as chairman of the NCAA Football Rules Committee, played an important role in its development."

There were, of course, other sports and other stars. The four Princeton Olympians who competed in the 1896 games accounted for eleven olive branches, the largest number won by any national contingent; in the 1930s miler Bill Bonthron was the nation's best; nearly twenty current and recent Princetonians, eight of them women, were trying for places in the 1984 Olympics at Los Angeles, where the U.S. men's track and field coach is Princeton's Larry Ellis, the first black coach in the Ivy League. Princeton's tennis teams have been the best in the Ivy League on and off for a score of years, and in 1983 a women's varsity player, Andrea Leand, reluctantly dropped out at the end of her freshman year to take advantage of her youth on the professional circuit. Using Princeton experience as a stepping stone to a career in professional sports is not common, but it's certainly not unknown. Back when baseball was more of the national sport than it is now, Princeton contributed one of its most colorful characters in the person of Morris (Moe) Berg, '23.

There could be no greater contrast between Princeton athletes than that between Hobey Baker and Moe Berg, except for their skill on the field. Berg was a first-generation American at Princeton, a poor boy in a rich boys' school, a high school boy in a prep school environment, a Jew in a WASP sanctuary. Baker was small and blond; Berg large and dark. Whereas Baker was at best a conscientious student, Berg was a brilliant one, graduating magna cum laude in languages. Nor did he make it easy for himself. The heavy academic schedule he chose included two and a half years of Latin, four years of French, two and a half years of Spanish, three years of Italian, a year of Greek, a year of German and a course in Sanskrit. No language was dead for Berg. On the diamond, Berg, playing shortstop, would trade signals with the second baseman in Latin, confident that a non-Princetonian would never understand them.

Though less famous than Baker, Berg was the star of a 1922 Princeton team that was so good it nearly beat the world champion New York Giants in an exhibition match. The caliber of his play is indicated by his batting average of .386 in 1923. Aside from baseball, Moe was a loner on campus, according to his biographers Louis Kaufman, Barbara Fitzgerald, and Tom Sewell. They attribute this partly to his fury when, invited to join an eating club, he was asked not to bring any other Jews with him, and rejected the bid. But several classmates quoted about Berg saw it more as a part of his nature—and an augury of things to come. "Moe was a man of mystery," said one. "No one could quite account for all the things he did and the places he went. He traveled alone most of the time and you never saw him with anyone."

After college Berg continued his language studies in France, received a law degree from Columbia—and earned his bread on the diamond. "The game was in my blood," he once explained. Transforming himself from shortstop to catcher, he played first for the Chicago White Sox, then the Boston Red Sox. He was a favorite of reporters, who were bemused by his Princeton background and facility with languages, and called him "the most intelligent man in sports." The air of mystery he exuded on campus stayed with him, possibly because he spent most of his time off the field reading and studying. "I mean Moe Berg was as smart a ballplayer as ever come along," Casey Stengel said of him. "But, I'll tell ya, nobody ever knew his life's history. I call him the mystery catcher. Strangest fella who ever put on a uniform."

Thus it seems only natural that during World War II Moe Berg would serve in the Office of Strategic Services, the spy organization from which the CIA sprang. What isn't so natural is that Berg, the linguist, took a cram course in physics and became the chief spy for the Manhattan Project, where the A-bomb was developed. Instantly recognizable because of his size and athletic prominence in sports pages, Moe rather incredibly gumshoed around Europe in his black civilian suit and pried secret information about German atomic capabilities from scientists all over the Continent. Typical of Berg's peculiar talent is the case of an Italian theoretical physicist who had rejected all Allied appeals to discuss what he knew about atomic developments. Berg, however, had heard that the man was also a Petrarch scholar, and when he visited the scientist's home near Pisa he began to quote Petrarch in Latin. After three days of trading Petrarch's verses they were soon trading atomic knowledge. Berg continued in a number of sensitive government jobs after the war, but he never went back to a class reunion at Princeton.

Despite the fact that most professional athletes now have some college background, a Princetonian among them can still get the Berg treatment. At a Washington Redskins game last season a second-string quarterback, Bob Holly, Princeton '82, was given a rare chance to play. The announcer brought up his Princeton background and opined that at least Holly ought to be a "smart quarterback." But probably nobody in professional sports in recent years has flown the scholar-athlete flag as high as Rhodes Scholar Bill Bradley, a Princeton '65 star of the New York Knicks and now the Honorable William W. Bradley, Jr., U.S. senator from New Jersey.

Bradley at Princeton was as shining a star as Baker and almost as good a student as Berg. Like Baker, Bradley was credited with almost superhuman dedication to practice. On an ocean voyage to Europe with his family as a young man, Bradley spent the whole passage in the bowels of the ship dribbling a basketball. It paid off. He led the Princeton team to the highest national rank-ing Princeton had ever achieved in basketball—a third in the NCAA tournament in 1964—was an all-American for three years on varsity and was a gold medalist in the 1964 Olympics. He also hit the books hard and was known as something of a "Christer," a Princetonian term for churchgoing young men of moral recti-tude. He was nearly too good to be true. That Princeton might have represented something of a cheerless effort for Bradley is suggested in his account of his professional days, *Life on the Run,* where he admits with something of a sigh that he learned how to live in England and Europe, and his only passage in the book about the place where he earned all his glory is a curious one:

We [he was with teammate Dave DeBusschere] walk out of the coffee shop and start the long walk to Gate 48. A man stops me. He tells me that he went to Princeton (my alma mater) in 1958 and that he is a friend of a friend, who is in politics. He asks what I think of our friend's chances. When I catch up to Dave he grins and says in clipped military fashion, "Princeton '58," as if the graduation year was the first name spoken after the surname Princeton.

At the departure gate a few Knicks are already sitting in the plastic chairs attached to the floor of the waiting area. DeBus-schere makes his way to the seat next to Danny Whelan, the Knick trainer. He leans over and informs him that I had been stopped by "Princeton '58." Whelan, a man with foxlike features and

carefully combed white hair, has been a trainer in either professional baseball or basketball for twenty-five years. "Hey, Red," he
says to Red Holzman, the Knick coach, making sure I hear, "Bill
just met Princeton '58. Just think, Red, Princeton '58. From the
tables down at Mory's and all that rah rah. Makes you proud to
know a Princeton man, doesn't it? Did he wear white bucks and
a striped tie, Bill?"

A few waiting passengers seemed puzzled. DeBusschere looks
out the airport window, chuckling.

And so much for Princeton in the tough world of the pros.
Perhaps Princetonians do not belong there despite the athletic
atmosphere of their undergraduate years. One Princetonian who
had to lick his wounds from the rough and tumble of sport as
business is Bowie Kuhn, '48, who was fired in 1983 as commis-
sioner of baseball by a vote of the club owners. It must be said,
in passing, that Kuhn, who landed in the front office of baseball
by way of the law, did last fifteen years in a controversial position
and that his choice of career is another indication that Princetonians view athletics as a serious part of life.

Though the glory of Princeton athletics in terms of its flagship, football, has faded from the sports pages in recent years, the
Tiger in terms of concern for athletic achievement burns as
brightly as ever. Something like 2 percent of the university operating budget of more than $300 million is spent to defray the
costs of thirty-five full-time coaches, uniforms, equipment, travel,
upkeep on playing fields, tennis courts, two large gymnasiums,
swimming pool, ice hockey rink, lake and boathouse—all within
walking distance of any student's room. That these facilities are
put to good use cannot be doubted. In the 1982–83 season
Princeton's male intercollegiate teams took an Ivy League second
with a winning average of .623 in a selected composite of eleven
sports, and won championships in basketball, cross country, and
lightweight crew, as well as the National Intercollegiate Indoor
Tennis Championship. Princeton women came out first for the
fifth time in six years with a winning average of .765 and Ivy
championships in field hockey, ice hockey, indoor track, outdoor
track, soccer, softball, tennis, and volley ball, not to mention the
national championship in squash.

The interest and involvement of Princeton women in sports has astonished the administration. "We've had to add about one sport per year in the last seven or eight years to accommodate women," Myslik says. Conservative in this as in everything, Princeton lets a sport develop first as a "club varsity" before officially sponsoring it. The club sports are student-organized and student-run, but, as contrasted with intramurals, play teams from other schools. Two recent additions to the regular intercollegiate varsity program through this system are women's ice hockey and softball; women's golf is still in the club stage.

Female involvement in sports took an interesting turn a while back when a Princetonian became the first woman's sports writer for the *New York Times*. Though not particularly interested in sports, Robin Herman, a member of Princeton's pioneer 1973 class of coeds, was interested in journalism. As the first full-time woman sportswriter on the *Daily Princetonian,* Herman insisted on covering sports like her male colleagues. Enter a sort of *dea ex machina* in the form of an evidently feminist member of Princeton's psychology department who wrote the *Times* asking why she never saw a woman's byline on a sports story. The newspaper replied that they never had a qualified female applicant, whereupon the psychologist got in touch with Herman, whose byline she had seen in the *Princetonian.* By then used to being a pioneer, Herman applied, was hired, and wrote sports for a number of years until she became a free-lancer.

With women crowding the playing fields, about the only facility that can be said to be underused is Palmer Stadium, the forty-thousand-seat horseshoe arena erected in the days of Princeton's gridiron glory and now seldom more than half filled, making it impossible for the university to count on any significant support for its massive sports program from gate receipts. This decline in Princeton's football fortunes is the result of a deliberate act—Princeton joined with the other Ivy League schools in 1954 to subscribe to a code that says, in effect, every athlete should be a fully qualified and normally treated member of the student body. As part of this agreement, scholarships are to be given on the basis of financial need alone, not athletic promise, and such academically disturbing demands as spring football practice are prohibited. Ever since this agreement, no Ivy League school has played headline-grabbing football, but there is a startling statistic that few people know: football players in the Ivy League graduate at a rate of about 95 percent of those admitted, a rate comparable to that of the whole student body, whereas nationally only about 30 percent of college football players earn a degree.

Nobody in the Ivy League would dispute the right, or even duty, of a gifted individual to make his or her career in professional sports, but what is disputed is the wisdom of an institution to call itself educational and favor, or use, athletes for publicity and profit. This makes life difficult for people like Myslik and his coaches. "We recruit like crazy," Myslik says. "We have to try harder as the cost of a Princeton education gets up in the middle five digits to keep our athletic quality what it is. When you're talking about fifty or sixty thousand dollars for four years as compared to not paying anything at some pretty good schools, that's a real challenge to convince a kid to come here. When the financial aid department here processes applications, they don't know anything about the kid. They find out what the family income is, grind it into a computer and come out with an answer." Still, Myslik argues that, pound for pound, skill for skill, Princeton football teams are bigger and better than those great gladiators of yore. But, because of the Ivy League restrictions, among other things, "everybody else's skills elsewhere have been honed to a degree that far outdistances us, and so, comparatively speaking, our football skills have gone way down."

If football is of no financial help in staying in and only of marginal help in getting in—athletic skill is an elusive personality factor weighed on the scales with academic achievement in the admission process—why would anybody play football, a time-consuming and grueling sport, at Princeton? For an answer, I sought out Kevin Guthrie, '84, whose performance as a pass receiver won him in his last season the Poe Cup for football excellence. In physical attractiveness and size—he weighs only 165 pounds—Guthrie was not unlike Hobey Baker or a copy of the Fitzgerald fantasy of Princeton football players as "slender and keen and romantic." I had some doubts about the romantic bit because I had seen Guthrie knocked out during the course of a spectacular, diving catch in the Bucknell game a few weeks before; but I knew he was well grounded in Princeton tradition as the son of one of my classmates, General John Reilly Guthrie, '42, USA (Ret.). He had something else, too, that distinguishes Princeton athletes: his future had yet to be determined by a Rhodes Scholarship for which he had applied (he was an engineering major) or a professional football contract on which he had already received feelers. And he was something more: one of fifteen or so Princeton members of the Fellowship of Christian Athletes, which may account for his frankness. Coming as they do from somebody on the bridge of the "flagship," these words of Kevin Guthrie say a lot about athletics in the elite society of Princeton today:

"I think the most significant problem here—at least in football, and this is different from other sports—is that football players have always been supported by accolades. You are rewarded by newspaper articles, or whatever, and whenever you do well you are always rewarded with glory. Consequently, a lot of football players are motivated by that. You know, players thrive on that, and a lot of the motivation is from an egotistical perspective. People come to expect it when they play football, and they get used to it in high school.

"The Princeton recruiting effort is substantial, and a lot of people from other areas of the country know little about the Ivy League except that it isn't on TV. They're flown in here for a weekend, have a good time, have expectations of 'college football,' and when they come here it is a shock. I went to public high school in Virginia. It didn't matter there whether you were first string or fourth string. If you were on the football team, people knew who you were. At Princeton, people don't even know who you are if you're first string. If you're second string, it's not even worth being out there. A lot of people ask why there's so much attrition in football here, why in freshman, sophomore, and junior years we lose players along the way. I think the major reason for that is that the motivation for football is egocentric and when you're not starting, you're wasting your time. I didn't quit because I never had to go through what most Princeton players do, which is sitting on the bench. I learned early that football should be something you do for yourself, that there are a lot of things you can learn in interacting with other people in a team sport.

"Here there's no preferential financial or academic treatment —being a football player has a negative connotation for the professors. But if you're playing football at Penn State, you have a scholarship, and you're not going to quit. The second thing is that, if you're playing football for Penn State, it gives you a certain amount of visibility in the school. You might get a lot of pressure, but there's a significant amount of pressure here, too, from alumni who remember the days of glory and want to see Princeton in national prominence. I don't say the alumni shouldn't pressure for Ivy League championships, because that's what it's all about. But in terms of beating, say, Penn State or somebody in the top twenty, it's all over. But pressure is something you put on yourself, and I don't think football as a sport results in less pressure here other than the fact that you don't have one hundred thousand fans a game.

"Some of the things that sound like I'm whining about them are positive aspects of sports at Princeton. I don't want to be considered a football player first and a human being second. So I'm a human being first, and a lot of people don't even know I'm a football player. I mean, for example, sophomore year I played a lot and caught a lot of passes and junior year I did the same thing, and people would ask me, 'Oh, do you play a sport?' I'd say, 'Yeah, I do, I play a sport.' And they'd say, 'What sport do you play?' And I'd say, 'Football.' I had a certain amount of exposure, but they'd say, 'Oh, you play football. Do you play lightweights?' When you first come here, that's very hard to handle, but I think it's an important lesson to learn—to play football for glory is not a good reason. I think I've gotten more out of that lesson and the way it's taught here than I would have at any other school. You must learn it, or you will not survive."

For this Princeton alumnus, there was nothing more exciting on the tube than some of the come-from-behind games Princeton won in the 1983 season and some of the heartbreakers they lost by one or two points. It is particularly enthralling when it is known that the young men who are playing are human beings first and that the glory is in the action and not the results. Football will last at Princeton where it started, but only because the university believes in football *per se,* along with some forty-six other sports, as part of what Myslik describes as "providing good athletic experiences for undergraduates." In the religion of Princeton, there is no place for the kind of idolatry that goes with Super Sunday.

# Chapter Eight

# BEYOND "THE BOMB" AND INTO THE STARS

Hidden away in some drawer in Princeton is a collection of playful mathematical equations that could yet again change the world. The thing is a kind of joke, the campus guide says, as she leads a visitor past a functional brick building that has all the charm of an old New England hat factory. "Einstein once had an office in here," she says. "He'd roam the halls, drop into any empty classroom, and begin scribbling equations on the blackboard. Naturally, the next professor who used the room would wipe them off. The university was afraid something might be lost, so they assigned a graduate student to follow Einstein around and copy them down. They're still around somewhere, but of course nobody knows what they mean."

Whatever the meaning of those equations, the visitor gazes meditatively at that building, which contrasts starkly with the elegant Gothic and ivied colonial structures that give Princeton the feel of a medieval college. It somehow symbolizes the hard edges of much of the thinking that has gone on for two centuries in an institution that has been more often thought of as a seminary or country club, and the characteristic glimpse of Einstein at work is typical of the informal, casual way in which such thinking is done at Princeton. The visitor is reminded that here, or nearby, a very human being developed many of the seminal ideas for the atomic bomb, the computer, the space ship, and even, an era ago, the telegraph.

As a concrete symbol of the soaring growth of the sciences at Princeton since Einstein's time, the relatively new Fine Hall, with its thirteen-story tower, houses the university's mathematicians only a few minutes' walk from their old factory. Necessarily left behind in what is now Jones Hall are mathematical formulas in the leaded windows and, over the fireplace in the lounge, Einstein's enigmatic quotation: "God is subtle, but He is not malicious." For the current users of Jones Hall, this residue of another discipline could also be seen as symbolic of a continuing concept at Princeton: the essential unity of all forms of scholarship.

Many who visit Princeton for the first time might get the impression that the tail is wagging the dog there when it comes to the place of science in the spectrum of human knowledge. These would be the people who, approaching Princeton from either New York or Philadelphia on Route 1, a few miles east of the university, mistakenly turn off at a sign proclaiming the Forrestal Campus of Princeton University and stumble upon the space-age Plasma Physics Laboratory. Or, coming into town from Kingston, on Nassau Street, they might wander first into a ferociously modern complex called the Engineering Quadrangle on the eastern edge of the campus. If they drive in from the south on Washington Road, looking for a college, they could well find themselves on the doorsteps of tower-topped Fine Hall and its equally new companion for the nurture of physicists, Jadwin Hall. All these structures are eye-popping, and none of them suggests a place with the pockmarks of Revolutionary cannon balls on the walls. Only when newcomers try to find their way around the giant E-Quad and discover little logic in the supposedly alphabetical numbering of offices might it start to dawn on them that something of Princeton's historic preference for theory over immediate practicality is yet alive.

Actually, the presence of palaces of science in or on the edges of Princeton and the wonders they sometimes display is nothing new. For an institution supposedly founded to manufacture Presbyterian ministers out of boys versed only in Latin and Greek, Princeton quickly became involved with the physical sciences. Even while they were still meeting under the roof of their second president, Aaron Burr, in Newark in 1751, Princeton undergraduates took up a collection to pay for amazing demonstrations in the mysteries of electricity by one Lewis Evans. By 1771 there was installed in Princeton's single building, Nassau Hall, an orrery with which students, by turning a winch, could simulate the movement of the planets in the form of little brass and ivory balls around a gilded brass sun. Thereafter, some instruction in mathematics and science was always available and always under attack by the more pious Princetonians. Arriving in 1788 to teach these subjects, astronomer Walter Minto felt obliged to make the following remarks:

> It is said by some that science tendeth to make men skeptics in every thing which is not susceptible of mathematical demonstration and therefore that instead of being useful it is in the highest degree dangerous to the interests of morality and religion. It is the property of errors to clash with one another, but truth can never be opposed to itself. Mathematical truth, therefore, is perfectly consistent with every other species of truth. Instead of these sciences being hurtful to religion and morality, they will be found to be of the greatest advantage to them. Natural philosophy in particular, by leading us in a satisfactory manner to the knowledge of one almighty all-wise and all-good Being, who created, preserves and governs the universe, is the very handmaid of religion. Indeed I consider a student of that branch of science as engaged in a continued act of devotion.

It wasn't, however, until Joseph Henry, the most famous American scientist after Benjamin Franklin, joined the Princeton faculty in 1832 that the university could be said to have entered the big leagues of science. Henry, who later left to become the first secretary of the Smithsonian Institution, has his name immortalized in "the henry," the active unit in self-inductance, a phenomenon he discovered. Whether or not they understood what he was up to, the Princetonians of his time must have been impressed by the shows he put on. The first scientist to wind insulated wires around an iron core to create an electromagnet, Henry built the largest such device in the world, a magnet that could lift thirty-five hundred pounds. He also strung wires from his office in Philosophical Hall to his nearby campus home, and using his own invention of the magnetic relay that Morse would later claim as his in connection with the telegraph, Henry would signal his wife when it was time to put lunch on the table.

It would be hard to live within the sight of such scientific accomplishment and go on thinking that science stood in the way of God. So it fell to the lot of the college's eleventh president, the Reverend James McCosh, Scotch-educated and quintessentially Presbyterian, to found Princeton's first school of science in the early 1870s and, of all things, to come to the defense of Darwin's theory of evolution in 1888. "My first position is the certainty of evolution," McCosh wrote to the amazement and anger of many trustees, alumni, and probably students. "There is a general progression in nature. The theory that the world was once a vapor from which the earth evolved is not inconsistent with the Scriptures, for they speak of its being 'void without form.' I have regretted for years that certain defenders of religion have been injuring the cause by indiscriminately attacking development, instead of seeking to ascertain what the process is and turning it to religious use. They have acted as injudiciously as those who in Newton's day described the law of gravitation as atheistic."

McCosh rode out the storm that his pronouncement caused, and from then on there was no question that Princeton would pursue scientific truth as religiously as it had the theological verities. Indeed, the open and rather relaxed scientific "climate" of Princeton was undoubtedly one of the factors that later gave rise to the establishment of America's most famous think tank, the Institute for Advanced Study, a few miles west of the campus. Though not officially connected to the university, the institute is clearly a stepchild; Albert Einstein was housed in old Fine Hall until the new building was finished in the early 1930s. Between the university and the institute, the Princeton community has drawn to itself a galaxy of the scientific luminaries of this century —Einstein, Oppenheimer, von Neumann, Wigner, Spitzer, to name only a few.

What these scientists have wrought might give the Reverend Mr. McCosh some second thoughts about his enthusiasm for development. As an examination of that most prominently wagging scientific tail—it represents some 38 percent of Princeton's total projected expenditures for 1983–84—the Plasma Physics Laboratory suggests Princeton's scientists may be more actively engaged in changing what God created than in merely admiring it. Indeed, the grand purpose of the PPL, as it is called, is to control the enormous power of fusion and thereby present mankind with an inexhaustible, and relatively inexpensive, supply of energy. Nothing so effectively illustrates the way of science at Princeton as the story of the PPL.

Princeton scientists seem to be notorious for thinking on their feet, as it were. Einstein, for instance, was an almost compulsive walker. Students in the early 1940s remember him vividly as he trudged around town in old sneakers *sans* socks, with his mane of shaggy white hair blowing wild in all weathers, and the story goes that anybody who tried to pick him up during the mile or so walk from his home to the institute would be rebuffed. That Einstein's mind was elsewhere during these walks was charmingly illustrated by a neighbor's observation to author Lincoln Barnett: "If I looked out the window I could see him returning from the institute at lunchtime. He would stroll up the street with an assistant and when they came to his house they would stand outside on the sidewalk talking. Very often they'd become so deeply involved in the discussion that Einstein would simply turn around and start walking back to the institute." Knowing his preoccupation, Princeton people learned to leave Einstein alone but, as an assistant told his biographer Ronald W. Clark, strangers would often stop him, and "Einstein would pose with the waylayer's wife, children, or grandchildren as desired and exchange a few good-humored words. Then he would go on, shaking his head, saying: 'Well, the old elephant has gone through his tricks again.' " In view of this, it is probably well for PPL that another famous Princeton scientist, astrophysicist Lyman Spitzer, Jr., did his heavy thinking in the anonymity of ski clothes on a mountain near Aspen, Colorado.

"It was in 1951," PPL spokesman Anthony R. Demeo, Jr., recalls, "and Spitzer, supposedly on this skiing vacation, got to thinking about a newspaper report that a German scientist working for Perón in Argentina had succeeded in controlling thermonuclear fusion for the peaceful purpose of making electricity. Though he doubted the claim, the report raised in Spitzer's mind a nagging question: would this be possible? When he was riding up the ski lift one day, the concept of confining a hot ionized gas in a magnetic field and heating that gas to temperatures high enough to bring about fusion occurred to him. That spring he went before the then Atomic Energy Commission and got a contract to fund a study, and PPL was on its way to being born."

To laymen, the most impressive thing about the multimillion-dollar PPL operation that grew out of Dr. Spitzer's brainstorm is what it demonstrates about that most necessary attribute of the true scientific spirit—persistent patience. For thirty-three years Dr. Spitzer and the host of scientists he recruited have labored through experiment after experiment, many of them coming to disappointing results. Though they are now certain that the Spitzer theory will prove out in practice, the scientists at PPL estimate that it will take at least thirty more years—until about 2015—before electricity generated by the power of fusion will start running out of the wires of a demonstration plant. A leading scientist in another field points out that, historically, it takes seventy-five years for a seminal idea to bear full fruit, and in that light PPL's work is ahead of schedule. Still, even in these hurry-up days, it is impressive, and comforting, to know that there are institutions like Princeton and people like the PPL scientists who are willing to devote what amounts to two working lifetimes passing the torch from hand to hand, to a project that is of yet no earthly use.

The reason that they are willing to do so is another attribute of true scientists that makes them part of society's elite: a clear vision of the future. "Where there is no vision, the people perish," says Solomon, and, according to the PPL view, this will literally happen in our increasingly energized world without a new and plentiful source of power. Demeo recounts: "Not long ago a young woman said to me, 'You people have been working thirty-two years and you haven't made any energy yet! How can you stand it?' Well, it's not a long time—thirty-two years, or fifty years, or even a hundred years—when you think of the results. People seem to focus on their lifetimes and forget about history. But we've got to care, or we're going to run out of energy."

What they are trying to do at PPL is no less than to duplicate and harness the natural way by which the sun and stars create energy. It is significant in the context of Princeton that man's capacity to understand this process derived from Einstein's still most famous equation: $E = MC^2$. This was a way of saying that mass can be converted into energy, and a generation of physicists, working within that formula, learned that it can be accomplished by two methods—fission and fusion. In fission the heavy atoms of an element like uranium are split apart to release the energy that holds them together. In fusion—the sun's way—light atoms join together, giving off even more energy as they do so. The fission method is used in the atom bomb and nuclear power plants; fusion is the basis for the H-bomb.

Of all the elements involved in fusion, hydrogen is the easiest to handle. Indeed, the surface waters of the earth contain more than ten million million tons of deuterium, an isotope (or form) of hydrogen. The other isotope of hydrogen needed for fusion, tritium, can be obtained from lithium, which is available in deposits on both land and sea that are inexhaustible. So if hydrogen can be turned into energy the future is literally bright.

The nuclei of all atoms contain protons with a positive electrical charge and, except for one form of hydrogen, neutrons with no charge at all. Circling the protons like little planets around a sun are negatively charged electrons that make the atom electrically neutral. All forms of hydrogen have only one proton and one electron, but deuterium also has one neutron and tritium two. In a gaseous state and subjected to high heat, the electrons spin out of their orbit, and the result is ionized gas called plasma, composed of rapidly moving free nuclei and free electrons. Although the positively charged nuclei repel each other, they can be made to move so fast by still higher heat that they collide and fuse, forming a new and heavier element—in the case of deuterium combining with tritium, the result is helium-4. The byproduct of this change in the nature, or mass, of the elements is energy.

Although this process was well known to scientists by 1951, and particularly to a student of the stars such as Spitzer, the unanswered question was whether a device could be made to imitate it. Consider the heat involved. It was easy enough to calculate that the plasma had to be cooked to 100 million degrees Celsius, six times hotter than the core of the sun, but how could such heat be confined and for how long? Split apart, the positively charged nuclei, or ions, and the negatively charged electrons in the plasma move randomly in straight lines, which means that they would hit the walls of any containing vessel. The result would be either to melt the walls or cool the plasma below the point where fusion can take place, or both. In theory at least, there was an answer to this dilemma. If a magnetic field could be created within the container, the particles could be made to follow it, like cars on a racetrack, and thus kept away from the walls and in the field long enough, perhaps a second, for the energy given off by their fusion to be used as heat to create power.

In approaching the Atomic Energy Commission, Spitzer started out with the idea of setting up a magnetic field by wrapping coils around a figure-eight-shaped tube, a device he called a "stellarator." With funds in hand, Spitzer set up shop with a handful of assistants and graduate students in a cluster of quonset huts in the middle of a wilderness area called the Forrestal Campus, across Route 1 and far enough away from Princeton proper that no Gothic towers would be shaken if something went bang. The site had actually been used for hush-hush work on the Manhattan Project in World War II, and Spitzer's own work was classified and given the code name Matterhorn until the wraps were taken off in the Atoms for Peace atmosphere of 1958. Meanwhile, the theory of using a magnetic field proved very tricky in practice, and an ever larger band of scientists found themselves building ever larger and more complicated stellarators without getting plasma, much less fusion.

By 1961 Spitzer was ready to turn over the helm of what was renamed the Plasma Physics Laboratory to a fellow astrophysicist, Melvin B. Gottlieb. They were playing around by then with a model-C stellarator, but it was, as Demeo relates, "a period of doubt and pessimism. We weren't getting the times and temperatures that we should get and didn't know whether it was a fault of the concept or of the technology." What turned things around was proof of what many scientists had argued since the time of the first A-bomb: an attempt to keep ideas that any trained mind can conceive secret only inhibits scientific development. After declassification and in a period of relative goodwill, American and Russian scientists were exchanging knowledge in the thermonuclear field, and the Americans started to take a hard look at what the Russians called a tokamak—their acronym for toroidal magnetic chamber—a doughnut-shaped vacuum vessel in which the plasma is held in a twisting magnetic field. In 1965 Gottlieb was, in the tradition of Princeton scientists, thinking at play. As the story goes, he was in the swimming pool when he suddenly paddled over to the side and announced to a colleague: "We're going tokamak."

By 1975 a curious $14 million monster was built called the Princeton Large Torus, and by 1982 a $314 million replacement called Tokamak Fusion Test Reactor. These vast amounts of money, as well as a $125 million annual operating fund, are poured into Princeton by the Department of Energy for which the university acts as a contractor. Besides the TFTR, a two-story structure of pipes and wires and magnets that looks as if it had sprung from the fertile imagination of Rube Goldberg, the laboratory now consists of humming computers and a network of offices in a nearly luxurious modern building. There is a full-time work population of 1,350 and another 250 part-time. Yet until Christmas eve of 1982, by which time another astrophysicist, Harold Furth, had taken over from Gottlieb, there was still no certainty that all this money and manpower might not be wasted.

If there are years—generations, even—of frustrating patience required to bring off a scientific breakthrough, there are moments of high drama too, and Christmas 1982 provided them for the people of PPL. The probability was that they would at least get plasma in the TFTR sometime on December 23. The rest of the university had gone on holiday, but there was no question of shutting down PPL. So great had been the enthusiasm and excitement at PPL in the preceding weeks and months, in fact, that the administration had issued an order that nobody could work more than eighty-four hours a week, to prevent exhaustion.

The tension of the last few hours comes through in Dr. Furth's report to the press: "There was some probability that we were going to get first plasma at two in the afternoon. So I rushed around in the morning, bought four cases of champagne, and iced them in some large garbage cans which I locked in the cafeteria. Then if we got first plasma in the afternoon, we would be able to have the appropriate celebration. But there was trouble all afternoon and all evening. Around 1:00 A.M. of the twenty-fourth I started having visions of taking the champagne bottles back out of the garbage cans, drying them and putting them back into the boxes. It seemed like a rather cheerless thing to do. But I was under pressure because everyone had been working hard for months, and we decided to shut down at 2:00 A.M., no matter what. We just had to send people to their families over Christmas. As that time approached, it was clear that TFTR was just about to work, so nobody was really going to quit. It was a very tense situation, sort of like a poker game. You've got to know when to fold your hand, and you can make great mistakes either way. Being a very orderly people, we pulled the cord on the clock at 1:55 A.M. and went right on."

An hour later the tired and nervous watchers could see plasma moving on the TV monitors, and the champagne corks popped. Historic as that moment was, the plasma was still, in Demeo's words, "very cool, very crude." But he predicts now that TFTR will reach "break even," the point at which the heat being given off by fusion within the plasma equals the heat being applied to it. That is still a long way from the goal of an economical energy producer. "$Q=1$ is break even," Demeo explains. "$Q=1$ will be a condition that is proof of the scientific principle, but you have to reach, say, $Q=10$ to be economical. Where we really want to be is at ignition, $Q=$ infinity, when the plasma produces enough fusion energy so that it can sustain its own temperature, and you can turn off the auxiliary heating."

Getting to ignition requires a bigger machine, and PPL has applied to the Department of Energy for authorization to begin work on a Tokamak Fusion Core Experiment, the core of a reactor, which will be one and a half times larger than TFTR. But that still won't do the job, and Demeo explains why: "In this fusion reaction that occurs between deuterium and tritium, helium is produced. Eighty percent of the energy created by the mass that is lost is carried away by neutrons, which, because they are neutral, sail right out of the magnetically trapped plasma into a blanket, which will turn hot and from which the heat can be conducted away to make steam. We won't have that blanket with the new experimental reactor core. Meanwhile, though, 20 percent of the energy stays in the plasma in charged alpha particles, and when that energy gets high enough to keep the plasma at 100 million degrees we have ignition. This we know we can do in the next step and thereby demonstrate the physics of ignited plasma."

Considering the problems of developing a blanket to catch the neutrons and building a large enough device to turn heat into steam to run a generator, the year 2015 seems a rather optimistic prediction when the first bulb will light up with power from fusion. But will it then be safe? With all the present fears and arguments about nuclear power, society might ultimately reject the fruits of these long labors at PPL.

Demeo faces the question candidly: "It will be safer than fission, but how much is a question. There's no possibility of a meltdown, or a runaway. You have to *force* fusion to occur, whereas in fission if you get enough concentrated fuel together in one place at one time it's going to run out of control unless you control it. Fusion is the exact opposite to bring about. You have to get enough fuel together, and that's not easy. You have to get the plasma, and then you have to heat it. Even when you reach ignition, there's only a small amount of fuel in the vessel, and you have to keep feeding the fuel in. If you dumped in an enormous amount of fuel, you would put it out.

"With fission you produce a variety of radioactive by-products, but with fusion your only byproduct is helium. Yes, there is radioactivity. We have to handle tritium with care. Still tritium is lighter than air and, if it escapes, it is quickly dispersed. The blanket structure will become radioactive after a time. The hope is to come up with something that will become radioactive so slowly that it will last the life of the plant—twenty or thirty years. Then you just shut down the plant and let it sit, and a year later the radioactivity will be so low that you can touch it. It's really a matter of weighing risks. It's certainly going to be safer than walking down almost any street, and I wouldn't want to burn coal now with what we know about acid rain."

If the Plasma Physics Laboratory is the biggest scientific project, and one in which Princeton is clearly a world leader, it is far from the only impressive effort going forward at the university. Across a patch of woods from PPL on the Forrestal campus is the physical evidence of another discipline in which Princeton is held to be farther out, or higher up, than other institutions— aerospace engineering. There is a 3,000-foot airstrip, a 750-foot "long track" dynamic model testing facility; various wind tunnels, rocket test stands, combustion chambers; laboratories for research into guidance systems and other aspects of aeronautical science. Out of these and other facilities at E-Quad have come many of the guidance and control concepts of Mercury, Gemini, Apollo, and much of the work on the F-1 engine of the Saturn booster. Trained there, too, through studies for a bachelor's and master's degree, was the third man to walk on the moon, Charles Conrad.

Mechanical and aerospace engineering is only one of the four departments in the School of Engineering, in which a student can major in chemical engineering, civil engineering, electrical engineering, aerospace engineering, and computer science. In all, there are 900 undergraduates, 250 graduate students, 90 faculty members, and a research staff of 50, making up about 15 percent of the university population. Underway are 250 research projects, costing some $9 million. Not all of them are devoted to outer space. The titles of some projects twist the tongue and glaze the mind—"Effect of Grain Boundary Structure and Interface Orientation on the Performance of $CuInSe_2/CdS$ and $InP/CdS$ Solar

Cells," for example—but there could be nothing more down to earth and potentially usable than the results of a study called "Automobile Energy Efficiency" or yet another called "Field Measurement of Wood Cookstove Efficiency."

Engineering as taught and practiced in Princeton is sometimes criticized as too "theoretical"—it doesn't seem to attract the kind of support from industry enjoyed by rivals like MIT or Stanford. Dean Robert George Jahn, a professor of aerospace sciences, readily answers the critics: "It's true that the school tends to deal with fundamental processes in the applied sciences as opposed to pragmatic issues," he said. "No doubt this is less attractive for support of a more prosaic nature such as the design for a corporation's product or some manufacturing process. But the ratio of experimental work to theoretical work in this engineering school is probably higher than at most other places, and our track record for getting support for both our academic program and basic research is very good."

It is in the academic phase of its mission rather than research that Princeton's School of Engineering can claim to be special. As in every other department of the university, the main emphasis is on undergraduate instruction and, according to Dean Jahn, the profile of the engineering student is similar to that of the A.B. with whom he or she mingles in the colleges and clubs and on the playing fields. With something of a twinkle, Dean Jahn points out that engineering students on the average scored one point higher on verbal SATs as well as an expected fourth higher in mathematics. For a full third of their program, engineers have to attend classes in languages, economics, politics, English, and other liberal arts. A disproportionate number of engineers play on the football squad, and a recent concertmaster of the Princeton Orchestra was an engineer. Not surprisingly a sizable number of graduate engineers go on to law school, business school, medical school, and even theological seminary. "If you think of us as just one of the departments in a liberal university, you won't be far wrong," says Dean Jahn. "A number of our students simply look on engineering as a basic form of education."

In one way, the School of Engineering hasn't kept pace with the university, but is ahead of the pack of most engineering schools—20 percent of its students are women. That is a fairly sharp rise since Dean Jahn took over in 1971, when there were *no* women. Probably no figure is more representative of the new elite that Princeton is fashioning than the woman engineer, and Dean Jahn is actively recruiting them.

"I think the motivation to get women is quite pragmatic. I think it's clear that women can be important in the engineering work force. It's clear that they have much to contribute by their perspective and backgrounds in the comprehension and solution of a whole pattern of problems in modern engineering. From a selfish point of view, women double the pool of intelligent students you can reasonably attract, so it upgrades the academic quality of the place. If you can dispose of any heritage of discomfort about being involved in this profession, what women find attractive with us is the style of education, which isn't so much geared to shop practice as it is toward basic comprehension of the fundamental processes. There they are equally interested and equally trained, and we have no basis of distinguishing them any longer.

"In the practical sense, women don't regard themselves as female engineers and we don't treat them any different than other students. In fact, one of them said the other day, 'Look, we don't want to be known as women engineers; we're Princeton engineers.' In one way you might not think of, women engineers *are* different, however: they're tops in the job market. Quite frankly, this is due to the need for corporations to comply with affirmative action regulations. The market is more intense because there are fewer women engineers so far. For instance, we have only three women on our faculty now just because there haven't been women in engineering long enough to get through the Ph.D. and out into teaching."

Together with the School of Architecture, the School of Engineering is often pointed out with a slight sneer as one of only two "trade" schools in an otherwise liberal institution, yet it seems obvious that its academic philosophy isn't much different from the purer sciences like mathematics and physics. What goes on among the mathematicians in Fine Hall or the physicists in Jadwin Hall would probably elude the layman until the results are glaringly apparent. It is not without significance that Princeton physicist Henry D. Smyth became the author of *Atomic Energy for Military Purposes*—the world-famous "Smyth report"—after the Bomb went off. The ranks of Nobel Prize winners in physics have been crowded with graduates or faculty members of Princeton, from Arthur H. Compton in 1927, through Eugene P. Wigner in 1963, to Val L. Fitch in 1980. As for mathematics, it is enough to say that, as early as the 1930s, Danish scientist Harold Bohr called Princeton "the mathematical center of the world."

Whether Princeton mathematicians will ever turn those discarded Einstein equations into signposts toward a new scientific frontier or not, it is reasonable to bet that the work going forward in the rather casual, human atmosphere will have a lot to do with altering the future of mankind. One certain frontier to be explored is the inner one, and to that end Princeton is erecting still another multimillion-dollar facility to house a department in molecular biology. And then there is that twinkling universe overhead.

Listen to Dean Jahn as he discusses his own favorite subject, space: "From a technical standpoint, I think the two most viable enterprises in space are the establishment of a manned space station in orbit and utilization of a portion of the moon's surface for pragmatic purposes—manufacturing, mining, communications. But my own personal interests are the continuation of an interplanetary program. I think we are going to ultimately have the same urge to put a man on Mars as we did to put a man on the moon. The basic knowledge is already here, but you're talking now of the containment of a crew in an aircraft from three to four years, and that is a different scale of enterprise than we've been talking about heretofore. It's just a different order of magnitude, a larger scale of expense—really a matter of will."

If the visitor by now thinks that science is running away with Princeton, and running away with the world as well, let him take comfort in the Princeton version, which is so intricately intermingled with other disciplines and seems to retain a vestige of the Presbyterian reluctance to do away with God. This attitude was expressed most eloquently by the late Professor Hugh S. Taylor, head of Princeton's chemistry department and later dean of the graduate school. Writing before the Bomb but when the horrors of World War II were already apparent, he said:

> We are, I think, abundantly convinced that man cannot live by scientific bread alone. We, too, subscribe to that cry, as it were, of anguish, with which the late Professor [Isaiah] Bowman prefaced, in his *Sacramental Universe,* his final lectures to a Princeton audience: "The age in which we live is notable for two things, man's progressive triumph over nature in the field of theoretical and applied science and his tragic inability to order his own life. Every year adds appreciably to our knowledge of the physical world; every year brings home to us the baffling inscrutability of human nature as revealed in our disordered civilization." We recognize with Christopher Dawson that we cannot "look to science for a power which will unite and guide the divided forces of society." We agree with him that "science provides, not a moral dynamic, but an intellectual technique." It is entirely indifferent to moral considerations, and lends itself with sublime impartiality to any power which knows how to use it or how to abuse it. Had we not known this the history of the last sad years would have abundantly instructed us. That is the reason why in every university of free men, letters as well as science must have freedom and the fullest of facilities.

Princeton has been trying to take these words to heart and may therefore represent, in a world that hasn't improved much since Professor Taylor spoke, a small, bright light of hope.

## Chapter Nine

# DOES GOD GO TO PRINCETON?

$I$t was probably inevitable that, in 1981, Princeton University's then director of admission, James W. Wickendon, would find among the thousands of applications for the freshman class one from a candidate called God. It may have come because by then it was widely known that Princeton was accepting any highly intelligent young person—be it woman, Jew, Chinese, Chicano, black, Indian (both American and Asian), and even WASP. That the candidate was fully aware of this state of affairs was evident in a scribbled note next to an optional question on the application form relative to the applicant's ethnic origin: "You name it!" In addition, both male and female sexes were checked off as to gender, in an indication that the candidate wasn't taking any chances.

He/she needn't have worried. The Scholastic Aptitude Test

scores, both verbal and mathematics, were perfect 800's. The explanations for lesser scores on the College Entrance Examination Board's achievement tests were plausible. For the 770 grade in biology, God apologized: "I was marked wrong on the evolution question and have tried to convince ETS their answer is wrong, but without luck." As to the 760 mark in physics, it was noted: "I was marked wrong on the relativity question, but ETS and Einstein are wrong." Above all, the extracurricular activities listed were far more impressive than those of the average high school football captain or class president. Among them: 168 hours a week "arranging the weather," fourteen turning "day into night" and a similar number turning "night into day," countless hours "listening to prayers." Instead of slinging hash or serving as a lifeguard, the candidate spent the summer of 1980 causing a spectacular eruption of Mount Saint Helens, and his/her plans for a career could not be faulted: "Redeem all humanity."

But what really made God stand out from the other applying overachievers were the answers to questions on age and the reason for choosing Princeton. Stating birth date as "B.C.," the candidate asserted that he/she had been in the Princeton class of 1764 and implied a desire for a second chance, having been graded D in biology and only B+ in theology. A personal statement on the application read:

> Since people like to think of me in different ways and all are correct, it would be inappropriate for me to describe myself, my values or my ideals, but I would like to explain why I wish to attend Princeton. As you probably know, I attended in the eighteenth century, and I would like to return so I can experience first hand what college life is presently like and so I can take courses in a more relaxed manner. It does not seem right to me to listen in on courses when I do not attend and have not been admitted: and equally importantly, I do not have a chance to write the papers or take the tests to make sure I am really learning and understanding everything. I am quite sure I will be able to attend without causing too much commotion on campus, and I look forward to an opportunity to learn at one of the world's best universities and the chance to match wits with some of this nation's brightest youth.

The admissions people suspected God of trying to take unfair advantage of an old Princeton myth in asserting prior attendance. Particularly in recent years, when Latin has no longer been compulsory, Princetonians have taken to translating the university's motto, *Dei Sub Numine Viget* (loosely, "Under God's power she flourishes"), into "God went to Princeton." Whether he/she got in is hard to tell, since the response to a request for physical description was "invisible." There are quite a few unhappy alumni who would argue that it is harder for their academically average sons and daughters to get admitted to Princeton today than God. But as many, or more, in the Princeton community would claim that the invisible presence is probably there. Nothing in the rapidly changing Princeton of recent years has evoked more passion and invective, aroused more genuine concern, than the institution's religious posture. God's application turns into more than a joke.

This preoccupation with religion at Princeton is understandable in the light of the institution's history. Princeton was founded in 1746 by a group of reformist Presbyterians who followed what they called the New Light. There were four clergymen and three laymen in the group, six Yale men and one Harvard graduate. Their clear purpose was to recruit and train preachers for their own view of Presbyterianism—more freedom from the church hierarchy, more personal commitment than Calvinist legalism—but in order to get a charter from the Anglican governor of New Jersey, appointed by the king of England, they slipped in a clause promising an equal education to young men of every denomination. In practice, they staffed the college and larded the Board of Trustees with Presbyterians, most of them ministers.

The first two clerical presidents were also founders, Jonathan Dickinson and Aaron Burr, Sr. They literally ran the fledgling college in their homes, in Elizabeth and Newark, until in 1756 Nassau Hall was built in Princeton, then little more than a stagecoach stop between Philadelphia and New York. Teaching all the courses, raising all the funds, and erecting the largest stone building in the colonies wore Burr into the grave a year later at the age of forty-two. The dismayed trustees turned to Burr's father-in-law, the most famous divine in America—Jonathan Edwards—who exhibited a faith in science unusual for his time, but not for Princeton presidents, by submitting to an inoculation for smallpox. Unfortunately, this faith was unwarranted, and he died of a fever brought on by the treatment two months after taking office. For a century, men of the Presbyterian cloth dominated Princeton's presidency. To get the real article, Princeton's trustees twice went back to the cradle of Presbyterianism, Scotland, and brought back their most famous presidents until the layman Woodrow Wilson—John Witherspoon (1787–94) and James McCosh (1868–88). Witherspoon helped free America politically from Britain by his leadership in the Revolution, and McCosh helped free America mentally by his support for Darwin's theory of evolution.

That the devils of freedom were lurking behind the pious facade of Presbyterianism might have escaped early undergraduates of the college. The picture of their lives related in Thomas Jefferson Wertenbaker's *Princeton 1746–1896* is rather bleak in today's terms. Here are a few glimpses of Princeton in the eighteenth and early nineteenth centuries:

> The trustees and the presidents of the first decades never forgot that the education of young men for the ministry was the prime purpose of the founding of the college, and shaped the work from the very first with this in view. The courses in Latin, Greek and Hebrew opened the door to inexhaustible fields of religious learning; every student had to know the Bible from cover to cover; the emphasis on elocution helped to equip the future minister for the all-important task of preaching; the presidents themselves conducted courses in theology. . . . The college prided itself upon its discipline. "The utmost care is taken to discountenance vice and to encourage . . . a manly, rational and Christian behavior in students," said the trustees. . . . Nassau Hall, to some of its young denizens, must have seemed like a prison. No student was to be absent from his room without leave from the president or a tutor save at stated hours, or make any "treat or treatment," or invite any young woman to his chamber, "nor jump and hollo nor make any boisterous noise in the hallways."

By 1804 the scene hadn't improved much. Wertenbaker quotes a letter from an undergraduate of the times named James Iredell:

At six o'clock the bell rouses us to morning prayers. From this till breakfast, which is always at half past seven, I study the recitation. The time between breakfast and nine I spend either in conversation or reading. At nine the bell rings for the students to retire to their rooms, except the two lower classes, which must attend in the recitation room where they are confined until twelve. From this till dinner, at one o'clock, I generally read. At two we again go to the recitation room and stay till five, when the bell rings for evening prayers. From this till supper, at six o'clock, I study or read, and also from supper till seven. Between seven and eight I usually take a walk and from eight till ten read. At nine the tutor visits the rooms to see that the students are all in.

Princeton was slow in relaxing its demands upon students to be both pure and pious. Parietals, among which was a rule against women in rooms during the hours when their presence would be most fun, were strictly enforced at least until World War II, and compulsory chapel (or attendance at another religious place of choice), though reduced gradually from twice a day to twice a month, was an imperative for underclassmen well into the 1960s. The efficacy of enforced religion may be judged by the fact that, back in the nineteenth century, when the *Daily Princetonian* started to publish in the morning, it warned undergraduate subscribers that reading the paper in chapel, and particularly rustling its pages, might force a return to an afternoon edition. Even in the face of such ennui and despite the fact that the specific training of ministers had long since—in 1812, to be exact—been elevated to the graduate level and assigned to a separate institution, the Princeton Theological Seminary, the keepers of the Princeton flame remained reluctant to abandon totally the religious character of the institution.

One of the reasons may be the chapel itself, a magnificent building that may be one of the few places of worship in the United States worthy of being called a cathedral. Ever since the college outgrew Nassau Hall, there has been a chapel off center campus to vie with the colonial building as the heart of Princeton. The third of these, the present structure, was opened in 1928, and with its Gothic, cruciform design, vaulting arches, and towering stained-glass windows, it is more reflective of the Catholic or Anglican traditions than Presbyterianism. It is, however, unmistakably Christian in architectural character, as have been most of the services conducted within its walls until recently. Some vision of a different mission must have been in the designers' eyes, however, for in addition to religious motifs in the windows are such figures as Witherspoon the Teacher and Madison the Statesman, as well as representations of the seven arts. Outside, on a drainpipe on the southeast corner, architect Ralph Adams Cram, a Yale man, added a humanizing touch of collegiate humor with the gargoyle face of a Yale bulldog.

The change—what might be called the pluralization of the chapel—came about in a typically Princetonian manner. The institution does not discard either traditions or people lightly, and it waited out the twenty-five-year tenure of one dean of the chapel, Ernest Gordon, a firm Church of Scotland man most widely known for his experiences in the infamous Japanese war prison camp on the Kwai River. When Dean Gordon's retirement approached, a few years back, august committees of faculty and trustees were appointed to take a hard look at how the chapel, and its dean, should function in what was becoming a new Princeton. Characteristically, these committees did not want, as the saying goes, to throw the baby out with the bath water, so their reports suggested, in sum, that the new dean be a man of strong personal religious commitment, but that he preside over a more open chapel. A quote from the trustees' report gives the gist of this difficult compromise: "We wish now to affirm the importance of maintaining a chapel congregation which will continue to use the chapel for the purpose for which it was built: to worship God, as revealed in Jesus Christ. We believe that his congregation should take its place—no greater place, no lesser—alongside other congregations worshipping in accordance with their own religious beliefs."

Mere discussion of any change in the chapel's essentially Protestant orientation stirred up an angry buzzing in heavily WASP-

ish alumniland. Particularly from the older classes, letters ex-
pressing grief, shock, and horror flowed into the *Princeton
Alumni Weekly* and other publications. Consider this fairly representative one from a graduate of 1927:

> With the campus a moral morass (wide-open sex, drug and alcohol
> abuse, stealing, the honor system in shambles, library books muti-
> lated or stolen, visiting lecturers abused when attempting to pre-
> sent a conservative point of view), it would be tragic, I believe, to
> eliminate or downgrade the one person who represents Christian
> morals and religion across campus, the Dean of the Chapel.
> . . . What has made Princeton great through the generations so
> that Princeton men have been able to contribute so much not only
> in the service of the nation but also in the service of the world?
> I would say well-developed minds coupled with strong Christian
> moral fiber.

Nevertheless, the university authorities pressed on with what
the new dean of the chapel, Frederick Houk Borsch, an Episcopal
clergyman and graduate of the class of '57, calls an "experiment."
The reason is that the administration was overcome by history,
perhaps of their own making. Although Princeton has long wel-
comed ex-officio chaplains, furnished by their denominations as
"missionaries" to the campus, their ministry now overwhelms
that of the chapel. On any given weekend, according to Dean
Borsch, there may be 300 Jewish students involved in their own
religious activities, 500 Catholics attending mass, and only 150
undergraduates at chapel services. In all, the dean estimates that
there are about a thousand religiously active students, or less than
a quarter of the student body. The unchurched may share the
view of a faculty member who told Dean Borsch: "Leave me
alone. I'm a happy pagan."

What has happened at Princeton is almost revolutionary in
terms of the religious, ethnic, and cultural composition of the
community. To grasp it one has to go back to the Princeton I
attended. There were no blacks in my entering class (or indeed
the entire university) in 1938 and, of course, no women; the 1983
entering class was composed of 17 percent minority members and
35 percent women. Only 9 men in my class of 674 listed their

religious preferences as Hebrew, whereas 20 percent of today's students may be Jewish. Now forming perhaps a third of the student population, even Roman Catholics were hard to come by forty-five years ago—less than 10 percent of the class. My class was rather typical of some two hundred classes before it. In the class of 1915, for instance, the man who was to become the nation's first secretary of defense, James V. Forrestal, reportedly felt himself to be in a snubbed minority, though he had formally renounced his Catholicism, which may account for the fact that, as chairman of the *Daily Princetonian,* Forrestal led one of the early editorial attacks on compulsory chapel attendance.

The Jewish experience of Princeton perhaps brings into sharpest focus the religious *angst* of the institution. In the 1930s, a Jew entering Princeton was sticking his head into what was probably America's tightest WASP's nest and was likely to be stung socially. More rich men have made it through the needle's eye into heaven than Jews in those days into Princeton's clubs, the accepted eating facilities for all upperclassmen. As discussed earlier, even such campus gods as Moe Berg had a problem. How insidious exclusion could be is apparent in a story that lingers in memory. There were on campus two brothers, two years apart, sons of a father with a Jewish name and a mother with a Christian name. The older brother, using his father's name, fared poorly in the club cut, whereas the younger brother, using his mother's name, easily got into one of the tonier clubs. The trick then was for a Jewish student to take on protective coloration, as the story of the brothers shows, or to stand proudly apart, as Berg did.

An unintended but ironic illustration of the historical position of Jews at Princeton occurred when Rabbi Edward Feld, arriving to represent the Hillel Foundation some ten years ago, couldn't find the building, Murray Dodge Hall, where the university had assigned him an office. "I just joined one of those Orange Key guided tours of the campus and peeled off when they pointed out Murray Dodge," he recalls. "They've got some signs on buildings now, but I think it was sort of a studied thing then—if you didn't know how to find your way around you didn't deserve to be on campus." Hard by the chapel, Murray Dodge is a crouching, irregular jumble of age-blackened stone, one of the more curious

pieces in Princeton's strangely harmonious architectural amal-
gam. Today it is a lively place; it houses, in addition to the dean
of the chapel and his ordained female assistant, such thriving
unofficial subchaplaincies as Rabbi Feld's.

Because of his position as an outsider ministering to what were
once outsiders, Rabbi Feld, who still looks young enough and
rumpled enough to pass for a graduate student, is an unusually
perceptive observer of the Princeton scene. He had heard all the
horror stories of Princeton's past, including one about the Jewish
son of a wealthy cabinet member who was so disaffected that he
never, like Berg, attended a class reunion until, forty years later,
he was brought back into the fold following an outpouring of
letters of invitation and apology from classmates who had been
broadened by life. "My sense is that the people who were hurt
worst in those days were those who came from wealthy or famous
backgrounds and had no expectation of running into social ostra-
cism," Feld says. "They expected to pass, whereas the people who
came from poorer backgrounds and were on scholarships were
grateful for the educational opportunities. They were two very
different Jewish experiences.

"That is wiped out in Princeton today for the most part
because, for one thing, there is no single dominant culture. My
sense of Princeton then was that it was a single culture, and you
were either part of it or not. But today there are a lot of subcultures, each of which perceives itself to be under seige. Nobody has
the feeling that they are at the center of the Princeton experience. The people who aren't in Ivy think the people who are in
Ivy are crazy. Why would someone come to Princeton today, for
instance, and join an all-male club? You want to meet women,
and why would one cut oneself off from so much of campus
experience? Or take athletes, who once dominated the campus.
Today athletes feel themselves to be here by sufferance. The
assumption is that if you are on the football team, you aren't here
for academic reasons, and you have to explain how it is you're
here. You are certainly no campus hero.

"So I think Jews are as related to the university as any other
students. There are Jews in every club, Jews in every student

organization. Things really began to change in 1969 with the admission of women. A larger proportion of those first women were Jewish because they had to recruit quickly, mostly from the East. Although the man-woman ratio for the campus as a whole is 1.8, among Jews it is 1 to 1, and also among blacks. The pattern is that the men are still going to dad's school, but the women aren't going to mom's school. Still, there's a sense of Waspishness here. It's not inoculated by any official or other action; it's just here in the architecture. So I think that religious life among Jews is more active than it would be elsewhere in terms of numbers and percentages of Jews involved, because it is necessary to touch base with Jewishness. We get large turnouts for more social kinds of things than services per se, but we reach on a regular basis about 20 percent of the Jews on campus, and that's a lot."

Making blacks a part of the Princeton elite has been more difficult than integrating Jews. They are clearly one of Rabbi Feld's subcultures "under seige." But when it comes to religion the problems are more subtle. Most blacks are nominally Protestant but, as Dean Borsch says, "A lot of black students who come here can't find anything that represents their experience in the black church—even the black churches in town are different. They come to chapel and hear all that Bach and see that big building with the stained-glass windows and are somewhat at a loss. Is it that they're so far from the kind of gospel music and the kind of preaching they're used to?"

Such diversity is partly a deliberate administration recruiting effort and partly a case of drifting with the tides of the pluralistic, largely secular, social sea outside the Gothic campus. A significant aspect of this has been the switch in balance between prep school and public high school graduates in any given Princeton class. In my own class, I was in the minority as a high school graduate; today I would be part of a substantial majority. From a religious point of view, the former primary feeders of Princeton were, by and large, miniature Princetons, wealthy WASP's nests with compulsory chapel. For many of my classmates, Princeton's mild, once-a-Sunday church attendance requirement in underclass years represented something on the order of religious freedom, and few of us, myself included, really questioned the university's right to hold the cross aloft.

Both Dean Borsch and Rabbi Feld agreed in attributing what they see as an improvement in the quality, if not the quantity, of campus religious activity to a falling away from the faith on the part of the students' parents, which is to say my generation. Dean Borsch says: "There was more formal churchgoing in the 1950s than now, although there's more now than there was ten years ago. It's coming back to some degree. There's more consciousness on the part of those who do involve themselves in organized religion of what they're doing and why they're doing it, rather than simply a following of tradition. You also get an interesting phenomenon—I wouldn't want to exaggerate it in terms of numbers—of students who come to Princeton and, well, how do they put it? 'You know I never had a chance when I was growing up to find out anything about religion.' Read behind that, 'My parents didn't go to church or synagogue. In college I'd really like to find out.' That's the reverse of what used to happen: 'My parents made me go to church so much I'll never go again.' It's not necessarily a rebellion against parental values but a looking for something other than what they found at home in terms of religious experience."

Rabbi Feld adds: "On our Hillel board the majority of students are more religious than their parents. They have by now been raised in secular homes for a couple of generations—or at least one—and they're largely ignorant of the religious vocabulary. I think there's a rampant pagan culture on campus—one of self-fulfillment and self-aggrandizement. There are also a group of people who are in search of an alternative, and they look for the possibilities in religious involvement. This tends to be behavioral and not theological. They are less interested in looking at what they mean in believing in God than in trying to find a kind of community to which they can attach themselves, because what they see out in society is scary."

If the chapel has been shifted off center in terms of religious belief and practices at Princeton, it is still physically and strongly visible at the core of the campus, and the dean's "experiment" in subtly altering its distinctive Christian character goes on. Aside from sharing the building on Sundays with Episcopal and Catholic congregations, the main effort has gone into making interfaith events out of the universitywide exercises, such as the opening of college and the baccalaureate ceremonies, which have been traditionally held there. One small change has been to move these ceremonies from 11:00 A.M. on Sunday—often called "the most segregated hour of the week"—to 2:30 P.M. More effective perhaps has been a different use of religious symbols, as described by the dean in an early explanatory statement to the Princeton community.

"What we have done at interfaith services in Princeton is to create a focus for our worship in the chancel of the chapel, which symbolizes the breadth of God's relationship with humanity. While the main cross remains in its traditional place, there has been added before the altar a screen made from leaded glass doors which years ago enclosed the bookcases in the library of Prospect [long the residence of Princeton's presidents]. In front of the screen are candles, symbols of our common search for truth and faith in God as the source of light and life. Their flame reflects in the screen the same amber light which shines from the hanging lantern lamps throughout the chapel. Also before the screen stands a table on which several symbols are placed. At the opening exercises there was a chalice, a symbol for Christians of the sacrificial life, death, and power for the new life of Jesus. Alongside it was a menorah, the traditional Jewish candelabrum, together with copies of the Jewish and Christian scriptures, the Koran and prayer books from the several faiths. In the past we have also used the dove, the symbol of the Spirit, and at future service stars, a shofar, a cross, and other symbols will be used. These symbols are expressive of the diversity of the human experience of God but, placed together, also remind us that it is the same God who wills to bring us to a higher understanding of human purpose and to an awareness that we are meant to be made loveable by his love and thus able to love."

Along with using a multiplicity of symbols has gone an effort to select, create, or edit a liturgy of song, scripture, prayer, and preaching that will be acceptable to a wide spectrum of the faithful and presumably those of the disinterested who are not active atheists. A pertinent sample might be the Prayer for Princeton: "O Eternal God, the source of life and light for all peoples, we pray that you would endow this University with your grace and wisdom. Give inspiration to those who teach and understanding to those who learn. Grant vision to its trustees and administrators. And to all who work here and to all its graduates the world wide give your guiding Spirit of sacrificial courage and loving service. Amen."

Dean Borsch feels that the university is taking the hard, rather than easy, way out in trying to accommodate its Christian tradition to a broadened religious atmosphere. "What has happened in so many universities and colleges is that a sense that the university had a religious tradition and supported religion as part of the life of the university has been dropped," he says. "If you go to most places, you will not find anything like our opening exercises. It *is* a religious service in the chapel. In other places such exercises are held in the gym with perhaps the chaplain saying a prayer. What's caused this in other places is not, in my opinion, secularism but pluralism. People didn't know how to handle the fact that they had different kinds of Christians and a number of Jewish people that they were now recognizing as part of their community. But our trustees opted to try to create a worship service in which thanksgiving and prayers could be made to God on behalf of the whole community and in which everybody could participate. The easiest thing would have been to create a service where people just watched, but we wanted it to be participatory. I think Princeton is being very conservative in trying to keep its tradition by trying to create an opportunity for the whole community to worship before God."

The dean is conscious that participating in *any* chapel service may be difficult, or even impossible, for some Jews or others who feel it violates their faith, but Rabbi Feld believes that the experiment is going rather well. "Looking back on the chapel controversy, it seems such a minor issue, and I think everybody was dealing in symbols. The chapel is a remnant of the old Princeton —there's no stronger symbol of that. The university opens and closes with ceremonies there, and the people for change were saying that this wasn't reflective of what's here, and the people who opposed change opposed it because it was the last thing they could hold onto. The women's issue had been lost, for instance, and there was really no rhetoric they could use against that since people want their daughters to be able to go to Princeton. But on the religious issue the rhetoric could still be effective—'We can't take down the cross of our Lord Jesus Christ!' But I think that insofar as the chapel welcomes everybody equally, the sting has been taken out. Here it was that you came to Princeton and the first event was a distinctly Christian service. That has changed; it is really an ecumenical service. More likely now, people only feel that it is slightly boring."

In the old days, the dean of the chapel could take comfort from looking down from his lofty pulpit on row after row of conscripted Christians—on a solid sea of faces that were all white, all male, all young, all scrubbed. It must have made things easier for him for, as Dean Borsch ruefully admits, "It's hard now to get a sense of intimacy in the chapel." Little knots of people, many of them "townies," straggle out the length of the long nave. The students are distinguished by their blue jeans and sneakers, not by their sex and color; there are as many black and Asian faces as white. There is the feeling that everybody is welcome, even though the dean resisted his first instinct to force "intimacy" by roping off the back pews. "I realized that there are a lot of people who sneak into the back about ten after eleven," he says. "It's almost a physical manifestation that they are on the edges of faith, and they might come back."

All in all, in Princeton today, the impression is that there is as much truth as humor in that application from God and in the standing joke that the chapel is "Princeton's $6 million monument to antimaterialism." Princeton does seem to be a place where an applicant who says that "people like to think of me in different ways and all are correct" would feel at home, and where there is at least an acknowledgment by the university that the spiritual is as important as the material in education, as in life.

# Chapter Ten

# "PRINCETON IN THE NATION'S SERVICE"

In 1977, in connection with its twenty-fifth reunion, the class of 1952 published a book in which one of its members, Don Oberdorfer, diplomatic correspondent of the *Washington Post* wrote, in part:

> When the United States mounted a naval operation last summer to bring American civilians out of wartorn Lebanon, the National Security Council's staff office in charge of the Middle East was in touch by cable and telephone with the senior American on the scene at the U.S. Embassy in Beirut. The two men had little cause to misunderstand each other, having been well acquainted for years as fellow members of the Class of 1952. Bob Oakley was at the White House end of the line; George Lambrakis was in Beirut as deputy chief of mission, acting as senior officer of the embassy during the long illness of one U.S. ambassador and following the murder of another.

Among those closely involved in the operation at the State Department was Hal Saunders, director of the Bureau of Intelligence and Research and one of Henry Kissinger's favorite Middle East experts. Alongside was the deputy director of the bureau, Roger Kirk. At the Navy's Operation Center in the Pentagon, Rear Admiral Bob Morris was helping to direct the evacuation ships, their escorts and the surrounding fleet in his post as Assistant Chief of Naval Operations in charge of the surface warfare division. . . . None of these classmates was the subject of headlines in this Middle East episode, but each in his own way had a role in shaping what took place.

If Oberdorfer were to write in the same vein about the same area today, he would undoubtedly have to add an equally involved classmate, James A. Baker III, White House chief of staff. If he were to loosen up a little and jump class lines, he would also have to include Donald H. Rumsfeld, '54, President Reagan's special envoy to the Middle East, and, at the top of the list of actively concerned Princetonians, Secretary of State George P. Schultz, '42.

To illustrate the nexus of Princetonians gathered around a single crisis in current national affairs would require a small city telephone book. Indeed, in Princeton's *Alumni Directory,* there are nearly three small-type, five-column pages devoted to Princetonians living in the District of Columbia, not to mention the surrounding suburbs. Presumably, many of them serve the government in a variety of ways. Whereas William D. Ruckelshaus, '55, head of the Environmental Protection Agency, must be mentioned in terms of present power and policy, several on Capital Hill who ought to be noted because of their opposition to present power and policy are Democratic Senators Paul Spyros Sarbanes, '54, of Maryland; Clairborne deB. Pell, '40, of Rhode Island; and William W. Bradley, '65, of New Jersey.

But for the names, class years, and positions held, similar paragraphs could be written about the Washington scene for almost any given period in the Republic's history. For instance, according to *A Princeton Companion,* "The United States House of Representatives has not been without a Princeton alumnus in its membership in any year since it first met in 1789." The class of 1954 alone contributed three members—Rumsfeld, Sarbanes, and William H. Hudnut, who later became mayor of Indianapolis. There have been only twenty years in our history when the Senate has been spared the advice of a Princetonian. Eight Princeton alumni sat on the Supreme Court, and one of them, Oliver Ellsworth, class of 1766, served as chief justice from 1796 to 1800. More than a hundred Princetonians have served as ambassadors, and at least thirty-five have served as cabinet officers. Of course there have also been two Princeton presidents—Madison and Wilson. In keeping the country running, Princeton's contribution of governors (more than forty), state legislators, mayors, judges, county commissioners, and uncounted civil servants may be more important. When it comes to stimulating the electorate, Princeton's contribution of two spectacular presidential candidates—Norman Thomas and Adlai Stevenson—may be one of its finest.

There is evidence that the involvement of Princeton graduates in public service grows directly out of their Princeton experience. It is impossible to attend Princeton without having the concept of service drummed into an undergraduate's head by every ceremonial utterance. There is the sense of literally following in the footsteps of men of conspicuous service. When you walk into Nassau Hall, you go up steps so hollowed by forerunners over the centuries, you're in danger of turning your ankle. When you stand in its atrium you see marbled walls inscribed with the names of 644 war dead (the seventy who died in the Civil War in even columns of thirty-five each from North and South). Entering the wood-paneled faculty room, adorned with portraits of prominent Princetonians, you see a portrait of George Washington, which he sat for when he came to Nassau Hall to receive Congress's thanks for his war services. A few steps away from the austerely colonial Nassau Hall, you can get something of the same feeling by entering the rotundalike auditorium of an architectural gem called Alexander Hall—a gaudy Romanesque revival building with mosaics and sandstone carvings, alive with the echoes of voices as diverse as those of William Jennings Bryan, Andrew Carnegie, Will Rogers, Eleanor Roosevelt, Albert Einstein, Art Buchwald, and Jerry Falwell. In 1896, four years after the hall was built, one of those voices was the ringing tenor of a thin, horse-faced profes-

sor of politics, Woodrow Wilson. Because of his eloquence and
popularity on campus, Wilson had been selected to give a keynote
address before a glittering assemblage of foreign scholars, American college presidents, and the president of the United States,
Grover Cleveland. The title he chose—"Princeton in the Nation's
Service"—was a brilliant articulation of tradition, one of those
happy phrases that would be sounded through in years to come
as an inspiration and motto for the university.

Wilson didn't present a new idea; he simply recited history,
dwelling mostly on that period after 1768 when, fresh from Scotland, the Reverend John Witherspoon, as president of the College
of New Jersey, turned the place into a veritable hornet's nest of
revolutionaries. James Madison sat under Witherspoon's tutelage
and Philip Freneau, the poet, as well as two veritable Yankee
Doodle Dandies, Aaron Burr and Henry (Light Horse Harry) Lee.
At the 1770 commencement Witherspoon's scholars made national news by wearing American homespun instead of British
cloth. (After the "Boston tea party," Princetonians staged their
own tea-burning bonfire.) Witherspoon became the only minister,
and one of three Princetonians (along with Benjamin Rush and
Richard Stockton) to sign the Declaration of Independence. He
was one of more than thirty Princetonians to serve in the Continental Congress. Although not among them, Witherspoon's sym-
pathies and support would have gone to the nine Princetonians
(more than any other institution of learning—Yale had five, Harvard three) who struggled to create a Constitution at the Convention of 1787.

It is doubtful that most of his collegemates would have predicted that James Madison, Jr., would become the hero of that
convention, "the father of the Constitution."

At a time when any Princeton student with anything on the
ball gave an oration at commencement, Madison sat silently
through his own in 1771. One of his biographers, Irving Brant,
speculates that this was due either to ill health brought on by a
scholarly regime so severe that young Madison seldom slept more
than five hours a night, or by such an aversion to public speaking
that he was unable to conquer it for a decade, and even then a
man who heard him would say that he spoke "so very low that

his meaning could not be comprehended." It certainly couldn't have been academic ineptitude, because President Witherspoon agreed to keep him on after graduation to tutor him in law and Hebrew. The *Federalist Papers,* which he coauthored with Hamilton and Jay, virtually sold the Constitution to the public. But despite his almost heroic "hitting of the books," Madison, like most Princetonians who later made a mark, wasn't a "grind." He was a founder of the Whig Society, a literary and debating group, which, along with the already existing Cliosophic Society, was the only form of extracurricular activity on campus. Joining Freneau and others in writing sometimes ribald doggerel, he kept his eye on something other than books long enough to note that there was "no place so overstocked with Old Maids as Princeton."

Madison was so popular with his fellow students that they came to his aid in unforeseen ways. Aaron Burr, for instance, who was something of a social butterfly, introduced the reticent Madison to the vivacious widow Dolly Payne Todd, thereby giving the country one of its most colorful first ladies. Mrs. Madison is remembered for, among other things, serving spiked ice cream in order to make boring White House dinners more tolerable for "respectable" ladies. At the crucial Virginia convention to ratify the Constitution, Madison was so tongue-tied that he called his fellow Princetonian, Light Horse Harry Lee, to put across the arguments he had devised in favor of the document.

Virginians Madison and Lee were among the first of the southern contingent to go to Princeton—hence the description "northernmost of the southern colleges." Madison was pointed in that direction by the Princeton-educated tutor on the family plantation, and Lee's father broke a family tradition of educating sons in England because of his admiration for John Witherspoon.

Fellow Virginian or not, no one could have been less like Madison than Light Horse Harry Lee. The thirteen-year-old Lee arrived at Nassau Hall in 1769, already bright enough at studies to win prizes for translating English into Latin and, prophetically, for declamation. Even at that tender age he was something of a dazzler. He enjoyed singing, bull sessions, flashy clothes. Compare Madison's silent, invisible performance at commencement to Lee's in 1773, as described by a classmate: "The stage covered with gentlemen and ladies, amongst whom was the governor and his lady; and that he might not appear singular Lee was stiff with lace, gold lace."

If John Witherspoon's belief that education should "produce a spirit of liberty and independence" inspired Madison to flights of political philosophy, it armed Lee for military feats. While still in his twenties, Lee became a major, then a colonel in command of his own small "partizan" force of three hundred cavalry, at whose head he rode wearing, according to author Burton J. Hendrick's *The Lees of Virginia,* "a tall leather helmet, with horsehair plume streaming in the wind, green jacket, white lambskin breeches, shining boots reaching to the knees." The speed with which his command could move earned Lee the nickname "Light Horse" and fame for what now would be called guerrilla raids, including the capture of an entire British garrison at Paulus Hook. He was sent south to serve under General Nathanael Greene, and was credited by Greene with the strategy that regained the lower south and bottled Cornwallis up in Yorktown. A later student and admirer of Lee's military exploits was his even more famous son, Robert E. Lee.

It is ironic, in view of the turn history took, that Harry Lee, debating in favor of Madison's Constitution in the Virginia Assembly against the greatest orator of the time, Patrick Henry, said he would not hesitate to use force to save the union. He almost got his chance when Washington, always fond of Lee, appointed him major general in command of fifteen thousand troops to suppress the "whiskey rebellion" in western Pennsylvania and Virginia; but the rebels gave up without a fight. Lee served as governor of Virginia, and later in Congress. On Washington's death in 1799, he was chosen to give the eulogy. Off his golden tongue rolled that immortal phrase "first in war, first in peace and first in the hearts of his countrymen"; but though he could speak gold, he couldn't earn it. Ten years after he spoke those words, he lost his shirt in western land speculation and was thrown into debtors' prison. He could look through the bars at an open square where once Washington had dismounted, strode up to the talisman, and cast his *viva voce* vote for General Lee as his congressman.

A penchant for pursuing dubious land schemes instead of earning an honest living was one of the characteristics Lee shared with another of John Witherspoon's star pupils, Aaron Burr, Jr. Burr, also thirteen when he unpacked his bag in Nassau Hall the same year as Lee, entered into what amounted to a legacy. His father, the Reverend Aaron Burr, Sr., was a founder and second president of the college, the builder of the hall itself, and his maternal grandfather, the Reverend Jonathan Edwards, was the third president. In one ghastly year when Burr was only two, his father died of overwork, his grandfather died from a smallpox inoculation, and his mother died of a broken heart. But Esther Edwards Burr left behind in her journal a shrewd assessment of her infant son: "Aaron is a little dirty Noisy boy very different from Sally [Burr's older sister] almost in everything he begins to talk a little is very Sly and mischievous Has more sprightliness than Sally and most say he is handsomer, but not so good tempered he is very resolute and requires a good Governor to bring him to terms."

Burr biographers Herbert Parmet and Marie Hecht attribute Burr's brilliance and instability mostly to the Edwards side of the family. Grandfather Jonathan, a fiery preacher and missionary to the Indians in western Massachusetts, was the leading philosopher-theologian of the day, but a strain of madness in the family caused one distant relative to do his sister in with an axe, and another killed her son. Wherever he got it, Burr was looked upon at Princeton as the brightest scholar of the century. Studying, like Madison, eighteen hours a day, he also gave time to the Cliosophic Society, rival to Madison's Whig Society. Burr digested what Princeton had to offer in three years. Unlike Madison, Burr was a star performer at his commencement in 1772. His delivery was reportedly "excelled by none" as he charmed his audience with an address called "Building Castles in the Air," eerily foreshadowing his life.

Like Lee, Burr was a glory seeker. His war service as a colonel involved some courageous and irregular episodes of espionage in the New York area. After the war he settled down to practice law in New York, was elected to the state legislature, became New York's attorney general and then U.S. senator. In 1800 he received enough electoral votes to tie Thomas Jefferson in the election for president; the decision went to the House of Representatives, where Light Horse Harry Lee, in one of his last acts as a congressman, voted for his old Princeton classmate. To no avail. Burr was relegated to vice president—then, even more than now, a political dead end. So Burr began campaigning for governor of New York. Some of the statements Federalist Alexander Hamilton said in opposition to him could not, in Burr's opinion, be borne with honor. At a time when dueling was still widely accepted as a way of settling such affairs, Burr sent Hamilton a challenge, and on July 11, 1804, across the Hudson at Weehawken, New Jersey, Burr's bullet mortally wounded Hamilton in an exchange of pistol shots.

The event turned Hamilton into an instant martyr and Burr into a fugitive from indictments in both New York and New Jersey. Still vice president, Burr showed up in Washington and was twice entertained at dinner by President Jefferson, who was no friend of Hamilton's. Burr presided over a Senate impeachment trial of a Supreme Court justice as a last act of office. With his political career in ruins, Burr, like Lee in similar circumstances, looked to the West, the land of opportunity. No historian has yet figured out what Burr was doing at the head of a ragtag army floating down the Mississippi; whether, in fact, he planned to separate Louisiana and the Southwest from the United States and make himself an emperor. He was tried for treason in 1807 on President Jefferson's orders. From a Princetonian point of view, he was in good company; his codefendant was Jonathan Dayton, Princeton 1776, a former U.S. senator from New Jersey; his attorney was Luther Martin, Princeton 1766, one of the founders of the Cliosophic Society in which Burr had been active as an undergraduate. Burr was acquitted.

Revisionists are now suggesting that history has been unkind to Aaron Burr; there is no doubt that life was. After licking his wounds in Europe, Burr returned incognito to New York in 1812. His only daughter, Theodosia, drowned when the ship on which she was sailing to meet her father sank; and a short while later her son, Burr's only grandchild, also died. Burr's relationship with Theodosia was unusual for the time. A staunch believer in education for women, he saw to it that she and some of her friends were superbly tutored. Known as a ladies' man, he charmed them by paying attention to their minds. (He would undoubtedly have been one alumnus to applaud Princeton's decision to go coeducational two centuries after his time.) Burr lived another quarter century, practicing law in New York. He lacked money, but was always hopeful about a western land scheme, and he often represented the poor. There is a story that he kept a box on his office table that grateful clients would put money in and from which needy clients would help themselves.

Princeton, at least, was kind to Burr. When he died his body was taken there to lie in state in the chapel and he was buried at the foot of his father's and grandfather's graves with all honors, including a eulogy by President James Carnahan, a military band, and pallbearers from the Cliosophic Society. Madison tried to be kind to Lee, too. He offered to make him a general in the War of 1812, but Lee was so exhausted by his financial tribulations, and the beating he suffered in a riot related to the war, that he had to decline. In 1813 Lee left his family to try to recover his health in the West Indies. Returning home five years later, he was deposited by schooner on an island off Florida with his sole possessions—an old trunk and a cask of wine. He died and was buried there, far from Princeton, and no member of his family saw his grave until the fortunes of another war permitted another General Lee to visit it.

Little wonder that Wilson devoted much of his speech to these early Princetonians, since few alumni seemed to have achieved high office in the intervening years. Wilson could not have known then that he would become the next and most famous Princetonian of all to enter the nation's service. Even today Wilson remains a strange political phenomenon in that the reputation that sent him to the White House was earned almost entirely in academic circles, most specifically at Princeton. Even stranger that much of that reputation outside of Princeton came from battles he lost rather than won, just as his enduring stature among American presidents comes from another cause he lost in his lifetime, American participation in the League of Nations.

As with most later achievers, Wilson showed flashes of promise as an undergraduate in the class of 1879. Although he didn't earn high grades in courses he didn't value, and almost made a vice out of outside reading, and though some fellow students remembered him as austere and standoffish, he managed to get elected speaker of the Whig Society, secretary of the Football Association, president of the Baseball Association, and managing editor of the *Daily Princetonian,* then as now the loftiest nonathletic post on campus. Despite his obvious interest in sports and time spent in exercising, Wilson seems to have been kept off the actual playing fields by a certain awkwardness as well as health problems that would remain with him all his life. One of these apparently led to an editorial crusade.

In a diary notation of March 20, 1877, Wilson wrote: "I was obliged to leave English recitation this morning on account of some trouble in my bowels and they have been irregular ever since." Wilson's destination on that hurried departure from class would have been a malodorous block of brick latrines, called the *cloaca maxima* by undergraduates and located just south of the gleaming white Grecian Whig and Clio Halls. His unwanted familiarity with this place caused Wilson to fume in print: "We had thought that all that would be necessary in order to bring about a thorough overhauling and cleansing of the three wells on campus was to mention to the authorities the need for such action, trusting that their good sense would show them that they ought to act immediately. But it is always a mistake to trust their good sense, we have found."

Editor Wilson was also impatient with campus horseplay, calling snowballing an "unmitigated nuisance" and noting: "Not a day passes but someone's cherished tyle [undergraduates wore derby hats], procured regardless of expense at Dunlap's or Terhune's, is crushed into a shapeless mass. We can be saved only by an awakening of public conscience or a general thaw." Most of Wilson's editorial fire was devoted to calling for a more winning spirit in athletics, and one of the few suggestions of his later uncompromising character and deep social concerns comes through obliquely in an editorial apology: "We were too severe in our strictures on a gentleman who has recently come among us as a private instructor in education. Our statements were overdrawn. We were attacking a principle and not a person—the principle of the unwisdom involved in getting any but the very highest talent at our command when instruction in any branch is desired."

After earning a doctorate at The Johns Hopkins University and teaching at Bryn Mawr and Wesleyan (where he also coached football), Wilson returned to Princeton as a professor in 1890. As noted, his abilities earned him a place on the Alexander Hall platform and unanimous selection as president by the trustees in 1902, when they called for the resignation of a rather lax president, Francis Patton. Apparently a pleasant personality but a poor administrator, the Reverend Mr. Patton had let "college life" in the form of exclusive eating clubs, athletics, hazing, and highjinks get out of hand to the point where, in Wilson's view, the sideshow was livelier than the main tent. Wilson corrected all this with a reformer's zeal and with such success that Princeton became a nationally recognized leader in educational experimentation.

He started selective admission, turning away a quarter of those who applied, and flunking out as many as forty-six students at the first mid-year exams for failing to pass half their courses. There was some howling, and one student, according to Wilson biographer Henry Wilkinson Bragdon, bitterly complained: "Princeton is becoming nothing but a damned educational institution." In spite of a temporary drop in enrollment, Wilson stuck to his guns with full faculty support. Then, contrary to prevailing practices at Princeton and elsewhere, which allowed students a free choice of electives, Wilson instituted a required curriculum in the first two years, followed by concentrated work in a major discipline. In 1905 he enriched the faculty and impoverished the exchequer with his preceptorial system. At the same time, he set in motion a massive building program—three instruction halls, four dormitories, a gym, and other odds and ends—that would transform Princeton from an architecturally eclectic hodgepodge to a place of predominantly collegiate Gothic. Though the devoted son of a Presbyterian minister, Wilson was credited with breaking the hold of conservative Presbyterians on the Board of

Trustees. Princeton was formally declared a nonsectarian institution in 1906, and Wilson appointed the first Jew and the first Roman Catholic to the faculty.

He was an educational inspiration, a shining hero to the young, enthusiastic faculty he was building. Then he made a mistake when he tried to inaugurate the Quad Plan. To the one-third of upperclassmen rejected as "unclubable," Wilson was looked upon as a champion of social reform. To the rich alumni, many of whom were more sentimental about their clubs than their college, Wilson's plan was a red flag. They retaliated with strong rhetoric and, even more effectively, withheld money to the point where the trustees felt forced to reject the Wilson plan. It is generally accepted that Wilson's bitterness over his defeat by the privileged turned him into the "fair dealing" politician who would start a social transformation of American society that culminated in Franklin Roosevelt's New Deal.

But that was only the first of Wilson's rebuffs. Everybody, including Wilson, agreed that Princeton needed a graduate college to make it into the university it proclaimed itself to be. An effete, elitist Latin scholar named Andrew Fleming West was dean of such graduate instruction as there was. West met and so impressed President Grover Cleveland that when Cleveland retired from the White House he and his wife went to live in Princeton in a place called "Westland." Cleveland's interest and prestige earned him a place on the university's Board of Trustees, where he sided with West when the corpulent, luxury-loving dean squared off with the lean, ascetic president on where the graduate college should be located. Wilson wanted to give up his own residence at Prospect, in the heart of the campus, as a site for the school on the principle that graduate students, like faculty, should mingle with undergraduates to their mutual educational benefit. West wanted *his* school to be an elegant Gothic quadrangle set in splendid isolation where the lofty graduate students would dine together in black gowns and explore the higher reaches of the mind.

Once again Wilson was roundly beaten by money. A major donor, William Cooper Proctor, class of 1883 and president of

Proctor and Gamble, sided with West and threatened to withdraw his gift if the graduate college wasn't located on the golf
course half a mile off campus. A stalemate ensued until Isaac C.
Wyman, class of 1848, a wealthy Salem, Massachusetts, bachelor,
whom West had been secretly cultivating, died and left a pur-
ported $3 million (which turned out to be only about $800,000)
for the graduate college, with West as one of two trustees. West
reportedly laid a sprig of ivy from Nassau Hall on Wyman's coffin,
and Wilson told his wife bitterly: "We've beaten the living, but
we can't fight the dead." A verse from Princeton's faculty song
covered the situation nicely:

> *Here's to Andrew Fleming West,*
> *a Latin scholar self-confessed.*
> *He lives to see a lifetime's hope*
> *constructed out of Ivory soap.*

Wilson caved in, and even congratulated West on his fund
raising, but began at once to listen to politicians who were urging
him to run for governor of New Jersey in 1910. His position at
Princeton was simply no longer tenable and, in fact, after moving
to the White House in 1912, he seldom came back. Today the
graduate college, with its striking Cleveland Tower, stands by the
golf course where West wanted it with the negative effects of
isolation from the life of the college that Wilson foresaw. Wilson
would undoubtedly approve the present Quad plan, but whether
he would be equally pleased with Princeton's other great innova-
tion—coeducation—is to be doubted from an incident recounted
by Raymond Fosdick in *Chronicle of a Generation*. As the father
of three daughters, Wilson might have been expected to be recep-
tive when the mother of a student urged him to institute coeducation. But, according to Fosdick:

> He asked, "Why?"
> "To remove the false glamour with which the two sexes see
> each other," she replied.
> "My dear madam," Wilson shot back, "that is the very thing
> we want to preserve at all costs."

Despite administrative defeats, Wilson's words and later accomplishments set a high-water mark of public involvement for
Princetonians that is still visible. Fosdick, who sat under him,
says: "For me Woodrow Wilson lit a lamp which has never been
put out. All my life I have remembered him as the inspiring
teacher who introduced us to the kingdom of the mind, and held
before our eyes what [Alfred North] Whitehead later called 'an
habitual vision of greatness.' " A contemporary and friend of
Fosdick, Norman Thomas, class of 1905, said: "No man made a
deeper impression on my youth than Woodrow Wilson. I was his
admiring pupil at Princeton. I even tried, unsuccessfully, to
model my public speaking on his." However inspired by Wilson,
neither Fosdick nor Thomas looked upon their mentor as "liberal." Later, Wilson's social reforms would fall far short of those
Thomas advocated as a six-time Socialist candidate for the presidency, and Wilson's rigid character would evoke from Thomas,
a man who softened his social gospel with self-deprecating wit, the
comment: "All his public life he was inclined to take strong
opposition or criticism as a sin against the Holy Ghost."

There was little about young Norman Thomas that would
have caused his classmates to imagine his future as a radical
gadfly, a goad to the capitalistic conscience. Fosdick, who later
became president of the Rockefeller Foundation, considered himself a more liberal undergraduate than Thomas, and, indeed,
Thomas listed himself as a Republican in the senior *Nassau Her-
ald.* In his senior year Thomas was pleased to join the tony
Colonial Club, about which he said: "It didn't make a snob of me,
but it did in later years give me a curious confidence that if I
espoused unpopular causes it wasn't some personal incapacity for
ordinary social success that drove me to them." Thomas may
have been invited because some sort of success seemed assured for
him: with a straight-A average, he was class valedictorian. In
addition, he and Fosdick, as members of Whig Hall, were the
school's leading debaters. The other thing they shared was a not
so genteel poverty, and on one occasion they signed on to debate
against each other on French politics, a subject unfamiliar to
both, for the sake of winning the Baron de Coubertin award, a
gold medal valued at $150, which they agreed the winner would

sell for cash. Fosdick won, hurried to a New York jeweler with his prize, and discovered that it was a gold-washed alloy worth seventy-five cents. Thomas learned a lot more about poverty when, while studying for the ministry, he worked in a New York settlement house and was radicalized for life by the experience. He thereby turned his guaranteed success into failure, which he wistfully expressed in his fiftieth reunion class book: "I've failed —doubtless to your general satisfaction—in the chief purpose of my career: to create a viable party democratic socialist in principle."

Despite his intellectual estrangement from his classmates, Thomas was sentimental about Princeton, attended reunions, and noted late in life his "satisfaction that Princeton and the things it stands for have endured." His "capitalistic college," in turn, honored him with a Doctor of Letters in a ceremony that became comic. Thomas was last on the list, and the gentleman who was handing out the awards began to sit down without mentioning him, until he was stopped by a whispered reminder. Afterward he apologized, saying that the Thomas citation had been paperclipped to another. Thomas shot back: "I know, a capitalistic clip." The fact that Thomas never broke with Princeton more than justified the title Murray B. Seidler used for his biography—*Norman Thomas: Respectable Rebel*—and raises some provocative thoughts about that other Princeton also-ran, Adlai E. Stevenson, '22, who reluctantly bore the brunt of keeping Democratic ideas alive in the golden conservative Eisenhower years.

Aside from trying to unhorse one of the most popular generals in history, Stevenson, even according to admirers, helped defeat himself by an intellectual honesty that would not allow him to threaten doom or promise the moon. This is a very Princetonian attitude, and it may or may not be a virtue. When you study a conservative curriculum devoted to the long view of history and the arts and sciences, it's hard to get too passionate about *any* cause of the moment. When the person whose politics you hate turns out to be the admired captain of the team you're on, or your most likeable clubmate, it's hard to take the view that *anybody's* all wrong. The virtue of thinking this way, of feeling it in your

bones, is that Princetonians of opposing views can usually maintain mutual respect, keep up a civilized dialogue, work for the
common good. Just as they can get together to conserve Princeton, Princetonians can usually reach a compromise to keep the
corporation, or the Republic, or whatever, going at some sacrifice
to personal pride and prejudice. The possibly crippling aspect of
this attitude is that it induces a caution that can be mistaken for
apathy or cowardice. My own political convictions began shifting
sharply to the Left as early as 1946, but it wasn't until 1964 that
I voted for a Democrat. My wife, chiding me, asked, "What took
you so long? *I* voted for Roosevelt," and I unthinkingly replied,
"I guess it's because I went to Princeton."

Wives have a way of shaking husbands up, as did Mary
McCarthy, the novelist, who married Edmund Wilson, '16, one
of Princeton's true literary lights, and himself so far out politically that he once flirted with communism. Although related to
the arts rather than politics, Wilson's letter about this incident,
written in 1944 to his lifelong friend and former teacher Dean
Christian Gauss, is one of the most revealing descriptions of the
Princeton attitude:

> I have been thinking about the whole [Princeton] group [of writ
> ers] and I believe that, in certain ways, Princeton did not serve
> them well. I said this to Mary, who has had considerable opportu
> nity to observe the men from various colleges, and she said: "Yes,
> Princeton didn't give them quite moral principle enough to be
> writers." Instead, it gave us too much respect for money and
> country house prestige. Both Scott [Fitzgerald] and John [Peale
> Bishop] in their respective ways, I think, fell victim to this. I don't
> want to be pharisaical about them: I was more fortunate than
> either of them, not in gifts, but in the opportunity to survive,
> because I had enough money for study and travel in the years
> when those things are most valuable, but not so much that . . . I
> didn't have to think about earning some. One's only consolation
> is that Princeton did give us other things that were good—a sort
> of eighteenth century humanism that probably itself was not un
> connected with the rich patron relationship of the University to
> somebody like M. T. Pyne [class of 1877, longtime trustee, donor
> of buildings and prizes]. And then, if we had gone to Yale, though
> we should probably all have survived in the flesh, we might never

have survived in whatever it is that inspires people not to take too seriously the ideal of the successful man.

Adlai Stevenson's warmest admirers insist that, though he took his causes seriously, he could never take himself seriously. Except for being chosen managing editor of the *Daily Princetonian,* his undergraduate career was undistinguished—a "gentleman's C" average and only third place, with eight votes, in the class poll for "biggest politician." Evidently, his classmates didn't take him seriously either. As William E. Stevenson, no relation but a classmate who became president of Oberlin College and ambassador to the Philippines (with Stevenson's help), noted in *As We Knew Adlai,* "Of the 27,314,992 people who voted for Ad in 1952 only a comparative few were classmates."

This should have come as no surprise to William Stevenson. The Republican hue of Princeton alumni is so visible as to hardly need pointing out. Polls of my own class over the years have shown the Republican majority at more than 70 percent, and in one of our yearbooks it was concluded that "the Independent voters of the class of 1942 will judge each candidate on his own merits, weigh all the evidence carefully, and vote for whatever candidate they wish as long as that candidate is Republican." At graduation the class of 1942 defined its political inclinations as 61 percent liberal, 37 percent conservative, and 2 percent radical; recent polls of undergraduates show them strongly Democratic or liberal. Ironically, Princetonians who have achieved fame in *elective* office have been mostly Democrats, starting with Madison, who was the forerunner of the Democratic party, through Wilson and Stevenson and the roster of senators on which Democrats outnumber Republicans two to one.

Princeton's respect for sons who go politically astray and fail in the process is noted in Stevenson Hall, a Stevenson window in the chapel, a library in one of the colleges named for Norman Thomas. Its respect for sons who succeed in terms more acceptable to the Princeton majority stands in a monument to John Foster Dulles, class of 1908, Eisenhower's secretary of state—the Dulles Library of Diplomatic History. As an undergraduate, Dulles was something of a studious mole who earned a Phi Beta Kappa key and stood second in his class, but who failed to be elected to a club. "A publicity handout prepared by Dulles's personal public relations adviser in 1944 (during his developing prominence as a lay church leader in the fight to establish the United Nations) contained the statement that it was Dulles's 'own wish' not to accept membership in one of the social, class-conscious eating clubs," writes Townsend Hoopes in *The Devil and John Foster Dulles.* "The handout attributed this stance to Dulles's sympathy for the position of the university's president, Woodrow Wilson, who held that on moral grounds the clubs ought to be abolished because they were breeding grounds of snobbery and an anti-democratic spirit." Hoopes notes wryly that when Dulles became a wealthy New York corporation lawyer he quietly accepted an invitation to become an alumni member of Cottage Club. As secretary of state, Communist-fighting Presbyterian Dulles exhibited little of Stevenson's caution, perhaps because he knew that the men of his class were behind him.

One of the more enigmatic and tragic Princetonians in the nation's service was the first secretary of defense, James V. Forrestal, '15, now memorialized by the complex a few miles from the university called the Forrestal Campus. There is some indication, according to biographer Arnold A. Rogow, that Forrestal transferred to Princeton from Dartmouth as a sophomore because of its prominence during the Wilson presidency, which led him to believe that he would there meet "people who counted for something." Like so many undergraduates who went on to fame, Forrestal worked his way up to the editorship of the *Daily Princetonian,* but his Princeton life was not a very happy one, owing to an estrangement from his family and a crisis of faith in which he renounced his paternal Catholicism. They may account for the fact, as discussed, that Forrestal launched the *Princetonian* on one of its early crusades against compulsory chapel attendance. A stubborn character, reflected in his pug-nosed, tight-lipped features, may have caused Forrestal to withdraw in the spring of his senior year without a degree, rather than retake an

English course from a professor whose lectures he had cut because he was convinced the man disliked him.

Forrestal nevertheless accomplished his original objective of "meeting the right people" and provides one of the best examples of the Princeton connection, or "old boy (now girl) network," in action. During Forrestal's senior year, an earlier Princetonian, Dean Mathey, '12, was sent by his New York investment firm, Dillon, Read, to look for promising recruits. Wasting no time, Mathey asked: "Who's the editor of the *Princetonian?*" and then sought out Forrestal. After he floundered around a year or so in newspaper work, Forrestal followed up on that meeting, joined Dillon, Read as a bond salesman, and became president of the firm at forty-six, earning a comfortable fortune and making the useful contacts that allowed him to enjoy a distinguished public career in World War II and beyond. Perhaps the issues of faith and family that plagued him at Princeton still tortured him on the dark night when he ended that career by plunging to his death from the window of a Washington hospital.

Lawyer Dulles and financier Forrestal were part of a Princeton tradition of service, still in evidence in the person of Secretary of State George P. Shultz, '42. Historically, Shultz may well be the epitome of the Princeton public servant, having served previously as director of the budget, secretary of labor, and secretary of the treasury. His success in the private sector as a professor of economics and, most recently, president of the Bechtel Group, Inc. is no less glittering. It is indicative of the secretary's loyalty to Princeton that he was willing to give time to talk about his Princeton experience in one of the most challenging weeks of his career, when the Grenada invasion immediately followed the bombing of marines in Beirut.

As an undergraduate George Shultz was a standout; he won letters in football and basketball, was chairman of the Class Memorial Fund Committee, a member of the Quadrangle Club. But what he recalled when he was asked about the meaning of Princeton in his life was "high standards of excellence and the expectation of achievement." Like so many graduates, he was conscious of the "Princeton in the nation's service" theme, and he became interested in public issues when he majored in the School of Public and International Affairs. The secretary did not, however, feel that the unseen hand of the "Princeton connection" had much to do with pulling him up the ladder in his subsequent career.

By contrast, White House Chief of Staff Baker claims he virtually owes his political career to a variant of the Princeton connection—the Ivy League connection. Baker, a practicing attorney in his native Houston, Texas, moved in a small Ivy League social circle that included Vice President George Bush, a Yale man, and it was Bush who persuaded Baker to give time from a lucrative corporate practice to Republican party affairs. In addition, the Princeton experience has, Baker says, made it possible for him to move with understanding between the contrasting Texan and eastern cultures and to get along with people of differing political views.

Baker, the son of a Princetonian and a handsome and genial man, by his own account was nonpolitical on campus. The record bears him out. He played tennis and rugby, was a member of Ivy, and the class history notes that in junior year "the efforts of Jim Baker and an all Junior '21' club kept party spirit alive throughout the fall." This particular organization was described thus in the *Bric-a-Brac* of 1952: "Twenty-one members of the junior class who believe in upholding the long-suffering cause of serious, altruistic drinking amidst the press of educational life compose the club." Another of Baker's undergraduate associations, the Right Wing Club, would seem to have some prophetic political meaning: "The purpose of the club is simply to have a good time and see that its guests do also." But Baker, a crossover major in history and classics, emphatically says: "I got a fine education." As for the service theme at Princeton, he says succinctly: "I feel honored to serve my country at a high level."

Whether the fact that the fate of America has been so long and so often in Princetonian hands is a good thing is not for any Princetonian to judge. After all, two of the nation's superspies were CIA chiefs Allen Dulles, '14 and William Colby, '40. President Bowen takes the position that the service theme should apply not only to national service, or even to specific governmental efforts on any level, but should embrace all forms of relatively selfless contributions to society. In that sense, any Princetonian who serves even a minor role on a community or church committee would have to cordially agree.

Chapter Eleven

# BUT DO YOU HAVE THE BUDAPEST STRING QUARTET?

N ot long ago a citizen of the Princeton community got into a discussion with a friend from a similarly pleasant place along the New England coast about the relative merits of their respective locations. The New England man went on and on about the joys of living near the sea; about the pleasures of having not one, but two golf courses, as well as a hunt club a mile from his door; about the convenience of a comparatively brief commute to his office in the city. When he'd heard his friend out, the Princeton man asked quietly, "But do you have the Budapest String Quartet?" The discussion ended right then: there *is* a different dimension to life in the Princeton area.

Although the flattening cultural steamroller of twentieth-century suburbia is coming ever closer, Princeton has so far stood out in character against that bleak horizon much as its university's Gothic towers rise incongruously above the New Jersey flats.

Princeton truly fits the often-raised but rarely tested cliché: it is incontrovertibly a place of the mind. Many years ago, the *Saturday Evening Post* ran an article about the community entitled "Life Among the Egg Heads," and that same title still serves as well today. Among the twenty-six thousand residents of the municipalities of Princeton Borough and Princeton Township there have always been a disproportionate number of celebrated thinkers, writers, artists. They were initially drawn to the area by Princeton University, which physically and otherwise has dominated the town since 1756, when the largest building in the colonies, the still-occupied Nassau Hall, was erected. But in the past fifty years there has grown up around the university a ring of educational institutions and, beyond them, in contiguous communities, a much wider ring of think tanks, research facilities, and business installations, which depend upon heads instead of hands. Although there exists a hard corps of service people to provide such hands as even eggheads can't do without, it would be fair to say that more mental giants pass through Princeton's Palmer Square in a day than ever walked in the Agora of ancient Athens.

Physically, Princeton's greatest attraction was initially, and still is, its location. Before there was a university there was an important stagecoach stop here, halfway between New York and Philadelphia. Commuters who choose Princeton as a "bedroom community" today can thus reach their offices in either of two major metropolises with equal difficulty (about two hours door to door). The university's founders, after shuttling their college over a ten-year period between Elizabethtown and Newark, evidently picked Princeton for much the same reasons—to draw students equally from the then already populous areas. To describe Princeton physically is to dredge up the famous crack about a rich man's estate: "It shows what God could do if He had money." Over several centuries man's hand has made Princeton a forested, ivied oasis in a featureless plain; but it is remote from any natural wonder, such as mountain or sea, and its dripping winter weather keeps the infirmary dismally busy. Still, there are irreproachable spring days in Princeton, and it can be said that the mind functions infinitely better when it isn't subjected to natural distractions.

Because it grew almost to maturity in the days when the horse was the only means of transportation, Princeton is a cluster of large houses on relatively small lots, many of the houses still standing from pre-Revolutionary times. Most of old Princeton, as well as most of the university, lies within Princeton Borough; but, except when paying taxes or voting, the community pays little attention to the archaic subdivisions. So entangled are they that the line between borough and township runs right through a number of buildings, including the Princeton Inn, now part of the university. A few years ago, when it was still an inn, a guest died and the policeman arriving to investigate shoved the body a few feet down the hall, called his counterpart from the other community, and washed his hands of the case. In any event, the heart of Princeton in the borough has a lived-in charm that seems to increase as old dwellings change hands— "You can't get a decent house in Princeton for under $100,000" is an oft-quoted truism. The colonial motif was fortunately carried over into the twentieth-century remodeling of the town's commercial center, Palmer Square, just off Nassau Street, and strict zoning, along with the continuing value perceived in ancient buildings, has kept out high-rises other than the university towers. Beyond comfortable walking distance from the university, houses and properties in newer developments are indistinguishable from any other suburb, yet still quite expensive; it isn't cheap to feed the mind.

No doubt the most famous mind ever to reside in Princeton was Albert Einstein. For the last decades of his life the great discoverer of relativity lived in an undistinguished old house from which he could walk to the university and to the Institute for Advanced Study. In 1936, writing to his good friend Queen Elizabeth of Belgium, Einstein caught the essence of Princeton better than most of the resident novelists and poets: "I am privileged by fate to live here in Princeton as if on an island that in many respects resembles the charming palace garden in Laeken. Into this small university town, too, the chaotic voices of human strife barely penetrate. I am almost ashamed to be living in such peace while all the rest struggle and suffer. But after all, it is still best to concern oneself with eternals, for from them alone flows that spirit that can restore peace and serenity to the world of humans."

Einstein still hovers over Princeton as a sort of shabby ghost. His appearance was the essence of what was hoped for in a man of the mind. A less than casual dresser—sockless, bare ankles protruded below his baggy pants—and with utter disdain for barbers (his tangle of long gray hair stood out like a Marx Brothers' fright wig), he walked in oblivious thought in all the public places, particularly on Nassau Street, which fronts the campus on one side and is lined with stores on the other. Einstein's usual destination was a now vanished establishment known as "the Balt," where he could get his favorite food for the mind—ice cream. A vivid picture of the Einstein-Princeton relationship is found in the story of his arrival, as told by his biographer Ronald W. Clark.

Because he was already world famous in the early 1930s, Einstein was snatched off the liner bringing him from Europe by tugboat at the Battery and smuggled by car to Princeton to avoid reporters. "Einstein's boat was not yet at the pier in New York," the Reverend John Lampe, then a divinity student at Princeton Seminary, told Clark. "Yet Einstein walked through the doorway [of the Balt] just as the waitress behind the counter handed me my special ice cream cone! The great man looked at the cone, smiled at me, turned to the girl, and pointed his thumb first at the cone and then at himself. I wish I could say that I had the generosity or presence of mind to pay for Einstein's first typically American treat. But that would not be the truth. When the waitress handed his cone over the counter, Einstein gave her a coin and she made change, muttering something like 'this one goes in my memory book.' Einstein and I stood there together, then, nibbling our ice cream cones and looking out the window into Nassau Street. Neither of us said anything. We finished the cones about the same instant and I think I held the door for him as he stepped out."

The name of Einstein is evoked in curious ways. It is probable that, tolerant though he was, Einstein would wince at learning that the entertainment lounge—"live entertainment, top 40 in nature"—of the Hyatt Regency on Route 1 has been called "Al-

bert's" in his honor. But he well might like the use to which
Margen Penick, a former president and member of the Princeton
Planning Board, put his image. The most controversial development in Princeton is still another remodeling of Palmer Square,
a stone's throw from Einstein's old haunt, the Balt. Trying to
explain to developer Arthur Collins her objections to some of his
plans, Mrs. Penick said: "You know, Arthur, really, the personality of Princeton can be summed up in this kind of example. The
image is Albert Einstein walking down Nassau Street thinking
about something with an ice cream cone in his hand dripping
down his coat. We don't want any flashiness. We don't want to
change our history of what we are. We want to be smart, yet not
flashy."

In taking on Palmer Square, Collins was like a man putting
his foot knowingly into a bear trap. As a Princetonian, class of
1952, who had also earned a master's degree in architecture and
urban planning, Collins was well aware that the people of Princeton abhorred any change—even to move a familiar tree. Although
headquartered in Connecticut, his Collins Development Corporation had already built a housing development in Princeton; but
fiddling with the heart of the town was something else. "The town
is very insular, very conservative, very suspicious, very difficult
to work with," Collins says. Yet because of his background Collins felt that it was a job that somebody had to do.

Palmer Square was the conception and single-handed enterprise of a wealthy Princeton engineering graduate, Edgar Palmer,
class of 1903, who had a handsome home nearby. In the late
1920s he began to buy up for demolition and replacement old
commercial properties along Nassau Street and to the north, and
by the mid-thirties his creation was completed. A friend of John
D. Rockefeller, Jr., Palmer borrowed the structural design of
Rockefeller Center in New York and the building style of another
Rockefeller project, Colonial Williamsburg. As a centerpiece,
Palmer placed a reconstituted version of historic Nassau Tavern
two blocks in from Nassau Street behind an open square planted
with trees and grass and supplied with lounging benches. Around
this small park he built slate-roofed brick stores with apartments
or offices above, a movie theater, a post office. It was something

of an instant success, a lively place to which students and towns-people alike were drawn by the variety of merchandise, the "flicks," the amenities of the tavern. Indeed, it could be said that several generations of Princeton students spent more time in "the Nass" than in class; the tavern contained an all-male bar adorned by a Norman Rockwell mural of "Yankee Doodle" and was furnished with heavy tables from the former inn bearing the carvings of drinking Princetonians from times colonial. At his death Palmer donated his creation to Princeton as an income-bearing property.

Palmer Square gradually became more of a burden than a blessing to the university. High rents resulted in an influx of high-priced stores out of the reach of students. Shopping malls, many of them hideous, sprang up on the outskirts. Television and an inexpensive flowering of on-campus movies left the barnlike Playhouse nearly empty. It may be that the knell was rung for Palmer Square in 1970, when, a year after the university admitted women students, a determined group of local females "desegregated" the Yankee Doodle taproom. Some forty men and women, including members of the vocal NOW (National Organization for Women), marched in, sat down, and waited to be served lunch. Rather fainthearted in their approach; they had already eaten, but their strategy worked. The management not only let down the bars but turned the taproom into a dining room where students were soon outnumbered and outpriced. By 1980 the university decided it could make more money by investing the value of the property in securities and put Palmer Square on the block for $17 million.

When Collins appeared with an offer to purchase and presented a $70-80 million plan that would, in effect, double the capacity of Palmer Square, the university jumped at it. There had been originally about some seventy interested developers, Collins recalls, but only two at the end competed because of the many complexities. There was no ordinance that allowed changes, such as building a "bridge" over a back street to connect a new annex of rooms to the tavern, and Collins and his associates had to go "hat in hand" to several local boards for building permits. The sort of thing they ran into can be judged from a *Home News* account of an early Planning Board meeting.

"Board President Margen Penick, who cast the only negative vote, nevertheless that night called the Collins plan 'ninety-nine percent wonderful' and described her vote as a 'symbolic' protest against the planned removal of a grassy area and a spruce tree. And Elizabeth Hutter, the one abstaining member, said, 'I couldn't bring myself to vote against the plan,' adding that she also couldn't have voted for it as long as the lantern building would take up space where the lawn is now."

Compromising by dropping the "lantern building" and with the staunch support of the then mayor of Princeton Borough, Robert Cawley, Collins won his permissions one by one and a new Palmer Square is now emerging. In truth, it will look much like the old Palmer Square. No buildings will rise higher than the present structures on the corners at Nassau Street; parking for a thousand cars will be underground; condominiums will be tucked around back of the stores; traditional style will be reflected if not duplicated. In this project, at least, Collins is a sentimentalist, and his clear love for Princeton was, according to university officials, a major factor in their decision to sell to him.

"I wanted to go to Princeton because I loved the campus so much," Collins says. "Even though I didn't know it at the time, I was architecturally inclined, and when the father of a friend of mine took us down for a look around four or five years before I was ready for college, I fell in love with the beauty of the place. Now I'm back at Palmer Square, and I'm still thinking about the things I thought of when I was very young—the relationships of things—and I'm doing the same thing at Palmer Square. But I'm dealing with it on a much more educated basis. If we can catch some of the beauty of the campus in Palmer Square, we'll have a much better people catcher in the end."

In Collins's eyes is a place not only commercially revitalized with stores and eating places that will bring the gown back to town, but a place that will draw the outside world in to enjoy Princeton. His hopes may not be in vain, because the town is already something of a tourist attraction. A young woman who grew up in Princeton reflected: "I never really thought of it as a university town, but as sort of a tourist place. You hardly ever see students from any of its schools on the streets but you sure see a lot of sightseers." What brings the gawkers to Princeton, aside from its manmade beauty, is history. It was, after all, one of the cradles of the United States.

On appropriately named Mercer Street, for instance, the visitor can see the oak tree under which General Mercer died on January 3, 1777, during the victorious battle of Princeton, which may have turned the tide of the Revolutionary War; at Nassau Hall there is a dent in the wall made by a cannonball fired by a battery under the command of Alexander Hamilton in an effort to dislodge the British who had taken refuge there. Inside Nassau Hall members of the Continental Congress sweated out the summer of 1783 until they heard the good news of the peace treaty signed in Paris. Down the road is "Rockingham," where General Washington stayed during part of that session, and in Nassau Hall's faculty room there hangs a portrait of Washington by Charles Wilson Peale, inserted into the same frame from which a portrait of King George II had been symbolically ejected by one of Hamilton's cannonballs. Princeton's graveyard not only contains the remains of a long line of Princeton presidents, but such other figures as President Grover Cleveland and Aaron Burr, Jr., who killed Hamilton in one of history's most famous duels. Because of its predilection for hanging onto old buildings, Princeton has a Quaker Meeting House dating to 1726 among its colonial dwellings. Because of its size, Princeton's historical landmarks can be covered mostly on foot and in a day, and it is reassuring in what has become a disposable society to wander around a place where things endure.

It isn't the prospect of history-minded tourists that bothers the Penicks of Princeton; it is the non-Princetonian type of people who have come to stay and work in an ever-widening ring of commercial enterprises that are gobbling up the farmland around the town. Occupying for the most part low buildings glued to landscaped acreage are such installations as Squibb, RCA, IBM, McGraw-Hill, General Electric, Educational Testing Service, Institute for Defense Analyses, to name a few. The people who work there are likely to view Princeton as just another pleasant place, whereas the inner circle of Princeton citizenry are either actively affiliated with the university—the town's largest employer—or have returned to live or retire there as a result of sentimental memories of undergraduate days. There are more than one thousand alumni resident in both Princetons, according to the 1982 *Alumni Directory;* multiply this by a factor of three to include their families and the result is a hefty 11 percent of the twenty-six thousand total population in both communities and, of course, a high percentage of those of voting age. Many Princetonians must have shown a broad-mindedness in contributing to the elections over twelve years of a Lehigh graduate, Mayor Cawley, who works in a research establishment on the outer ring. This support may have been given because Cawley admits it is the presence of the university that makes Princeton what it is; paradoxically, he shares some of their fears about an influx of too many people like himself.

"In ten years at most, Princeton will be totally surrounded by development," he predicts. Although Cawley strongly favored the Palmer Square development, he sees the peripheral development turning Princeton into an island in a sea of traffic, and perhaps changing the character of the population. "So far Princeton has differed from other suburban communities, because the commuting population is relatively low," he says. "It really wasn't a commuting town. Princeton has been a center of population for a long time and until recently has been isolated as an entity of its own." In another way, Princeton Borough differs from most suburban communities and departs from the image of a place stuffed with Princeton graduates; it is heavily Democratic. In the township where the new people are squeezed in, it is half Republican. Cawley attributes the Democratic weight to "service" people—Princeton makes strong efforts to subsidize housing so that they *can* live in town—and the university faculty. This makes the long reign of Cawley, a Republican, unusual, but perhaps faculty vote independently, however registered. As to the faculty's politics, it is educational to listen to the alarm bell rung by the ultra conservative Concerned Alumni of Princeton (CAP), an organization founded by Princetonians living in Princeton: "A majority of Princeton's faculty is liberal to radical, evidence of which was seen in 1968 in the unscientific straw poll . . . that showed about seventy-one percent for Humphrey, seven percent for Nixon. . . . "

In the fall of 1983 liberalism, if that is the correct word, triumphed when Democrat Barbara Sigmund, a stunning woman who wears a white eyepatch, soundly defeated Richard Wood-bridge, Princeton '65, to take over Cawley's vacated job. Some doubt as to her Princetonian sensibilities comes from a campaign quote: "We are not simply the golden ghetto of F. Scott Fitz-gerald mythology." What concerned her, among other things, was the state of the ancient and leaky sewers beneath Princeton's elegant surface. Woodbridge's campaign verged on nostalgia when he said: "You can go downtown and know who you're buying your food and your newspaper from. I'd like to keep the town accessibly small." He did, however, turn around and agree with his fellow Republican Cawley by adding: "But Princeton is not an island and is part of a rapidly developing region."

One Princetonian who is undeniably happy about that state of affairs is a man named Robert Wolfe, a philosophy major in the class of 1969 who is manager of the Princeton Forrestal Center, the flagship of dreaded development, a 1,600-acre tract of land owned by the university and situated in Plainsboro Township across Route 1. Some 275 acres are reserved for the Forrestal Campus of the university where besides such facilities as the Plasma Physics Laboratory, an airfield, and a "long track" (ob-jects are moved through air instead of having air blown by them) for aerospace engineering, there is storage space for infrequently used library books. The rest is being developed under contract with the university by Sweet Associates, of which Wolfe is a partner, to lure even more research and development operations into the Princeton area.

Wolfe's present position is somewhat ironic. After earning a graduate degree in business at Stanford, he turned down offers in real estate development—he didn't want to be involved in "rape of the land"—and indulged his philosophic bent by working in the business department of Stanford and then Princeton. While he was in the latter position, the decision was made to develop

Forrestal, and Wolfe went along with it because, he says: "I agree with the general aims of the development here. The one given was that the area *was* going to develop, so the concern became maintaining the quality of development, doing an environmentally sensitive development, while at the same time earning as much money for the university as if it had been invested in stocks and bonds."

Wolfe claims success on both counts. As to money, Forrestal Center is doing better than the securities market, even though only 25 percent is completed. As to the environment, one would hardly know anything is there when driving past it on the highway. To be left untouched forever are 470 acres, including woodlands and wetlands and highway frontage. The tenants include some fifty companies, with as few as two and as many as a thousand employees. "We're zoned for light industry but choose not to have any," Wolfe says. "There's a fine line between what is research and light manufacturing. We do have some companies that have six Ph.D.s in white smocks in a lab who produce a product in a test tube once a month that is shipped out parcel post. Is that industrial? Maybe it is. Otherwise it's all office and research work."

Physically, in Wolfe's opinion, the Forrestal development is doing a lot to allay the fears of the citizens in Princeton town. "Within the natural strains of growth, our objective is to maintain or improve the quality of life—and make money," he says. "From my perspective, the Forrestal Center would be copied in the area only if it made money. It's too easy for other developers to look at it and say: 'Well, Princeton can afford to do that, but we can't.' They couldn't say that if we made a lot of money—and we are. Now we are seeing other big land masses along Route 1 being developed, and I think very nicely, and, though we can't prove it, it's better than if Forrestal had never been around."

Wolfe's welcoming attitude about the people Forrestal is attracting separates him from others in the Princeton community. Instead of diluting the brainy blood, they are enriching it, in his view, and his evidence seems to support him. For example, the chief researcher of a small biotechnology company gives lectures at the university, and the company has funded a postdoctoral fellowship. In another instance, Prudential, the largest lessor of property at Forrestal, gave $400,000 for Princeton's architectural and engineering schools to research designs of energy-saving buildings. Out of that emerged two buildings at Forrestal, which are projected to use one-sixth of the energy of a pre–oil embargo building, one-third that of a post–oil embargo building. So far relationships between the Forrestal installations and the university have been largely on an individual rather than institutional basis, but Wolfe points to the existence of the university as a big drawing card and foresees that Forrestal Center will eventually bring about closer ties and mutual benefit between Princeton and the private sector. "The old timer is saying that he's here because it's Princeton, and he's mad that other people want to be here," Wolfe says. "But what should the university do—be less of a nice place so that other people don't want to come here?"

Historically, "other people" in the brain business have always been attracted to Princeton for much the same reasons as the research and development people. Some have been there so long that their own walls are encrusted with ivy, and most have international reputations. The oldest, and literally next door to the campus, is the Princeton Theological Seminary, founded in 1812 in a not wholly successful effort to separate Presbyterianism per se from an increasingly nondenominational university. As the leading seminary of that denomination, Princeton attracts to its student body of eight hundred people from many other denominations, including Roman Catholics, and some seventy international scholars. One reason may be that it has "the best theological library in the Western hemisphere," a facility that is available to university students on an interlibrary exchange basis. With departmental approval, seminary and university students can enroll in each other's courses, and there is some exchange in teaching. But on the whole the institutions are so separate that the *Daily Princetonian* not long ago assigned a reporter, a senior who had never set foot on the seminary campus, to do a feature on life among the future divines.

Across Nassau Street and down a few blocks is the Westminster Choir College, founded in the late twenties in a Dayton, Ohio, Presbyterian church by a colorful character named John

Finley Williamson, and removed to Princeton in 1933 at the suggestion of a seminary professor, Dr. Charles R. Erdman. But, as Williamson said later in a comment that sounds ironical in view of today's Princeton: "We were not *invited* to come to Princeton, we were merely *allowed* to come, and many were dubious about having coeds in Princeton. Too, we were warned that no young lady should ever be seen on Nassau Street without a hat." In pre–World War II days they were *never* seen on Nassau Street, however dressed, partly because then, as now, they were so busy singing in choirs that traveled the world or with the New York and Philadelphia symphony orchestras and others. As one of the nation's leading centers for training church organists and choirmasters, Westminster draws an international student body, puts on concerts and festivals, and offers instrumental instruction to Princeton citizens on a private basis. One citizen who took advantage of the Choir College was Albert Einstein, who often trudged over from his home on Mercer Street, sockless and carrying a violin case, to play in the string ensembles.

It is Einstein's workaday establishment, the Institute for Advanced Study, built about the same time as the Choir College, that remains the loftiest citadel of the mind in all of Princeton. A collection of new Georgian brick buildings, the institute is found along a narrow, winding road behind untended fields. Professors at the institute are required to do nothing whatever except think, and the result is an atmosphere best captured by Princeton author John Davies in a *Princeton Magazine* article:

> The most distinctive feature of the cloister is its ambiance. Visit, for contrast, any academic building in nearby Princeton University. The first secretary to report apparently turns on a sort of educational muzak, compounded of student voices, shuffling feet, ringing bells, buzzing phones, clacking typewriters, and everywhere the professors looking at their watches like Lewis Carroll's White Rabbit, always on their way to lecture-seminar-conference-exam-correspondence and the external busywork prominently displayed on their hour-by-hour calendars. The appearance of activity is prodigious. The air is much like that at neighboring RCA or Squibb or General Electric, run by "businessmen" (etymologically, "busy men") meeting in committees, engaged in interaction,

directed by chairmen and deans, concerned with problems and reports and projects, deadlines and decisions and results. The Institute, on the other hand, is run by scholars (etymologically, men of *schola,* leisure) for meditation, the contemplative life. It resembles nothing so much as a well-run mortuary in the off-season. There seems to be no sound at all, at least no *hum.*

Over the last fifty years, an opportunity for soundless thinking has brought into the Princeton community a galaxy of intellectual stars. Although often perceived as a place of theoretical science because of Einstein, von Neumann, and its one-time director, J. Robert Oppenheimer, the Institute has also given thinking space to Thomas Mann, T. S. Eliot, diplomat George Kennan, art historian Irwin Panofsky, and Czech logician Kurt Godel. So prized is abstract thinking in silence that at one time, according to Davies, the scholars voted to have John von Neumann remove his first, clanking model of the electronic computer from the premises.

Unhappily, life isn't always serene for Institute people out of office-thinking hours. For most of his tenure, Oppenheimer, creator of the atom bomb, was shadowed by the FBI while he tried to fight off charges of Communist affiliation that eventually cost him his security clearance. The strain led to heavy drinking; and tragedy, including the suicide of his daughter, stalked the family. But the funereal atmosphere of the Institute must have been less apparent in Oppenheimer's day, for the director was known to use strong language in argument. On one occasion, his biographer Peter Goodchild reports, this so provoked a mathematician that he called the Oppenheimer home, Olden Manor, "Bourbon Manor." Before his death from cancer in 1966, Oppenheimer was heaped with honors—the Atomic Energy Commission's annual award, presented by President Johnson, a doctorate from Princeton University—but he indicated how difficult the life of the mind can sometimes be when he described himself to a reporter as simply "a survivor."

If these adjacent educational institutions are devoted to developing the mind, there are others devoted, for commercial reasons, to measuring the mind, investigating what is in the mind, and broadcasting the product of the mind. The Educational Testing Service, located on a sprawling park much like the Forrestal Center, creates among a multitude of other tests the decisive Scholastic Appitude and Scholastic Achievement tests for its client, the College Boards. Located on a Princeton back street, the Gallup organization, administered by the founder's son, George Gallup, Jr., '53, works through affiliates in thirty-five countries to find out what people are thinking about everything under the sun in "90 percent of the surveyable world." Everybody knows that academics have to "publish or perish," and standing on its own corporate feet is the Princeton University Press, which publishes about 130 titles a year for academic and library buyers all over the world. "We are publishers of scholarly books," says Director Herbert S. Bailey, Jr., '42, citing such ambitious press projects as the publication of the papers of Thomas Jefferson (fifty volumes), Woodrow Wilson, Henry David Thoreau, and of course, Albert Einstein.

Neither is culture in short supply in a place of the mind. The Budapest String Quartet *does* come to Princeton, and often there are better-than-Broadway quality productions at McCarter Theater—Shaw's *Saint Joan* and O'Neill's *Ah, Wilderness!* were two recent successes—not to mention smaller playhouses scattered around the countryside. On any given day there may be as many as half a dozen open lectures or seminars on campus, ranging from "Zaire's Debt Crisis: Managing and Manipulating Interdependence" to "Cooling of Superhot Photofragments and Photoexcited Molecules." On a winter night a lecture by a prominent architect drew a capacity crowd in which gray-haired men and fur-coated matrons outnumbered blue-jeaned students. Closer to home, any dinner or cocktail party is likely to include some expert recently back from China or Israel, with the latest inside news, or somebody composing a symphony or writing a book, and the table conversation always seems to drift toward vital issues or intellectual chat after the guests have dispensed with what Collins is doing to Palmer Square. Over the back fence the person having trouble with his crabgrass could well be a Nobel laureate. To hold your own in Princeton, you've got to be mentally alert day and night.

There are people who think all the heady interaction among the eggheads can be a bit much. One of them was Helen Blackmur, the wife of writer and critic R. P. Blackmur, who served for many years on the Princeton faculty. In *Poets in Their Youth,* Eileen Simpson quotes Mrs. Blackmur as saying: "I hate Princeton. It suffocates me. Richard does nothing but sit in that damn Balt and jaw. His book on Henry Adams will never be finished. It's being killed by talk." For Simpson's then husband, poet John Berryman, who was a writer in residence, the action wasn't enough. Comparing Princeton to his summer retreats, he wrote: "Whereas Princeton was academic/suburban/bourgeois, Wellfleet and Truro on Cape Cod were literary/radical/bohemian." Obviously—and a good thing, too, for Princeton, where it's getting harder and harder to shoehorn another person in—there are thousands of people out there who can get along without the Budapest String Quartet.

# Chapter Twelve

# IS THERE LIFE AFTER PRINCETON?

One of the most incisive comments on a Princeton education appeared not long ago in the pages of the *New Yorker*. It was a captionless cartoon showing a cemetery with a gravestone bearing the full legend: "James C. Crampton. Born 1909. Princeton 1932. Died 1983." As might be expected, the cartoonist, Henry Read Martin, has a firm grasp of Princeton as a member of the class of 1948 and a resident of the Princeton community. F. Scott Fitzgerald tried to convey a similar message in *This Side of Paradise* when he had an exasperated girl tell his hero, Amory Blaine: "Oh, you and Princeton! You'd think that was the world the way you talk!"

Even if Princeton is not the world, it would seem to form a larger part of the world for its sons, and now daughters, than any other institution of its kind. On a December day in 1940, Fitzgerald, in a scene he could hardly have invented, was making notes on the football team in the margins of the *Princeton Alumni Weekly* in his Hollywood home when he rose from his chair, clutched at the air and fell dead of a heart attack. The enduring grasp of Princeton can be perceived from an obituary last fall in that same publication, where it was reported that an elderly alumnus was laid to his final rest wearing his class of 1921 tie.

The fact is that no graduate ever seems to recover from attending Princeton. Whether one is sentimentally attached to the place or not, the alumni arm, which has been growing longer and stronger ever since it was founded under the aegis of ex-President James Madison, Jr., class of 1771, will reach out to touch every graduate. No Princetonian need ever face an empty mailbox. Along with the *Alumni Weekly* come periodic pronouncements of policy from administration and trustees, jolly notices about class reunions, appeals for donations to both the university and class funds. The odd Princetonians who manage to get themselves listed in their class rosters as having "no known address" have to be admired for their ingenuity.

On the whole, Princeton alumni appear to love so much attention. One proof of their sentiment is the record of annual giving by alumni, which in 1983 rose to $12 million, or about $240 per alumnus. Princeton administrators are cautious about making self-serving comparisons with other institutions when it comes to alumni loyalty, but E. J. Kahn, in a *New Yorker* article in the 1970s, reported that 60 percent of Princeton alumni gave something, as against 40 percent at Yale and 35 percent at Harvard. The reason may be more than sentiment. In the most recent edition of "The Gourman Report," a presumably disinterested study of more than one thousand eight hundred colleges and universities, Princeton's alumni associations were ranked second in the nation, a hundredth of a point behind Harvard's in maintaining strong ties to alma mater.

On campus there are an Alumni Council, charged with various activities to keep the sentiment alive, and an Annual Giving organization to turn that sentiment into hard cash. Although alumni giving represents a significant factor in the university's solvency, both President Bowen and Daniel N. White, '65, the director of the Alumni Council, emphasized the university's desire to maintain alumni interest and involvement in areas that have nothing to do with money. "Our business is to get the message out that, if you don't have the money, we're still interested in you," says White. The number of alumni who do participate in non-fund-raising activities is impressive: nearly three thousand in the Schools Committees, which recruits applicants; another small army in the "friends" groups—friends of athletics, friends of the library, friends of the chapel, and so on; and others on the advisory committees of academic departments and on the Board of Trustees. "The collective experience and wisdom of the alumni is an important resource of the university," White contends. "There's not much of major significance that happens in this university that doesn't involve alumni."

The Alumni Council and Annual Giving work off campus through an organizational structure lacking in many other places —the permanent class. Through most of its history Princeton has vigorously promoted class identity and cohesion. Until World War II freshmen had to wear identifying black dinks and were subjected by sophomores to various indignities. A nineteenth-century form of hazing—snatching away freshmen's canes— evolved into an annual wrestling, trampling, shoving match between members of the two classes, called the Cane Spree, in which virtually naked and greased freshmen would try to capture a high point from similarly stripped-down sophomores; in one of these mélées a student was killed. Today freshmen dress like everybody else, and the Cane Spree has been reduced to a ritualized wrestling match over a short length of stick between selected champions of each class. Even that's too much for some Princetonians, such as Eric Frey, who blasted the event in the *Daily Princetonian:*

> For most students Cane Spree is just an exciting athletic event that unites the classes and fosters school spirit; good, clean fun. But Cane Spree is more than fun. It is a tradition with a political and social message. It is a relic of a time when Princeton was an institution of an authoritarian hierarchy and discrimination. A time when silent obedience and conformist behavior were put above academic excellence and humane attitudes. A time when . . . first year Princetonians had to submit to senseless, violent

abuse by upperclassmen. Princeton is very different today.... The
university in the first half of this century was not a place we should
be proud of today. It was elitist, racist and anti-semitic. It fostered
academic mediocrity. To show that this institution has actually
changed, it is necessary to break with these traditions that cele-
brate the objectionable aspects of Princeton's past.

Whether enough Princetonians will share Frey's sentiments to
cause Cane Spree to be abolished—a doubtful proposition—the
Alumni Council's efforts to weld classmates to each other will
certainly continue. The Council once held an ice cream party for
freshmen interested in running for class office in order to, in
White's words, "educate the leadership in class responsibilities,"
and brunches with presumably stronger refreshments for senior
class leaders to introduce them to alumni, "which gives perspective to undergraduate class officers that they are part of a whole."
Annual giving actually begins with a senior class effort to raise
pledges. From then until death, a Princetonian's class allegiance
will be deepened by commencement reunions with special emphasis on every-fifth-year attendance.

A sociologist or psychiatrist could have a field day observing
Princeton reunions. Why would any group of men, and now
women, of increasing affluence, dignity, and responsibility—there
is hardly a class without a sprinkling of corporate chairmen, high
government officials, judges, distinguished doctors, professors,
clergymen—spend a weekend marching in funny costumes, sitting under hot tents where they drink far too much beer, talking
themselves hoarse over the deafening noise of jazz bands? Until
physical frailty makes it impossible, behavior at reunions can be
sophomoric in the extreme. *A Princeton Companion* gives the last
word on this to Norman Thomas, class of 1905, who, though out
of step with most of his classmates as both a clergyman and
quadrennial Socialist candidate for president, attended nearly all
of his reunions and commented: "Some things in life justify themselves emotionally without necessity for analytic reasoning. On
the whole, Princeton reunions fall in that category. In my moral-
izing moments, I may regret that reunions are too greatly inspired
by the prayer: 'Make me a sophomore again just for tonight,'

which prayer, with the aid of a sometimes excessive consumption of the spirituous, rather than the spiritual, often seems to be granted."

The "spirituous" Princeton reunions are, in fact, staged with the logistical planning and expense of a minor military operation. Eberhard Faber IV, '57, took a hard look behind the scenes of his class's twenty-fifth reunion for an article in a 1982 issue of *Fortune*, "Bringing Them Back to Nassau Hall." Twenty-three classmates on eleven committees spent one hundred hours in meetings and $200,000 to plan the event. The 524-page class book featuring biographies of 540 men (75 percent of the class) took years to produce at a cost of $45,840. When the class finally assembled wearing jackets ($100 each) with a motif of tigers peering through orange and black foliage, Thomas Kean, governor of New Jersey, was among them, and he might have agreed with a classmate who said: "I hope the colors run. Maybe then it will look like batik."

Whatever the reunions cost in expense and effort, they are clearly worth the while to a person in White's position, who says that alumni directors from other institutions would "like to have the problems I have." One of his—and the university's—minor problems is the existence of the Concerned Alumni of Princeton (CAP), discussed previously, which sometimes urges withholding of donations and generally functions as a hair shirt to the administration. The administration, bolstered by increased alumni giving in the face of criticism by CAP and other ultraconservative groups, now views such efforts as a "tragic" focusing on Princeton for all they deplore in society as a whole. This view is supported by the curious fact that *Prospect*'s staff, once all-Princetonian, is now largely recruited from a conservative undergraduate publication at Dartmouth and has moved on, as though from a farm team, to the big league of conservatism at the *National Review*. Edited by a Yaleman, William F. Buckley, Jr., the *National Review*'s publisher is a Princetonian, William A. Rusher, '44, a founder of CAP, and it often lifts CAP's quarrels with the alma mater to a national level. The flavor of its digs at Princeton over the years is nowhere tarter than in an article, "Advice to Princeton Alumni," that appeared in 1970 under the name of Al Capp of Li'l Abner fame. Fuming over the lack of administrative disciplinary action when, in May of that year, Princeton students staged a demonstration at the Institute for Defense Analyses, Capp wrote: "Princeton has only one problem: the lunatics are running the asylum. . . . Any administration of men over forty who consider students under twenty as smart as they are—is probably right. . . . Princeton has become a combination play pen and pig pen because it disregards one of the immutable facts of nature. And that is the inferiority of the college student to any other class. . . . "

One of CAP's continuing concerns is that, by diluting its male WASP composition with blacks, Chicanos, Asians, Puerto Ricans, and women, the university will no longer be able to command a remunerative alumni loyalty, which is attributed to those wanting to maintain a superior social class rather than an excellent educational institution. To this White says: "Today's attitudes toward class, toward the university, toward being an alumnus, toward tradition and spirit are very similar to those in my days. In fact, if there is any difference, it is much stronger, much more spirited, much more appreciative today. I think the four years here have become less of a boot camp or monastic existence. There's so much more diversity, more opportunity for people who don't necessarily feel part of the mainstream on campus to find satisfaction. The black alumni have been very active in supporting the university, and the women, just ten years out, are beginning to emerge."

Life after Princeton, then, at least in an organizational way, goes on being life *with* Princeton. But what concerns most undergraduates is what the rest of their lives will be like after graduation. The question was put starkly by a young black girl, a freshman, who asked: "Will it be worth it? Worth $14,500 a year?" If by nothing else, she can be reassured on a statistical and general basis.

Based on experience, it is relatively easy to compose a profile of the Princeton alumnus's achievements and lifestyle twenty-five years down the road: financial rewards by any standards but those of the very rich, secure and steady marriage and family; mildly adventurous recreation (yachting, skiing) and travel (Europe, the Caribbean, Asia); conservative but active in community affairs.

Whether this mostly bright picture can be attributed to a pre-Princeton background or to the knowledge and contacts acquired at considerable cost can't be factually determined, but one man's comment on his life after Princeton is representative of many: "The aura of the 'Princeton' label has helped me hold my own in the worldly world."

Through the years financial success would seem to be the primary goal of the largest segment of any Princeton class. Although different classes have slightly different ways of describing occupations, a comparison between the classes of 1942 and 1952 twenty-five years after graduation is instructive. Some 52 percent of the men of 1942 were engaged in pursuits that could be lumped under "business," which does not include such generally lucrative professions as law (10 percent) and medicine (8 percent) or the number of engineers and scientists (8 percent) in the profit-making professions. Sixty-one percent were earning more than $20,000 a year in 1967, when this was a respectable figure. Of the 1952 alumni, 37 percent were in "business," exceeding the combined total of those in law, medicine, and education. Sixty-two percent were making more than $40,000 in inflated dollars. (To go back to Princeton stability: 94 percent of the 1942 class were married, 53 percent to the same wife for more than twenty years; 95 percent of 1952 were married, 36.1 percent to the same wife for more than twenty-one years.)

Things scarcely change when it comes to the ambitions and performance of Princetonians. The first class with women, a special study of the class of 1973, was made ten years out and reported in the *Princeton Alumni Weekly* by one of its members, Robin Herman. "Banking, teaching, law, medicine, business, and advertising claimed most of the graduates, both male and female, with the heaviest concentration in law and medicine. Indeed, sixteen percent of the female respondents are lawyers, eleven percent are doctors." The results? A median income of $46,000 for men, $33,000 for women (enough to make an old-timer of '42 weep).

And Princetonians today seem even more intent on reaching that shimmering goal of financial success. Hearken to sophomore Valentina Vavasis: "There are a lot of people here who want to hit it big as far as money or power or prestige is concerned. It's not so much that past Princeton generations didn't want success in that way, but I think the difference now is that people say it and they're proud of it. And there's nothing wrong with it because they see how many opportunities are there that you wouldn't have if you didn't have money, like traveling and sending your kids to Princeton and things like that. I remember one girl who comes from a very wealthy southern family saying at dinner that she wants to be a social worker when she gets out of Princeton, and everyone was floored. They thought that was great and wonderful, but they were surprised because you don't hear that much these days."

The young people are surely entitled to their expectations. A flip through Princeton alumni records reveals names and titles in every class that confirm the image of money and power. To name only a few from the still active rolls: Laurence S. Rockefeller, '32, who, like his brother, the late John D. Rockefeller III, '29, was whimsically voted "most likely to succeed" by his class; Rawleigh Warner, Jr., '44, chairman of the board of Mobil Corporation; Donald C. Platten, '40, chairman of the board of Chemical Bank; Harold W. McGraw, Jr., '40, chairman, president, and chief executive officer of McGraw-Hill, Inc.; Charles Scribner Jr., '43, chairman of the Scribner Book Companies; Robert H. B. Baldwin, '42, president of Morgan Stanley & Co., Inc.

With people like that in position, the graduating Princetonian presumably has an edge if he or she chooses to follow the well-beaten path into business and the professions. As Robin Herman wrote of her class: "When the class of '73 left the university, it soon discovered the favor with which employers look upon Princeton graduates, a favor no less freely extended to women. The Princeton degree 'opened closed doors,' according to seventy-seven percent of the survey's male respondents and seventy-three percent of the women. Whether it was getting into graduate school, lining up a job interview, landing a job, being promoted or simply benefiting from 'networking,' the class of '73 found that being a Princetonian helps."

This seeming assurance of success to the contrary and notwithstanding, some Princetonians do fail. They may be among those with "no known address," and it is to be presumed that few of them eagerly report on their lives after Princeton. A sadly humorous exception is a man from the class of 1942 who wrote for the thirty-fifth reunion yearbook: "I have become the first and probably only one hundred percent 'self-unmade man' in our class, and possibly in the recent history of Princeton. Against overwhelming odds, I have achieved total failure and irreversible disaster. It wasn't easy. I overcame good health, moderate wealth, a small but adequate writing talent, a 200,000-word vocabulary, nearly flawless grammar and spelling, a good classical education, and thirty years of sound news and PR experience to achieve absolute unemployability in my field. I have also allowed my wife to squander my inheritance in just five years."

This disaster may have something to do with the fact that the respondent seems to have taken the path least traveled. Princetonians who pursue the arts, or the theater, or professional athletics, or even the media are still looked on as "sports" among their peers. Compared to corporation chiefs in any Princeton generation, they are indeed rare and have achieved what may be undue prominence in alumni annals. Among the sports: actors Jimmy Stewart, '32, and Jose Ferrer, '33, and producer-playwright Joshua Logan, '31, in the theater; classical composer Andrew Imbrie, '42, in music; literary lights Edmund Wilson, '16, F. Scott Fitzgerald, '17, John Peale Bishop, '17, W. S. Merwin, '48; journalists Louis Rukeyser, '54, and Hodding Carter, '57; *New Yorker* authors John Brooks, '42, and John McPhee, '53; cartoonists Whitney Darrow, Jr., '31, and Henry Martin, '48; New York Knicks star Bill Bradley, '65 (later, of course, Senator Bradley).

The fact that theater people and literary lights cluster around the shared years in college is significant in the Princeton story. Until recently, there was little in the conservative Princeton curriculum to instruct or inspire a student in the actual art of creation. Biographies of later famous Princetonian achievers in the arts show clearly that they caught fire from each other during extracurricular activities—Stewart-Ferrer-Logan, for instance, in the Triangle shows and Theater Intime productions; Fitzgerald-Wilson-Bishop on the *Nassau Lit.* Those headed for the media picked up both their taste and technique from the *Daily Prince-tonian* and other campus publications. Now, symbolically se-questered in a battered building a half block down Nassau Street from the main campus, there is instruction in drama, creative writing, painting. Though these are ancillary to a major in an accepted discipline, they will no doubt stimulate more "sports."

Author Joyce Carol Oates, who teaches creative writing, re-ports that she had at least two students who planned to submit novels as senior theses, and yet creative work—or professionalism in the arts—would still seem peripheral to the Princeton objec-tive in the light of President Bowen's comment: "I don't see these courses as professionalism. I don't think the purpose of Joyce Carol Oates's course is to train writers. I see it as a way of teaching a spectrum of students something about writing since writing is an enormous and fascinating aspect of our intellectual lives. Similarly with painting. One undergraduate I knew very well is now at Columbia Business School, but he is also a painter. Is he going to make his mark in the world as a painter? I don't think so. Do I think it is valuable in the business world to have people with first-hand appreciation of the arts? Absolutely. I think this is an important part of liberal education. We've tried in both writing and painting to tie these courses into the root departments—English and art history. We don't have people writing without reference to literature and the role of literature in society. One of the important changes in Princeton is that now the arts are much more strongly represented. We didn't give the arts their rightful place as subjects of study, and we've been trying to correct that balance."

It is possible to be a "sport" while undergoing the conforming Princeton experience and remain unscathed, as it were. One doesn't *have* to go along with the rest of the class into the minis-try, as was once the case, or into business, as now is the case. It can be imagined that lives after Princeton of those who do go it alone are indeed different from that shining composite picture of physical ease and moral security suggested by the statistics. Those of their classmates who knew the sometimes sordid details must have been astounded by the trio who took on the literary world in 1916 and 1917.

Scott Fitzgerald, by creating a romanticized Princeton in *This Side of Paradise,* became an instant critical and financial success. With his *Saturday Evening Post* stories bringing in enough money to blow it freely, he and his southern-belle wife, Zelda, came to represent in the flesh the "flaming youth" of the twenties. Their wild sprees and often childish pranks were legendary. They were thrown out of a Paris hotel because Zelda tied down the only elevator on her floor so that it would be ready when she was dressed for dinner. Scott was thrown out of Cottage Club after a weekend when he and Zelda, invited as chaperones for house parties, shocked even the undergraduates by their behavior. Zelda turned cartwheels down Prospect Street and came to breakfast at the club with a jug of applejack to make *omelettes flambées* while an inebriated Scott got into ungentlemanly brawls. But the critic Edmund Wilson and the poet John Peale Bishop were even more representative of the bohemianism of the "lost generation" that discovered the pleasures of free sex and bootleg booze than was Fitzgerald. Pertinent to the theme of Princeton bonding that never comes unglued is the story of how Wilson and Bishop both fell in love with (and evidently shared the favors of) the beautiful and notoriously promiscuous poet Edna St. Vincent Millay. Realizing that they were involved in an intolerable situation, Wilson and Bishop decided to break it off in a farewell evening recorded in Wilson's posthumous *The Twenties,* edited by Leon Edel: "After dinner, sitting on her day bed, John and I held Edna in our arms—according to an arrangement insisted upon by herself —I her lower half and John her upper—with a polite exchange of pleasantries as to which had the better share. She referred to us, I was told, as 'the choir boys of Hell,' and complained that our both being in love with her had not even broken up our friendship."

However different their lives from that of their classmates, Wilson and Fitzgerald, at least, came back often to Princeton. Wilson's purpose was mostly to share intellectual discussions with his former teacher and frequent correspondent Dean Christian Gauss; but Fitzgerald, his membership in Cottage Club restored, was more likely to wallow in the nostalgia of football games and parties. Although he never haunted reunions, an even more famous literary light, Nobel laureate Eugene O'Neill, never quite got Princeton out of his system. O'Neill, entering with the class of 1910, spent a little less than a year on campus. It was a tempestuous year. O'Neill, already a frequenter of bars and whorehouses, flunked several courses at midterms, and in the spring was walking back along the trolley tracks with some classmates after a bout of drinking in Trenton when they got the bright idea of knocking out the lights with stones. The dean let them off with a suspension, but an academically unenthusiastic O'Neill decided to quit altogether. Later he briefly attended Harvard and was honored by Yale, but biographer Doris M. Alexander quotes O'Neill as saying in later life: "My allegiance is always with Princeton. I like Princeton. I had a good time there, even though I stayed only a year."

It isn't necessary to last the course to be claimed by Princeton. One undergraduate, vintage 1939, spent only a few months on campus but became the most rabid Princetonian ever, attending every reunion and talking up the place in every gathering. He did not, however, have the benefit of higher education as did one part-timer whom Princeton does *not* claim, John Fitzgerald Kennedy. The man who could have been Princeton's third U.S. president withdrew in the freshman year of that same class of 1939 because of ill health, and later became fully identified with Harvard, class of 1940; but Princeton likes to quote his comment on his application for admission that "to be a Princeton Man is indeed an enviable distinction." Strangely, this distinction seems to have eluded author Booth Tarkington, class of 1893, as full-blooded a Princetonian as there ever was despite the fact that he spent only his last two years there and departed without a degree. He is quoted as saying in 1924: "The Ivy prestige is as ridiculous a thing as comes under my observation."

Perhaps Tarkington could get away with that because, unlike most of the "sports," he was *so* Ivy. He was, in fact, a member of the Ivy Club, a founder of the Triangle Club, a contributor to the *Nassau Lit,* the humor magazine *Tiger,* and the yearbook *Bric-a-Brac.* A professor of the time has left a picture of Tarkington as "the only Princeton man who had ever been known to play poker (with his left hand), write a story for the *Nassau Lit* (with

his right hand), and lead the singing in a crowded room, perform-
ing these three acts simultaneously." With his talent for friendship and showmanship Tarkington overcame any prejudice there
might have been about his Hoosier background and was greatly
admired by his classmates. And little wonder: although an oddball
in the sense that he earned his living by writing and never held
a job, Tarkington outdid them at their own thing. In the class
prophecy he was described as "our ten thousand a year genius,"
and ten years later: "Of all the class he has been the most successful. A success that none of us begrudges, a success that does not
make us envious, because it is a success honestly and fairly won
with the same gentle and lovable good humor that made him sing
'Danny Deever' for us over and over again under the old elms on
the steps of Old Nassau." By 1921, with the Pulitzer prize in hand
for his novel *Alice Adams,* and a reputation as the bard of American boyhood for *Penrod,* Tarkington was voted by booksellers the
most important author in the country. He was never bowled over
by being classed a Princetonian, but Tarkington had enjoyed his
time there and went back often; the university awarded him two
honorary degrees to make up for the missing A.B. degree. "Sport"
though he was, Tarkington died richer and more conservative
than most of the men of the class of 1893.

Curiously, the circumstances of being a successful Princetonian removed Tarkington from the pantheon of Princeton literary lights when the intelligentsia began to invade the campus
about the time of World War II. The vanguard of this onslaught,
which has now established a firm beachhead with its creative
writing program and Joyce Carol Oates, were Allen Tate and R.
P. Blackmur; others in the ranks were poets John Berryman and
Delmore Schwartz and Nobel Prize–winning novelist Saul Bellow. I personally learned that it doesn't do to be too Princetonian
if you seek literary laurels at a meeting when, in the presence of
Tate and Blackmur, we were gathering together the hundredth
anniversary issue of the *Nassau Lit.* Since Tarkington was still
alive I suggested that we ask him for a contribution; Blackmur
cut me, saying: "Oh, Tarkington—he makes two thousand dollars
a story from the *Saturday Evening Post.* We don't want him."
Fitzgerald, recently dead, would presumably have been all right;

his days of making that kind of money were long gone and he had undergone a cleansing artistic poverty. So, by the way, did Edmund Wilson, who once had a year so lean that his earnings amounted to only $1,800.

By and large, however, even those Princetonians in quest of something other than money seem to have a knack for acquiring it. One of these surely was Richard Halliburton, '21, whose consuming urge was to seek the thrill of adventure with a twinge of danger and a twist of romance. His undergraduate career was conventional enough—on the board of the *Daily Princetonian,* editor of the *Princeton Pictorial Magazine,* member of Cap and Gown Club; his obituary in the *Princeton Alumni Weekly* read: "Unconventional, unpredictable, and unassuming, Dick was not infrequently an enigma to many of his classmates." He was apparently an enigma to his conventional father, too, as a letter he wrote when he dropped out of junior year to make a vagabond junket to Europe suggests: "Dad, you hit the wrong target when you write that you wish I were at Princeton living 'in the even tenor of my way.' I *hate* that expression and as far as I am able I intend to avoid that condition. When impulse and spontaneity fail to make my 'way' as *uneven* as possible then I shall sit up nights inventing means of making life as conglomerate and vivid as possible. Those who live in the even tenor of their way simply exist until death ends their monotonous tranquillity."

There would scarcely be a moment's monotony for Halliburton, who swam the Hellespont and the Panama Canal, climbed Mount Olympus, the Matterhorn, and Fujiyama, marched with the French Foreign Legion, and crossed the Alps on an elephant. This was at a time when most Americans traveled vicariously; Halliburton easily supported his adventures with lectures and best-selling books, the first of which, *The Royal Road to Romance,* he dedicated to his Princeton roommates whose regulated lives inspired him to go and do otherwise. Halliburton's life ended, probably as he would have wanted it, while he was sailing a Chinese junk from Hong Kong to San Francisco in 1939. His last message was: "Southerly gales. Squalls. Lee rail under water. Hard tack. Bully beef. Wet bunks. Having a wonderful time. Wish you were here instead of me." The scorn he expressed for Princeton lives did not carry over to the institution itself: the money he willed the university's library for the purchase of materials in history, geography, and travel resulted in the Richard Halliburton Map Collection in Firestone Library.

Another unconventional Princetonian who sought—and found—another kind of adventure and made a fortune to boot was Temple Fielding, '39. On campus he distinguished himself as drum major of the band and captain in the ROTC, a circumstance that put him early into the army, where he was assigned to write a guidebook to orient new recruits to Fort Bragg. After war service, which included a stint behind the lines in Yugoslavia for the Office of Strategic Services, Fielding, at the suggestion of his wife, Nancy Parker, then a literary agent, decided to combine his personal enjoyment of travel with his guidebook formula. Fielding's success with his travel guides, which he sold off shortly before his death in 1983, made him a multimillionaire. His guides made him the most widely read travel writer in history. His readers spent liberally in the countries, cities, hotels, restaurants, and shops recommended in the guides. He was knighted by France, Sweden, Spain, and Denmark, which also gave the Fieldings a house for their personal use. On one occasion an Italian union called off a nationwide strike of waiters when it was learned that Fielding was traveling in Italy.

Fielding was pictured as a sybarite—a man who enjoyed high living, fine food, good wines, and beautiful women. He was all of that. He was known, for instance, as "Johnny Martiniseed" for his unremitting efforts to show European bartenders how to make that all-American cocktail; he created something of a sensation when he spent $10,000 to fly American friends to Copenhagen for his fiftieth birthday party. When he wasn't on the road he lived in splendor in a hillside villa with a spectacular seascape at Formentor, Majorca. His guide books included, where appropriate and approved, "feminine solace is available," a phrase that didn't have to be spelled out for faithful Fielding followers.

But behind the sophisticated facade that extended to his physical being—he was a well-built and handsome man who kept in shape with a regimen of isometric exercises and weight lifting —there was another Temple Fielding: a workaholic and a self-made man. Fielding wrote much of his own material and edited all of it, keeping to a seven-day-a-week schedule at Formentor, no matter how many of his guests were carousing around him. Six months of every year he and Nancy were on the road to make personal investigations of foreign territory. Fielding could be relentless when he experienced something he didn't like. At one point, his negative opinion closed down the Swiss resort town of Zermatt for two years after private detectives whom he hired found town officials culpable in a typhoid outbreak that killed a number of tourists. Despite his wartime exploits, Fielding feared flying. Once, aboard an Air France plane, he saw stewardesses taking cognac into the cockpit and wrote about it; in 1964 Air France banned liquor for employees. Fielding's frank criticisms brought on him at least forty libel suits for a total of $20 million in damages, but his accurate reporting saved him. Only once did he settle out of court, for $3,500.

Fielding's flashy life after Princeton drew the envy of some of his more regular classmates; and it is said that one of them "black-balled" him when he applied for membership in New York's intellectually minded Century Club; if true, it represents the dark side of Princeton's perpetual bonding. Apparently, Fielding didn't let it bother him. To the question "what have you learned since Princeton?" in his fortieth reunion book, Fielding responded: "May I turn the question from 'learned' (introspection baffles me with its pitfalls) to 'gained'? From a brash, broke, painfully insecure undergraduate, with what more could I be blessed than thirty-six years of glorious intertwining with my precious Nancy; our thirty-two-year-old Dodge [their son] becoming such a happy, warmly rounded, successful man, not because but despite us; the rays of sunlight cast constantly and generously by beloved friends; and the heavenly interlude between deadlines when we walk hand in hand through the Beautiful Foolishness of Things?"

The truth is nobody can predict who or what *might* come out of Princeton. A Princetonian—Charles Conrad, Jr., '53—has walked on the moon; another Princetonian—C. F. Martin, '16—makes the best acoustic guitars in the world; still another Princetonian—Dr. Jeffrey R. MacDonald, '65, a former Green Beret physician—languishes in jail after being convicted of charges of killing his wife and two daughters. Unrelievedly tragic though the MacDonald story is, there is a coda to it with respect to life after Princeton. A man who might be expected to be overcome with regret, MacDonald informed his biographer, Joe McGinnis, from his cell that one of his greatest regrets was having left college at the end of junior year to enter medical school, thereby losing a year of the Princeton experience. Whatever the lives they lead, it would seem Princetonians never seem to get over the fact that they once went to Princeton.

Should the ties of four college years persist throughout life when one is unlikely to see or even care much about the people and organization one may have spent thirty or more years with? This phenomenon is also present among former close comrades in arms, and may have something to do with that growing time in life when changes are arrestingly rapid, when impressions are vividly new. But it could also have something to do with a bonding in pursuit of transcendent objectives—the pure search for knowledge in one case, patriotism and the issues of life and death in the other.

Adlai Stevenson, '22, while still a contender for the presidency, stirred his audience when he returned to Princeton to address a senior class banquet: "And before you depart from this campus that you and I have known and loved, stay a moment, my young friends, and think a bit, inquire—these halls, this campus, our university, what do they mean? 'University' is a proud, a noble and ancient word. Around it cluster all of the values and the traditions which civilized people have for centuries prized most highly. The idea which underlies this university—any university—is greater than any of its physical manifestations; its classrooms, its laboratories, its clubs, its athletic plant, even the particular group of faculty and students who make up its human element as of any given time. What is this idea? It is that the highest condition of man in this mysterious universe is the freedom of the spirit. And it is only truth that can set the spirit free. . . . And now in the serenity and quiet of this lovely place, touch the depths of truth, feel the hem of heaven."

It is safe to say that most Princetonians have at some point felt the hem of heaven and, however hard-boiled they later grow, can never shake that exhilarating experience. Yes, one can have a life after Princeton, but never one without Princeton. It is tempting to leave this subject with Stevenson's high note still ringing in the ears, but understatement is something of a Princeton characteristic, which one alumnus was exhibiting when he struggled to recount what the Princeton experience had meant to him. A man more than ordinarily blessed with the financial success and family stability promised by the statistics, he came up with a surprising anecdote that hides a lot under its brittle surface. He was fox-trotting the wife of a friend around the country club dance floor with some flair when the music suddenly changed to a challenging Latin rhythm. He said it was beyond his abilities and proposed sitting the number out, but his partner blinked her eyes at him and cooed: "Why, Walter, of course you can tango. After all, you went to Princeton."

Let us leave it at that.

# Index

Women (*cont.*)
  on the faculty, 32–33
  in entering class of 1983, 152
  first class of, 40–42, 203, 204
  today, 34, 35–38
Women's Center, 37
Women's studies, 36–37
Woodbridge, Dudley E., 56–57
Woodbridge, Richard, 190
Woodrow Wilson School of Public
  International Affairs, 84

Working students, 88, 89–90
Wright, Thomas H., 56
Wu, Gordon Y. S., 43–44
Wu Hall, 44–45
*Wu Review*, 53
Wyman, Isaac C., 172

Yale, 58–60, 115–116

Zeitlin, Froma, 66